MW00721294

PARTISAN ODYSSEYS

Canada's Political Parties

In *Partisan Odysseys*, Nelson Wiseman sets out to survey the history of Canada's political parties. Uncovering distinctive motifs and events in Canadian party politics from pre-Confederation to the present, Wiseman shows how parties have adjusted, adapted, and reinvented themselves in response to significant social and economic changes as well as how they have, in turn, shaped or reinforced these social forces.

The book begins by tracing the rise of four different types of parties in the nineteenth century. By the end of the century, the Conservative and Liberal parties that continue to this day were firmly established. Among the topics covered throughout are nationalism, minority governments, third parties, and the reconfiguration of party positions. Wiseman concludes by examining changes in the way Canada's ever-evolving parties have operated and the rise of the modern party as a nimble, enterprising institution compared to its historical antecedent.

Substantial yet accessible, *Partisan Odysseys* will enlighten students, scholars, and general readers alike.

NELSON WISEMAN is a professor of political science at the University of Toronto.

Partisan Odysseys

Canada's Political Parties

NELSON WISEMAN

UNIVERSITY OF TORONTO PRESS
Toronto Buffalo London

ISBN 978-1-4875-0778-7 (cloth)   ISBN 978-1-4875-3695-4 (EPUB)
ISBN 978-1-4875-2539-2 (paper)   ISBN 978-1-4875-3694-7 (PDF)

Library and Archives Canada Cataloguing in Publication

Title: Partisan odysseys : Canada's political parties / Nelson Wiseman.
Names: Wiseman, Nelson, 1946–, author.
Description: Includes bibliographical references and index.
Identifiers: Canadiana (print) 20200178636 | Canadiana
    (ebook) 20200178652 | ISBN 9781487507787 (hardcover) |
    ISBN 9781487525392 (softcover) | ISBN 9781487536954 (EPUB) |
    ISBN 9781487536947 (PDF)
Subjects: LCSH: Political parties – Canada – History. |
    LCSH: Canada – Politics and government.
Classification: LCC JL195 .W57 2020 | DDC 324.271 – dc23

University of Toronto Press acknowledges the financial assistance to its
publishing program of the Canada Council for the Arts and the Ontario Arts
Council, an agency of the Government of Ontario.

Canada Council   Conseil des Arts
for the Arts   du Canada

ONTARIO ARTS COUNCIL
CONSEIL DES ARTS DE L'ONTARIO

an Ontario government agency
un organisme du gouvernement de l'Ontario

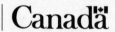 

Funded by the   Financé par le
Government   gouvernement
of Canada   du Canada

Canadä

MIX
Paper from
responsible sources
FSC   FSC® C016245
www.fsc.org

Contents

Introduction

This book argues that distinctive motifs launched by signal events characterize different eras in the history of Canada's political parties. An implicit theory undergirding the book is that political parties have adjusted, adapted, and sometimes reinvented themselves in order to respond to significant social and economic changes and cultural cues. Sometimes the parties have shaped or reinforced those social forces. Motifs or recurring elements in distinct eras of Canadian party politics speak to particular dominant ideas. The story begins by reviewing the rise of four different types of parties in the nineteenth century after the establishment of representative governments in British North America late in the eighteenth century and before the creation of the Canadian state. By the turn of the twentieth century two national parties that continue to this day, the Conservatives and Liberals, became firmly established. The book concludes by examining some changes in how the ever-evolving parties have operated.

Nineteenth-century party leaders, activists, and voters would not recognize today's political parties. The historical arc of Canada's political parties reflects the arc of Canadian history. Using largely secondary sources, this chronologically organized and easy-to-follow book, something of a primer, explores how the parties have emerged and addressed the conflicts and tensions of a society permanently under construction. Attention is focused on overarching themes and some of the ideas, personalities, social forces, and institutional structures that have driven the parties. Inevitably much is left in the shadows.

This book aims to enlighten non-specialist students of Canadian politics and general readers who have some knowledge or are somewhat innocent of Canadian history. Academic specialists will also find it interesting, encountering some things unfamiliar to them. Offering an accessible yet substantial understanding of the development of the parties, this study will be useful to politically engaged citizens, journalists, and anyone else who wants to know more about the history of Canada's political parties, how they came to be, and what and whom they have represented. On offer is a broad factual synthetic picture of the parties as historical and legal organizations. Specific aspects of any one party or of precise periods are not of primary importance; motifs structure the book to make the principal argument that the parties have changed in what they stand for and how they have operated as Canada and the values, concerns, and interests of Canadians have changed.

There are many histories of the leading parties and many biographies of party leaders, ranging from magisterial studies such as Donald Creighton's two-volume chronicle of John A. Macdonald's career to John English's equally admirable two tomes on the life of Pierre Trudeau.[1] Political scientists such as Richard Johnston, William Cross, and R. Kenneth Carty have provided richly textured quantitative and qualitative analyses of Canada's party systems.[2] An objective of this book, careful and granular in its historical approach, is to add value to and complement these insightful studies. Thick in description and examining a wide reading of materials, this book may be read as a history of the parties through the lens of Canadian history or as a history of Canada through the lens of the history of the parties. The story of Canada's political parties, like the story of Canada itself, is one of continuity as well as disruption, transition, and change.

A political party is a group of people with similar political goals and opinions whose purpose is to get party candidates elected to public office.[3] The world views, policies, leaders, strategies, and organizational forms of a party must adapt to changing times and to competitors. If a party does not, it fails and fades away. A party therefore must often recalibrate its message so that followers remain faithful and adversaries might be won over. Ideas drive parties because they serve as a compass, indicating a party's purpose and direction. The principles of a party feed the emotions and intellects of party supporters, many of whom have a sense of belonging to a tradition that will continue after they are gone. To remain relevant, however, parties must often re-examine and revise their ideological underpinnings and policy postures.

Party leaders may come and go, but their parties generally persist. Among their various functions in a democratic society, parties are the critical connective link between the public and its government; they are transmission belts between official and non-official wielders of power. Society, economy, culture, institutional structures, and leaders all contribute to shaping parties and the party system. At the same time, we must remember that the thinking propelling political parties and their

behaviour also influences society, the economy, how institutions operate, and culture generally. The causal arrow points both ways; party
and society are interrelated and interact. For example, the Depression
of the 1930s led to the emergence of new parties and a reorientation of
the older parties on issues of social policy and wealth distribution. The
arrow also points the other way, from party to society; the Liberal party's project for a charter of rights in the 1980s led to the rise of "Charter
patriotism" and "Charter Canadians" who see themselves as bearers of
constitutionally entrenched rights.[4]

Most of Canada's federal parties have endeavoured to be national
parties. The Liberals and Conservatives have long-established ped-
igrees, having emerged in colonial legislatures. Other parties, like
the Progressives, the Cooperative Commonwealth Federation (CCF),
Social Credit, and the Greens arose outside of Parliament. The Bloc
Québécois, composed originally of defecting Conservative and Liberal
MPs, was a federal party born in Parliament. So too was the Ralliement
des créditistes, composed of defecting Social Crediters. Styling itself
Quebec's national party, the Bloc Québécois has offered no candidates
in the rest of the country. The Greens are a relatively recent arrival in
Parliament. The Communist party, which once had an MP and several
MLAs, was for a time an outlawed party, its leaders imprisoned, its
publications shuttered.

A potent reflection of continuity in Canada's most successful party,
the Liberals, is the apostolic parade of its leaders; Paul Martin, who governed in the twenty-first century, served in the Cabinet of Jean Chrétien,
who served in that of Pierre Trudeau. Trudeau in turn served in Lester
Pearson's government, and Pearson served in Louis St. Laurent's.
St. Laurent was a member of Mackenzie King's government and King
a member in Wilfrid Laurier's, whose first Cabinet was formed in the
nineteenth century. Paul Martin Sr., bested for the party leadership by
Pierre Trudeau, had attended Laurier's funeral in 1919, the same year
Trudeau was born. Justin Trudeau, born to Pierre when he was prime
minister, came to lead a Liberal government a century later. Another
example of continuity is the legacy of Social Credit; although now long
gone, the party governed one province for thirty-six uninterrupted years
and another for two decades. The party's founder in the 1930s, Alberta
Premier William Aberhart, was the godfather of Preston Manning,
the founder of the Reform Party in the 1980s. Preston's father, Ernest
Manning, succeeded Aberhart as premier, and Preston's principal aco-
lyte, Stephen Harper, became a twenty-first-century prime minister.

Every party that began as a protest party has had a distinct regional
or sectional base of popular support. The Progressive Party represented

distressed farmers; the Reform Party championed an aggrieved region. The Reconstruction party captured a significant share of the popular vote in its one election campaign in 1935, outpolling the equally embryonic CCF and Social Credit parties, but it came and went quickly. It left no trace precisely because it had no regional or sectional anchor. The Progressives, the Reform Party, Social Credit, and the CCF have departed the political landscape in name, if not in spirit. The CCF's successor party, the New Democratic Party (NDP), firmly embedded itself in Canada's political culture; despite being a perpetual also-ran in federal elections, it has held the reins of government in a majority of the provinces and in one territory.

This book tells the story of these federal parties but also touches on some of the more prominent provincial parties like Quebec's Union Nationale and Parti Québécois. In places there are references to some of the provincial kin of federal parties such as the provincial United Farmers parties and the Alberta, British Columbia, and Quebec Social Credit parties. Repeated success in federal elections points to the strength of the Liberal brand and the party's resilience. However, Liberal success masks the party's vulnerability and the actual competitiveness of the Conservatives. Despite their election victories, the Liberals have experienced long-term erosion of support since winning power in 1896.[5] In the thirty-six elections between 1896 and 2015, the Conservatives won 47 per cent and Liberals only 40 per cent of the seats in English Canada.[6] In Quebec, Conservatives have won only 15 per cent of the seats since 1896, 45 per cent of them in three elections: 1958, 1984, and 1988. This made Quebec the most common pivot in determining which party governs in Ottawa.

The following synopsis is a roadmap of the study that follows. It runs from the turn of the nineteenth century to beyond the 2015 election, concluding with observations about some ways in which parties and voters have changed over time. The chapters explain as well as describe critical developments in the history of Canada's parties.

Chapter 1 traces the development of parties, presenting four types of parties that emerged sequentially in British North America in the nineteenth century. The growth of a democratic impulse and the struggle to create permanent, unified, national parties are recurring elements or motifs in this chapter. Institutional changes and socio-economic conditions at home and abroad informed the issues, parties, and party types that arose after the establishment of representative governments in Upper and Lower Canada in 1791 and, before that, in the Maritime colonies. Four party types – court, competing, coalition, and consolidated – took shape, with each party type dominant in each quarter of the nineteenth century. By century's end, a national party system loosely linking federal and provincial parties of the same name and orientation, Liberal and Conservative, had materialized. Ties binding them persist to this day. Contemporary Conservative and Liberal partisans continue to revere early leaders of their parties, John A. Macdonald and Wilfrid Laurier, referring proudly to some of their principles and accomplishments.

Chapter 2 examines competing nationalist narratives presented by the two parties at the turn of the twentieth century. They offered contrasting visions of Canada's place and affinities in the world, of the country's destiny as it could and should be. The central motif of party politics in this era was the debate between imperial federationists and continentalists. In an age corresponding with Britain's gradual decline as an imperial power and the rise of the United States as an economic behemoth, the salient issue was whether Canada was a familial part of a British global enterprise or a country whose primary interests lay in North America. The First World War resulted in Canada's exit from the cocoon of British colonialism, but English Canadians continued to value the British connection and the British Commonwealth despite the dissolution of the empire. As the economy became increasingly tethered to the United States and continental economic integration proceeded rapidly, partisans divided over Canada's identity and fate.

The motif in chapter 3 is the rise of third parties to challenge the established Liberals and Conservatives after the end of the First World War. The politically stormy 1920s and 1930s produced radical new parties, transforming the party system. The Progressive party reflected more than agrarian-driven politics; it challenged the partisan conduct of politics and the conventions of parliamentary government. However, the party withered, most of its MPs and supporters returned to their original home, the Liberal party. Nevertheless, the Progressives laid the foundations for other upstart parties. As regional and sectional grievances drove sharp changes in the behaviour of voters during the Depression, a more dynamic multiparty Parliament took hold, with ideology playing a more significant role. Some provincial farm organizations and labour-socialist parties federated to form the CCF. Proposing monetary reform as the tonic for economic ills, Social Credit arose first as a movement and then competed as a party, becoming the third largest in Parliament. The CCF and Social Credit grew beyond their roots, but the first-past-the-post electoral system undid the Reconstruction Party, and the Communist Party was never able to attract more than minor support.

Chapter 4 begins with all the parliamentary parties rallying to Britain's side at the outbreak of the Second World War. A change in public attitudes towards social welfare led the parties to accept that government had an obligation to provide for the economic security of citizens; the governing Liberals promised a new social order and the Conservatives promised social security from the cradle to the grave. The motif in this chapter is the success of the Liberals in situating themselves as ideologically equidistant from the Conservatives on their right and the CCF on their left. The Conservatives suffered from having less stable leadership than the Liberals and turmoil in their thinking. Both parties pilfered proposals from the CCF, whose fortunes rose and fell with public perceptions of the Soviet Union. Social Credit gave lip service to monetary reform but redefined its mission as opposition to socialism. French Canada remained in the Liberals' corner, despite the party's imposition of conscription and the emergence of the nationalist Bloc populaire canadien.

Chapter 5 scrutinizes the parties during the series of four minority governments produced by five elections over the course of eight years in the 1950s and 1960s. This era begins with the Conservatives winning power in 1957. The motif in this chapter is the competing conservative, liberal, and social democratic visions of Canadian nationalism. The CCF, rebranded as the NDP, and Social Credit played critical roles in determining the fate of Liberal and Conservative governments. Chief protagonists Conservative John Diefenbaker and Liberal Lester Pearson reshaped their parties. Diefenbaker opened his party's ranks to citizens of non-Anglo-Celtic or French ancestry. The prairies, at the time the country's most ethnically diverse region, became the strongest base of support for the Conservative party. Pearson recruited new Québécois voices during the Quiet Revolution and led a more urban-based Liberal party. For the first time, Quebec broke significantly with the older parties, electing a contingent of Social Crediters who, frustrated with their party's western leadership, broke away to form their own party, the Ralliement des créditistes. During this period, television revolutionized the coverage of parties.

Chapter 6 engages issues of language, national unity, and economy during a period when parties opened themselves to greater participation by party members. Trudeaumania in the 1968 election is the start of this era, and the motif in the chapter is the rise of Quebecois nationalism amid stagflation. Canada's centennial and her made-for-television prime minister caught the world's attention. In selecting Pierre Trudeau and Robert Stanfield as their new leaders, the Liberals and Conservatives departed from the managed leadership contests of the past. Trudeau, unpopular in English Canada, almost lost power in 1972 but succeeded in keeping the Liberals in office because of Quebec's overwhelming support. Trapped in a syndrome of opposition, the Conservatives were wracked by self-lacerating factionalism over leadership. The NDP took a nationalist turn, and Social Credit, in both English Canada and Quebec, virtually disappeared. Revisions to the Canada Elections Act greatly empowered party leaders, reducing the independence of candidates for office by requiring that they secure the signature of their party's leader in order to carry the party's name on the ballot.

The resounding victory of Brian Mulroney's Conservatives in 1984 starts the era in chapter 7. During his tenure, the Conservatives abandoned their long-held aversion to economic continentalism. Motifs in this chapter are the rise of neoconservativism and battles about free trade with the United States and the Constitution. Mulroney's ill-fated attempts to upstage Trudeau by securing Quebec's approval for the Constitution led to the implosion of the Conservative party and the rise of two new regionally based parties. Western Canadian Conservatives felt betrayed by their party and gravitated to the Reform party, which declared "The West Wants In" while the independantist Bloc Québécois served as the federal incarnation of the provincial Parti Québécois. The historic balance between Confederation's two parties ended. The Liberals became the major beneficiary of the collapse of the Conservatives in the 1990s, and the NDP reached its nadir. Unable to secure official party status in Parliament, it verged on irrelevance.

Chapter 8 begins with a fragmented Parliament in which the once Quebec-centred Liberals became Ontario-centred, benefitting from divisions among Ontario's conservative voters. The recurring element in this chapter is the entrenchment of regionalism. Regionalization of the parties intensified with the Bloc Québécois dominating Quebec, the Reform-cum-Canadian Alliance party supreme in the West, and the Progressive Conservatives competitive only in Atlantic Canada. The NDP was going nowhere but not going away, while the Bloc Québécois spoke exclusively for Quebec's interests in Parliament. The Liberals presented themselves as the only truly pan-Canadian party. After fighting and undercutting one another, the two partisan branches of the conservative movement reconciled. Dropping the qualifier "Progressive," the newly rebranded Conservative party led by Canadian Alliance leader and former Reform MP Stephen Harper billed itself as a merger but was more of an appropriation of the Conservative brand by Harperites. Infighting over the Liberal party's leadership and a major scandal opened the door to office for the refurbished Conservatives.

With the melding of the Progressive Conservatives and the Canadian Alliance, chapter 9 shines light on the conservatism of the old and new Conservative parties. The motif here is an uncompromising right-wing government opposed by a divided left that includes an uncharacteristically strong NDP. As Liberal support shrank during Harper's tenure as prime minister, support for the NDP rose dramatically; in 2011 the party leapfrogged over the Liberals to become the official opposition in Parliament. The humiliated Liberals suffered their worst-ever performance. Michael Ignatieff, who had returned to Canada to serve as Liberal leader, soon left the country once again. The NDP, which had never been a force in Quebec, became a Quebec-centred party in 2011 at the expense of the Bloc Québécois. Parliament's newest party, the Greens, began as a tiny party of one. Undermining predictions of their demise, the Liberals demonstrated their capacity to recover quickly in the 2015 election. Justin Trudeau swept into the leadership of his party and the prime ministership, partially because of popular memories of his father.

The concluding chapter looks at the nimble and enterprising modern party as a reinvented institution. Over time, parties transformed how they select their leaders, and the role of party members changed; party membership numbers now expand and contract like accordions. The financing of parties has also been remade, as have the ways parties relate to media. Links between federal and provincial parties of the same name have become more tenuous. Declining party loyalty and rising voter volatility have coincided with the increasing power of party leaders, reinforced by an unprecedented level of party discipline in Parliament. Indeed, more than ever before, leaders pull MPs along in their slipstream.

Political parties have been essential vehicles of Canada's parliamentary democracy. This study of the circumstances surrounding the emergence, development, and character of the parties points to their future; they will continue to mirror and shape Canada's diverse political culture.

PARTISAN ODYSSEYS

Canada's Political Parties

Chapter One

Four Party Types: Nineteenth-Century Party Politics

I don't care for office for the sake of money, but for the sake of power, and for the sake of carrying out my own views of what is best for the country.[1]

John A. Macdonald

Preston Manning, founder of the Reform Party and progenitor of Canada's new Conservative party, highlighted the ubiquity of political parties by identifying a group of plotters against Samuel de Champlain in 1608 as the country's first party.[2] However, the beginning of British colonial rule in the late eighteenth century is the signal event that begins the story of Canada's parties as we now know them. The distinctive feature of nineteenth-century politics was the creation of two permanent, unified, national parties in a context of an increasingly democratic political environment.

At the beginning of the nineteenth century, political parties were largely unknown to British North American settlers and the First Nations peoples who outnumbered settlers almost everywhere in what was to become the self-governing Dominion of Canada. By the end of the nineteenth century, First Nations peoples had been dispossessed of their lands and political parties were firmly established and well known. As Canada grew, political parties took root. Nevertheless, a climate of anti-partyism flourished throughout the nineteenth century; parties were thought to be uncompromising, dogmatic, and divisive forces.[3] Partyism prevailed because the parliamentary system imposed in British North America requires parties to function effectively.

Four distinct, chronologically overlapping types of parties appeared in the century after the establishment of popularly elected assemblies in the various British colonies in the late eighteenth century. The assemblies, representing voters, operated alongside executive councils

Table 1.1 Party Types in Nineteenth-Century Canada

Period	Party Type	Socio-economic Factors	Institutional Factors	External Factors
1800–1820s	Court party	Colonization Mercantilism Land granting Fish/fur	Constitutional Act Governor as monarch Family Compact Three solitudes	Jacobinism Louisiana 1803 War of 1812 Treaty of Ghent
1820s–1830s	Competing party	Timber Immigration Rebellions Canals	Assembly power Clergy reserves Durham Report Act of Union	Erie Canal Jacksonianism Whig government Reform Act
1840s–1860s	Coalition party	Anglo majority Grand Trunk Public debt Railways	Responsible government Dualism Political instability Confederation	Corn Laws Repeal Reciprocity Treaty Civil War Militia Bill 1862
1870s–1900	Consolidated party	Inter-Colonial Railway CPR Riel executed Newspapers	Electoral reform New provinces Pacific Scandal Provincial rights	Britain leaves JCPC Imperial federation Boer War

(cabinets) and legislative councils (legislative upper houses) appointed by the governor, who in turn was appointed by London. Institutional developments, socio-economic conditions, and external factors provided the context for the emergence of each of the four types of parties. Their rise corresponded roughly with the four quarters of the century. The party types are: the court party, the indisputable hegemon until well into the 1820s; the competing party, ascending in the 1820s and 1830s; the coalition party, a configuration critical to Canada's formation between the 1840s and 1860s; and the consolidated party, establishing itself in the 1870s as the Liberal and Conservative parties we know today (table 1.1).

The Court Party: 1800–1820s: Family Compact and Château Clique

The court party operated at a time in which one party ruled with little competition. It may be termed a quasi-party because the ruling party featured only some characteristics of a party. At the time, Canada's constitution was even more "court" than Britain's in that Canada's court party had a statist outlook and used patronage to fortify itself.[4] Britain's Constitutional Act of 1791 provided for two powerless assemblies in the newly constituted colonies of Upper and Lower Canada. The assemblies were feeble; while they could air grievances and criticize the governing court party, they had no legislative role. Similarly toothless assemblies operated in the Atlantic colonies, where British governors and their appointed councillors were preoccupied with whether to amalgamate or divide parts of them.[5] The system of government was based on the Westminster model but without responsible government, which requires the party in power to maintain the confidence of those elected by voters. Governors, who determined the composition of the governing court party, were only nebulously responsible to London.

In the Canadas and New Brunswick, governors and their appointed cabinets, as the court party, rewarded the decamped Loyalists fleeing the American Revolution with land grants. Westminster granted land directly in Prince Edward Island, and no land was granted in Newfoundland. Its settlers had no legal status, no titles to land, and no civil government; naval officers served as judges, the de facto court party.[6] Britain's 1803 Judicature Act made judges and courts critical components of the court party by extending their jurisdiction to all of British North America.[7] The court party, a small privileged group of military men, colonial administrators, ranking clergymen, judges, lawyers, and captains of commerce, wielded authority. This was consistent with the skeletal government institutions and the challenging conditions in the colonies. In Upper Canada, for example, both the government and legislature initially operated out of a two-room building that also served as a church. In Newfoundland the first resident governor died of the winter cold within months of his arrival in 1817.[8] In the comparatively well-established society of Lower Canada, a British court party replaced an earlier French regime.

The court party controlled public revenues. Until 1827, Upper Canadian land grants were exclusively for Loyalists, the military, and the Anglican clergy; in Lower Canada such grants benefitted the Catholic clergy. This system reinforced British tory principles of authority and hierarchy. As privileged patronage barons, court party members feathered their own nests. Leading clergymen and jurists served as cabinet members in all the colonies; sometimes they served in cabinets other than their own, as in Prince Edward Island, whose cabinet included both the chief justice and the Anglican bishop of Nova Scotia. Governors and their appointed cabinets as the court party had little need to build a political relationship with the popularly elected assemblies because they had no law-making power.

Primary producers – fishers, trappers, farmers, loggers – were in the majority of the population, but the merchant and professional classes dominated the assemblies as well as the appointed cabinets and upper legislative houses. Driving Upper Canada's economy until well into the 1820s was the fur trade directed from Lower Canada, where the woods industry had eclipsed the fur trade by the early nineteenth century. The capital generated by the fur trade, however, helped launch Canada's first bank, the Bank of Montreal, in 1817 and the city benefitted from its commanding economic location. The Atlantic colonists, dependent on the fishery and ports, handled American as well as British trade. They experienced the "prosperity of war," profiting economically from the War of 1812 between Britain and the recently created United States.[9] British restrictions on trade with the Americans and the Royal Navy's impressment of American seamen had triggered the war.

The colonies' three solitudes – the British and French in the Canadas and the Atlantic colonists – were culturally distinct societies. Nevertheless, one court party extended its influence into all of them and beyond. A PEI judge reassigned to Upper Canada described a single "Shopkeeper Aristocracy" as a "Scotch faction" and a "clan ... linked from Halifax to Quebec, Montreal, Kingston, York, Niagara and so on to Detroit."[10] Playing on fears generated by the French and American Revolutions, the court party's Upper Canadian leaders castigated their opponents, largely Whig Irishmen such as Robert Thorpe, William Weekes, and Joseph Willcocks, supporters of personal liberty and self-government. Authorities deemed them "supporters of unprincipled demagogues"[11] and as dangerous Jacobins, the most radical of the political groups formed in the wake of the French Revolution. PEI's chief justice hurled the same charge of Jacobinism at a group known as the "Club of Loyal Electors" that met in secret and criticized the governor and his land policies.[12]

Scottish-born newspaper publisher William Lyon Mackenzie, Toronto's first mayor, described the court party as controlling the governor "like wax, to their will."[13] His term for the court party, the Family Compact, came to be used as well in New Brunswick and Nova Scotia. There the same families often held offices for decades. The son of New Brunswick's first provincial secretary, for example, inherited the office when his father died in 1818.[14] In Nova Scotia, with few exceptions, genealogy linked all the cabinet and upper house members together between the 1760s and 1830s.[15] In PEI the governors appointed their relatives at every opportunity.

Origin was less of an obstacle to becoming a member of the court party in Upper Canada; many were from wealthy, highly esteemed

families, but others such as carpenter John McGill had humble begin-
nings. To quell upstarts such as Robert Gourlay, who called a convention to discuss popular grievances, legislation made such meetings
illegal. A sham trial conducted by members of the court party resulted
in Gourlay's deportation. The Upper Canadian court party included
brilliant figures such as John Beverley Robinson as well as incompe-
tents. Pettiness and folly characterized the regime; Methodists, for example, were nearly as numerous as Anglicans but the court party in
both Upper Canada and Nova Scotia denied Methodist clergymen the
legal right to solemnize marriages.

In Lower Canada's near hermitically separated English and French
societies – the Board of Trade had no French directors and the civil service was an anglophone preserve – the Château Clique, also known as
the merchants' party, served as the court party. Membership included
James Molson, the builder of Canada's first distillery and, crucially, its
first railway at a time when Upper Canada, with no access to the sea,
was an economic colony at the mercy of Lower Canada. Herman Ryland, clerk of the executive council, expressed the prevailing attitude
of many Lower Canadian court party members; suspicious of democracy and contemptuous of Catholicism, he defended aristocracy and
the royal prerogative – the right of the king subject to no restriction.[16]
A fledgling francophone Parti Canadien appeared, and its newspaper,
Le Canadien, aimed to counter anti-French Catholic prejudice, but the
Catholic hierarchy, fearful of revolutionary liberalism and Napoleon,
campaigned for the court party's candidates for the assembly.[17] Le Canadien is noteworthy, however, for in 1808 it became the first journal
to argue for responsible government, requiring the governing party to
gain the confidence of those elected to the assembly. This was not reflective of public opinion among the largely illiterate habitants. None-
theless, Le Canadien's propagation of the idea led Governor James Craig
to suspect the largely francophone assembly of seditious Jacobinism.

The chaotic state of politics in the United States at the time buttressed
the court party's argument that democracy along republican lines represented mobocracy. Court party members extolled the virtues of a stable
hierarchical political regime. Meanwhile the Louisiana Purchase of 1803
demonstrated the new republic's expansionary ambitions. The Americans claimed that the forty-ninth parallel was Louisiana's northern limit,
which Britain accepted in 1818.[18] The Treaty of Ghent ending the War of
1812 between the British and the United States maintained the British
colonial mercantilist system, a popular form of national economic protectionism at the time. The treaty also validated the court party's authority. In confirming British North America's eastern border with the

United States, the treaty contributed to the emergence of a British North American identity separate from yet still intimately linked to Britain.

Before the 1830s the British government and its colonial governors feared that political parties would undermine authority and lead to a weakened imperial connection.[19] This attitude, shared by much of the public, impeded the rise of a competing party. However, in 1837–8 escalating tensions between the elected assemblies and the governors' councils led to outright rebellions. The slowness of political reforms in the Canadas motivated the rebels. In Upper Canada the aim of the rebels was responsible government; in Lower Canada the aim included national independence. Responsible government implies competing parties vying for power. The competing party, however, came into focus even before the coming of responsible government, which proved to be the yeast for its rise.

The Competing Party: 1820s–1830s: Grits, Reformers, Patriotes

The competing party type arose in the century's second quarter in a context of growing resentment, rebellions, and a changing economy. The union of the two Canadas, Upper and Lower, followed. The backdrop included rapidly developing infrastructure, particularly canals such as the Welland and the Rideau. The opening of the Erie Canal in 1825 had provided an American outlet for Upper Canadian wheat, which now exceeded the value of Lower Canadian wheat. Obstruction of the preferred upper St. Lawrence route, however, meant Lower Canada continued to control import duties.

Mass immigration from Britain mightily advanced the competing party's strength, particularly in Upper Canada. Its population exploded from 77,000 to 952,000 between 1811 and 1851 at a time when liberal democratic ideas were gaining influence and authority in mother Britain.[20] Peasant stock Irish timberers led the most notable labour disruption of the 1830s, fighting for higher pay and the exclusion of French Canadians from such work.[21] Such developments contributed to divergent economic, social, and political interests of the two Canadas. Simultaneously, the competing party in each of the British colonies borrowed from the tactics and rhetoric of its counterparts in the other colonies.

Discrimination against Methodists and post-revolutionary American settlers – disqualified from voting and prohibited from inheriting real estate – only swelled support for the competing party. As ideas of religious equality gained currency, so too did the competing party's criticisms of reserving Crown lands for the Anglican clergy and having senior clergy sit in the cabinet. Controversy regarding the Crown reserves formed the framework for issues that arose with respect to other classes within society.

In the early 1820s, Upper Canada Governor Peregrine Maitland (who later became Nova Scotia's governor) favoured autocratic absolutist government, rejecting liberal ideas as abstractions. Upper Canada's derided "Jacobins" became the forerunners of the competing party, which came to be known as Grits and Reformers. Their rebellious efforts gathered steam in the late 1820s and crystallized in 1837 as the waves of revolutionary feelings that swayed throughout continental Europe in the 1830s echoed in the Canadas; Mackenzie and his supporters proposed an armed march, the arrest of the governor, seizing Toronto's armoury, and forming a provisional government.

The competing party had a distinct American flavour in its composition, supported by Upper Canada's post-revolutionary American settlers after they were given the right to vote again. Although the competing party embraced the British constitutional model, it was in the mould of the American "country" party – republicans who had agitated for elected rather than appointed officials.[22] Many of the competing party's leaders and followers pointed to American political practices and institutions as superior models of governance. Indeed, Mackenzie founded his newspaper, the *Colonial Advocate*, on the anniversary of the American Declaration of Independence, and those who participated in the 1837 rebellion adopted a declaration based on it.

The undoing of Upper Canada's high tory right began in 1825 with the election of many government opponents. Re-elected with larger numbers still in 1828 and flexing their newfound muscle, the Reformers who controlled the assembly jailed future premier Allan MacNab for refusing to answer questions regarding the hanging in effigy of the governor.[23] The Reformers lost the 1830 election to the Family Compact's Tories, but the governing style of the Tories and their royalist attitudes, which exceeded those of the king in their opposition to responsible government, were inconsistent with changing times, as reflected by the election of Britain's liberal Whigs in 1830. The Whig government transferred power over revenues from the colonial cabinets, composed of the court party, to the elected assemblies. This proved particularly crucial to the fortunes of the competing party. Unlike the court party of the past, however, the competing party was no hegemon; the Tories won Upper Canada's 1836 election. Nevertheless, the continuing vitality of the Reformers demonstrated that a competitive party had taken hold.

The partisan battles in all the colonies were similar: would the assemblies or the cabinets chosen by the governors control revenue? In the Maritimes, the separation of the formerly fused cabinets and upper legislative chambers in the 1830s coincided with the competing party agitating for places for assemblymen in the cabinets in all three colonies. It was a tactical gambit in the quest for responsible government. Maritime Loyalists, a more educated and refined lot than Upper Canada's frontiersmen, remained passive during the rebellions of 1837–8 that rocked the Canadas. In Newfoundland, representative government did not come until 1832 and was particularly liberal in providing for manhood suffrage unfettered by property, rent, income, or literacy requirements.[24] Capital generated by the fishery propped up Newfoundland's Protestant and conservative merchants' party, while the Liberals, composed largely of Irish Catholics, became the party of popular agitation.[25] Ethnic and religious differences in the Atlantic colonies correlated with party support, but those differences were not as fraught as they were in Lower Canada.

Before the Constitutional Act of 1791 created elected assemblies, there had been much resistance in Quebec to elected bodies because elections were thought to imply inevitable taxation.[26] The Parti Canadien that emerged as the competing party became the Patriote party in 1826, and although its leader, Louis-Joseph Papineau, reflected a streak of liberal *rouge*, he was no revolutionary ideologue. He was a monarchist professing a conservative liberalism.[27] The dominant Patriote outlook was even more profoundly conservative, seeking to protect the pre-liberal institutions of the old regime – the seigneurial system, an institutional form of land distribution established in New France in 1627, and tithing for the Catholic clergy. The liberalism of the Patriotes paled in comparison with the liberalism of Upper Canada's largely rural-based supporters. The essential goal of the urban, largely professional Patriotes leaders and their followers was national independence, not personal liberties.[28]

Unlike the Parti Canadien, which had appealed for the support of the English as well as French, the radical nationalist turn of the Patriotes after 1828 alienated the English. Drawing on ideas from Rousseau, Jefferson, Jacksonian democracy, and radical British liberalism, Papineau now attacked the constitutional system Britain had imposed on Lower Canada. He called for elections for all positions of power, including the governorship, and forbade his party's members from taking government posts at a time when only one of the eleven cabinet ministers was a francophone. Papineau did not want to contribute to legitimizing the regime.

Lower Canada's court party could no longer weaken opposition to it by dividing the opposition, as Governor Craig had done in the first decade of the century. After the assembly passed a nationalist manifesto inspired by Papineau known as the Ninety-Two Resolutions – a list of grievances and demands – their rejection by the British government energized the competing party. It now "had a defined ideology, a programme constantly modified to fit the conditions of the moment, a complex hierarchy in the smallest of localities in all regions, a well-tried strategy, and a dazzling leader."[29]

The quest for self-government drove the competing party in the Atlantic colonies as it did in Upper and Lower Canada. Nova Scotia's assembly, effectively empowered by 1830 to determine its own rules of procedure and the qualifications of voters and members, further strengthened the hand of the competing party led by Joseph Howe. He openly derided the shortcomings of Governor Maitland, who earlier had served as Upper Canada's governor.[30] Howe's evolution from "Mild Tory to Reforming Assemblyman"[31] reflected the relative ideological caution of Maritime reformism; his "highest ambition" was to secure Nova Scotia's representation in Britain's Parliament.[32] In New Brunswick, party politics played out differently once the assembly got control of revenues and Crown lands in the 1830s. Here, representative disorder, local jealousies, and quarrels prevailed, with assembly members behaving as greedy free agents. The local potentates most adept at parish-pump politics and dividing the spoils resembled a new Family Compact.[33]

In Upper Canada, Mackenzie, who had been in Washington shortly after the inauguration of Andrew Jackson, produced a legislative report that encapsulated the complaints of the 1837 rebels.[34] They could point to Britain's liberal Reform Act of 1832, which had extended the right to vote in the mother country. In response to the rebellions in both Canadas, Britain's Whig government dispatched Lord Durham, known as Radical Jack, to enquire into prospects for an "enduring tranquility."[35] He prescribed joining the two Canadas into a single province and instituting responsible government.[36] The 1840 Act of Union united Upper Canada and Lower Canada under one government, creating the Province of Canada, but Durham erroneously assumed that the French could be anglicized, becoming loyal subjects appreciating the benefits of British rule. His recommendation for responsible government permitted Upper Canada's competing party to claim vindication; gaining official approval for what they had long demanded stymied the accusations of court party members that they were traitorous disloyal republicans. The privileged court party, once a bastion of arrogance was now in permanent retreat, humbled and rendered ineffective. Responsible government, finally attained in 1848, sounded its death knell.

The Coalition Party: 1840s, 1850s, 1860s: Liberal-Conservatives

In 1829 Mackenzie had proposed to a non-committal Papineau that they form a joint committee to study uniting the Canadas. However, it was the turmoil of the 1830s that hastened union. Union ushered in the era of the coalition party. This party type followed on the heels of the 1837–8 rebellions and the coming together of Canada's English and French Reformers to pursue a common objective: responsible government. With their leaders exiled, the dispersed Patriotes reconstituted themselves as moderate reformers under the leadership of Papineau's protégé Louis-H. LaFontaine, while Robert Baldwin led Upper Canada's Reformers. Corresponding extensively in 1839–40, LaFontaine and future Reform premier Francis Hincks shared their belief in organizing parties based on principles rather than ethnicity or class.[37]

The coalition party was an exigency of union. Baldwin and LaFontaine's coalition government of 1842 proved too strong for the remnants of the court party, who continued to oppose responsible government. Coalition parties and governments prevailed, but both proved unstable and decomposed readily. Between 1841 and 1867 the new united Province of Canada had at least eighteen different administrations, and none lasted four years. Half of the governments came to office by virtue of floor crossings in the assembly and without fresh elections. In a legislature constructed with equal representation from Upper and Lower Canada, constitutional conventions, or unwritten rules, emerged that embedded dualism and the sharing of power. A double-majority principle required majorities of assemblymen from each of Lower Canada and Upper Canada to concur on major pieces of legislation. The ministry became a co-premiership, and many departments had two ministers, a francophone from Lower Canada and an anglophone from Upper Canada. This made coalition parties a sine qua non for sustaining the union and shepherding legislation, but political instability undermined this sociologically sound arrangement.

With responsible government attained, other more divisive issues came to the fore. Once the population of Upper Canada's anglophones exceeded that of Lower Canada's francophones in the 1850s, Upper Canada's Clear Grits, radical agrarian populists who were a reincarnation of the old radicals of the competing party of the late 1820s, demanded representation by population, rejecting equal regional representation. Deeming Baldwin too moderate, they forced his resignation and called for the secularization of the Crown lands reserved for the Anglican clergy, repeal of the law of primogeniture, free trade with the United States, and popular election for the three branches of the legislature. The Clear Grits made common cause in the legislature with Lower Canada's francophone *Parti rouge*, radical anti-clerical liberals in the European mould who endorsed American annexation of Canada. The alliance was tenuous, as the Grits were hostile to Catholicism and feared French domination. Nevertheless Grit leader George Brown came to accept the institutional dualism of French and English.

The coalition of conservatives that emerged in 1854 was a similarly uneasy alliance. It featured high Tories, Montreal's anglophone business elite who had signed an Annexation Manifesto in 1849, and moderate Tories like John A. Macdonald, the dominant political figure in the second half of the century. Macdonald's party designated itself the Liberal-Conservatives. As the most disciplined party, they were in government on their own or in alliance with others for all but two years between 1854 and 1867. Macdonald's aim was to build a big tent party, "to enlarge the bounds of our party," he wrote, "so as to embrace every person desirous of being counted as a progressive Conservative."[38] His government succeeded by making some concessions to the Reformers and forming an alliance with the francophone ultra-Catholic *Parti bleu*, grouped around George-Étienne Cartier and railway construction interests.

This coalition party arose in a context of international and domestic socio-economic changes that profoundly affected colonial politics. Union of the Canadas facilitated British finance and technical expertise for infrastructure development. The Irish famine and changing orthodoxies in economic thought led Britain to repeal its mercantilist Corn Laws in 1846, jeopardizing the exports of the British North American colonies. Britain then negotiated the 1854 Reciprocity Treaty with the United States on behalf of the colonies, reducing import duties and tariffs charged on goods exchanged. Largely Irish immigrant labour expanded the network of canals – by 1850, Lake Ontario steamships could reach Montreal, dramatically expanding trade – and built a galaxy of railways. A bill introduced by Cartier created possibly the world's costliest railway, the Grand Trunk, in which he was an investor and for which he acted as legal advisor. The Grand Trunk's yards and shops in the 1850s became the nucleus for the formation of a large, working-class residential district in Montreal.[39]

The American Civil War reverberated in the colonies as the United States emerged with the largest standing army in the world. American jingoists were predicting that the Stars and Stripes would soon fly from the Rio Grande to the North Pole. Simultaneously Britain, having withdrawn most of its military forces in 1855, looked to its colonials to contribute more for their own security. Taken aback at the defeat of Macdonald's militia bill of 1862, which was a response to border tensions roused by the Civil War, the British pursued greater disengagement from the colonies. Then the abrogation of the Reciprocity Treaty in 1866 by the Americans prompted leaders of the various colonies to think more positively about creating an east-west economic axis. These developments led to Confederation, which the British said would strengthen the credit rating of the new colony and ease its public debt woes; the Province of Canada's debt had doubled between 1855 and 1862.[40] Confederation represented a coalition of parties as well as colonies. It seemed logical that Macdonald's aptly named Liberal-Conservatives serve as the new dominion's first government.

Before Confederation, coalition parties had also appeared in the Atlantic colonies. As in the Province of Canada, they were elite accommodations, brokered arrangements among leaders and notables rather than reflections of popular will. And as in Canada, the coalition parties in the Atlantic region were troubled, uneasy, weak, wobbly, and relatively short-lived, because the parties were themselves loose, undisciplined amalgams of crusading interests subject to constantly shifting loyalties. In 1840 Nova Scotia's moderate Tories and Howe's Reformers had formed a coalition government that lasted until 1843. It faltered because the Reformers really believed in party government as it operated in Britain, and they knew that they would prevail in elections, given their upper hand in public opinion.

After Nova Scotia's coalition government fell apart, Howe labelled his party Liberals, which led the Tories to rebrand themselves as Conservatives. Howe, realizing the practical necessity of organizing as a party, compelled his opponents to organize similarly. The result was two more disciplined parties. After Whig-cum-Liberal Lord Grey became Britain's colonial secretary in 1846, he endorsed Reformer-cum-Liberal Howe's view of coalition government, rejecting it as unstable. A coalition party of sorts, however, re-emerged less than two decades later when Nova Scotia sent five delegates – three Conservatives and two Liberals – to negotiate at the Quebec conference on the road to Confederation. The delegates softened the roughest edges of their partisanship and bonded as a coalition party to negotiate in Nova Scotia's broader public interest, although most Nova Scotians opposed Confederation.[41] Macdonald's success in convincing the anti-confederate Howe to join his Liberal-Conservative government in 1869 spoke to his coalition-building skills, as did the inclusion in the government that year of Hincks, the co-founder in 1841 of the bi-national Reform Party in the Province of Canada.

In the quest for responsible government, New Brunswick's first premier, Charles Fisher, had embraced the idea of coalition government in the 1840s. A Reformer and friend of Howe's, he believed coalition was the best route to achieving responsible government, because "the growing influence of the liberals would in ten years give the liberals all without any violent movement."[42] Neither of the colony's embryonic and at times self-styled Liberal and Conservative parties had recognized leaders so, when responsible government came, the governor assembled some members of both parties into a kind of coalition government known as the "Governor's Party."[43]

In Newfoundland, responsible government came later, in 1855, but as elsewhere Liberals favoured and Conservatives opposed it. After 1861 the governing Conservatives realized that sharing the spoils of power was essential to avoiding insurrection or terrorism on the part of the Liberal Catholic minority, so they invited some Liberals into the cabinet. To de-radicalize Liberal partisans, the Conservatives established a system, which took on the status of a convention, of awarding patronage posts on a roughly proportional basis to Catholics and Protestants. Henceforth the parties were ad hoc coalitions of power-seekers, "cabals of politicians whose association with one another signified nothing more than their common desire to capture the government."[44] In Prince Edward Island, behind the times politically, two coalition governments appeared in the 1870s. One was the result of an election, which pitted a "Sectarian School" party against a "Free School" party, after which five Conservatives and four Liberals formed the government.[45]

The Consolidated Party: 1870s, 1880, 1890s: Conservatives and Liberals

The repatriation of British troops from their garrisons in Quebec, Ontario, and New Brunswick provided a backdrop to the development of a new distinct Canadian identity. After Confederation, the issues of union, land, and religion abated somewhat and the coalition party type gave way to the consolidated party. It emerged in the 1870s in a context of nation-building challenges. The economically integrative Inter-Colonial Railway, which Maritimers had demanded as a condition of Confederation, was completed in 1873. It promised expanded central Canadian markets for Maritime industries, but the reverse happened as Montreal industrialists captured the Maritime market.[46]

Electoral reform contributed to the rise of two consolidated parties. In the first three post-Confederation federal elections the governing

Conservatives staggered the dates of the elections in various constituencies for their own benefit; the adjacent constituencies of Toronto and York, for example, voted six weeks apart with open voting conducted over two days and the results of the first day's vote known before ballots were cast on the second day. After a federal Liberal government eliminated these gross abuses in the late 1870s, general elections took on a more national character, making the parties appear more like national parties; Canadians voted on the same day and the consolidated results, known almost immediately, determined which party would form the government.

In the consolidated party era, party strategy replaced factional intrigue. The Conservative and Liberal parties began to take shape as modern parties, striving to build national organizations that bridged the new federal-provincial divide. Initially with Confederation, MLAs could also serve as MPs. This boosted prospects for the consolidation of two national parties, Conservative and Liberal, contributing to the integration of the new federal parties with their provincial counterparts.

Macdonald's "Great Coalition" of Liberal-Conservatives, Brown's increasingly becalmed Clear Grits, and Cartier's *bleus* had all come undone. The newly refashioned Conservative and Liberal parties began to resemble national parties, as in England. Parties and factions with separate identities such as Reformers, Grits, the *rouge*, and Nova Scotia's anti-confederate Liberals came under the leadership of Liberal prime minster Alexander Mackenzie in the 1870s. These disparate elements shared a preference for provincial rights, their decentralist cause bolstered by constitutional rulings in the 1880s and 1890s by the Judicial Committee of the Privy Council, composed of British law lords.[47] Although they adopted the national Liberal party's label, the provincial Liberal parties were loosely organized, and the national Liberal party, as a federation of provincial parties, was more susceptible to internal dissension than Macdonald's Conservatives were.

Politics in Nova Scotia and Prince Edward Island exemplify how the coalition party gave way to the consolidated national party. In Nova Scotia more than two dozen Conservative MLAs had coalesced with four Liberals to endorse Confederation, while more than a dozen Liberals had united with four Conservatives to oppose it. These blocs contested the 1871 provincial and 1872 federal elections as the Confederate and anti-Confederate parties respectively. Although the anti-Confederates prevailed in both elections, both alliances crumbled by 1874 as Confederation became apparently irreversible. All the pro- and anti-Confederate Liberals and Conservatives returned to their original partisan homes with two of the formerly anti-Confederate Liberals joining Mackenzie's federal Liberal cabinet.[48]

A demonstration of the triumph of the consolidated party type in Prince Edward Island came in the 1878 federal election. Although PEI's Conservatives and Liberals sat together in government as a provincial coalition party, their cabinet ministers campaigned separately for their respective national parties.[49] The federal Conservatives eagerly welcomed Island Liberals as well as Conservatives into their fold, but the 1873 Pacific Scandal, in which Macdonald and other senior Conservatives received election funds in exchange for a contract to build the Canadian Pacific Railway, motivated PEI's provincial Liberals to throw their lot in with their federal namesakes.[50] Newfoundland, pinning its economic hopes on American rather than Canadian trade, spurned Confederation, but its two parties shared the names of the British and Canadian parties. Newfoundland's Liberal party took on the features of an organized modern party, as it had in Canada by century's end.[51]

The Conservatives, as the dominant group in the coalition cabinet that carried the Province of Canada into Confederation and as the government for most of the post-Confederation period, made use of the advantages of office. They dispensed largesse and patronage to secure and strengthen their party. Their privileged and superior position helped them cultivate alliances with political forces and parties in the new provinces of Manitoba, British Columbia, and especially PEI, where larger issues such as trade, finance, and communications began to displace local issues. However, the execution of Métis leader Louis Riel, followed by disputes over the funding of Catholic schools in Ontario, Manitoba, and New Brunswick weakened Quebec's dominant *bleu* Conservatives, strengthening the *rouge* Liberals of Wilfrid Laurier. He steered the party in a British liberal direction after becoming party leader in the 1880s. The French reacted against the federal Conservatives, who, as proud imperial federationists, dwelled on the sentimental and emotional attachments of Anglo-Canadians for Britain. They cheered Canada's membership in a globally federated, heterogeneous British Empire and they rallied in support of the mother country in the South African Anglo-Boer War.

In the provinces of Manitoba and British Columbia, admitted to Canada in 1870–1, as well as in those parts of the Northwest Territories destined to become Saskatchewan and Alberta in 1905, local politicians hesitated to identify with either national party. They feared jeopardizing their overriding priorities – completion of the CPR and securing federal assistance during the global recession of the 1870s and 1880s – if a national party other than the one they were inclined to support were to win office. Candidates in those provinces generally ran in support of the ministry and "any ministry would do.... They were always 'agin' the opposition."[52] With the completion of the CPR in the 1880s, Ontarian pioneers brought their Conservative and Liberal loyalties with them and served as architects of the West's provincial parties. By the 1890s they had allied with their federal kin, contributing to the consolidation of the two national parties.

Media also contributed to the entrenchment of the consolidated party type. By the 1890s every major city in the dominion, from Halifax to Victoria, had at least one Conservative and one Liberal newspaper. They served as unabashed party organs, hailing their preferred party leader and vilifying or ignoring the opposition party and its leader. Publishers and journalists had long been associated with parties, but during the consolidated party era the focus of press reporting was increasingly on the national parties and issues of national policy. Party-affiliated newspapers constituted more than half of the total circulation of newspapers nationally. In reward for their loyalty, the governing party showered newspapers that supported it with printing contracts. For example, when the Conservatives held office in the 1890s, the Saint John *Sun* received $55,000 from Ottawa but only $1,200 afterwards. The Liberals, in turn, gave the Saint John *Telegraph*, which had received nothing from the Conservatives, $45,000 in business after they took office in 1896.[53]

The careers of two premiers, Hugh John Macdonald and Oliver Mowat, exemplified the integrated federal-provincial consolidated party. Macdonald, the prime minister's son, became the leader of the Manitoba Conservative party in the 1890s after having served in the federal Conservative cabinet. Ontario's Mowat and three other provincial Liberals premiers joined Laurier's federal cabinet. Mowat's provincial party, which he had brought to power in 1872, helped sustain the federal Liberals during their years in opposition, just as Macdonald's governing federal Conservatives had helped sustain their provincial kin.

Patronage served as an important cementing agent of the consolidated party, as it had for the court party and the coalition party earlier in the century. Laurier's Liberals stood for policies different from the Conservatives', but their modus operandi in dispensing patronage as governments was similar. The "loose fish" and "shaky fellows" – terms Macdonald and Brown had used to describe MPs whose partisan allegiances could be easily swayed – became fewer. New parties such as Ontario's Patrons of Industry, a farmers' movement, and the anti-Catholic

Protestant Protective Association, both of which elected MPPs in the 1890s, faded quickly. They were victims of the consolidated party type, caught "between the two regular parties as a flock of sheep between two packs of wolves," noted journalist Goldwin Smith.[54]

Between the beginning and the end of the nineteenth century, a set of far-flung and diverse British colonies and territories came together; Canada emerged as a new state on the world stage. A succession of four distinct party types paved the path to and beyond the achievement of nationhood. At the beginning of the century, an unelected, hierarchical, and undemocratic court party had ruled. By century's end, after the appearance of competing and coalition party types, two stable, more disciplined, consolidated parties appeared; they linked party leaders and supporters across the federal-provincial divide. As national parties, the Conservatives and Liberals came to offer competing images of Canada and its place in the world.

Chapter Two

Imperialism, Continentalism, Nationalism

One Flag, One Throne, One Empire[1]

Imperial Order Daughters of the Empire

Confederation was the signal event marking the beginning of national party politics in Canada. Soon after, the Liberal and Conservative parties offered competing nationalist visions. Their contending narratives originated earlier; indeed, they predate Confederation, but empire versus continent became the central motif of party politics between the 1890s and 1930s, an era that corresponded with Britain's decline, Canada's independence, and the emergence of an American empire.

Britannia ruled the minds of both Conservatives and Liberals, but generally speaking the Liberals saw Canada's position in the world in North American and at times isolationist terms, while the Conservatives saw Canada as part of a global enterprise, the British imperial system with Canada as its leading affiliate. The expansion of Confederation made both visions viable; they coexisted in both parties but in different measure. Shining light on these rival accounts of what Canada was and could be reveals the power of the imperialist-continentalist debate driving party politics a century ago.

Motivated by opposition to a customs union with the United States in which there would be free trade between the two countries and a common tariff on imports, an Imperial Federation League formed in the 1880s. It advocated for an imperial parliament composed of Britain and the self-governing members of the empire. Conservatives of the imperial school depicted Canada's acquired territories, Rupert's Land and the Northwest Territories, as outposts of the British Empire.[2] Prime minister John A. Macdonald looked dubiously at some of the preachers of imperial federation but, like them, his Conservatives celebrated

Canada as an imperial citadel. Fancifully, some imperial federationists like philosopher W.D. Lighthall, the mayor of Westmount, thought Canada would become "the future and dominating portion of the British Empire."[3] An 1898 Canadian stamp conveyed the idea graphically: a map of the world with the British Empire in red, Canada in the centre, and the inscription "We Hold A Vaster Empire Than Has Ever Been."

"Imperialism," noted Carl Berger, "was a form of Canadian nationalism,"[4] but no less nationalist was the Liberal vision of Canada's destiny. Liberal intellectuals in the "Canada First" movement of the 1870s, which included future party leader Edward Blake, portrayed Britain as having betrayed Canada's interests in the Treaty of Washington of 1871 by opening Canadian waters to American fishermen and granting the United States free navigation in the St. Lawrence River.[5] The Canada Firsters argued that a more self-interested and independent Canada would strengthen rather than weaken the empire. Goldwin Smith, a self-described "Liberal of the old school"[6] steeped in Manchester liberalism, who had come to North America as a kind of envoy of the British Liberal party, revealed the mix of convictions that swirled about in late nineteenth-century Canada; intellectually vigorous and brilliant, he exhibited imperialist, nationalist, and annexationist inclinations at different times.

Conservatives and Liberals shared an exalted view of the virtues of the British constitutional system. They deemed it superior to that of the United States, and Britain's parties served as models for them, from their names to the social classes associated with them. As in Britain, those of established wealth, rank, and authority identified more readily with the Conservatives, while those of the parvenu and aspiring classes more likely associated with the Liberals. In both Britain and Canada, the Liberal party was less enamoured than were Conservatives with class distinctions.

The British cast of Canada's dominant political class produced a deferential attitude to things British; both parties spoke with solemn respect of Britain's guidance in the advancement of Canada. Nevertheless, both parties also parted from older dependent outlooks over time. Despite their praise for the merits of the British connection, neither party hesitated to distance itself from the parochialism and insularity of British society or British policy. Increasingly, Canadians saw themselves as an imperial people rather than as colonials and handmaidens to Britain. Macdonald, for example, who had once described Canadians as a "subordinate" people,[7] dashed British hopes that he would dispatch troops for Britain's Sudan campaign in aid of Egyptian forces in the 1880s. Liberal leader Wilfrid Laurier expressed a nationalism containing a "strong sense of North American pacifist isolationism," a sentiment shared by most Anglo-Canadian Liberals and virtually all French Canadians.[8]

Anglo-Canadians in both parties believed in the innate racial superiority of Britons and the civilizing effect of British colonialism. Most judge French Canadians a priest-ridden, backward, illiterate people, a drag on national development. Some in both parties, however, considered the French a natural ally. Conservatives could identify cultural qualities in the French Canadians that made them pillars of an organic, stable, and orderly society: their Christian faith, hierarchical values, loyalty to the Crown, rootedness in the soil, and suspicion of industrialization and urbanization. Some Liberals like Blake, who at first vilified French Canadians, came to accept them as a cultural nation and courted them by opposing a Conservative bill in 1884 to incorporate the fiercely anti-Catholic Orange Order, which Macdonald had joined before Confederation.[9]

Both the Conservatives and Liberals accepted capitalism as their economic paradigm, but those placing individual freedom ahead of the interests of collectivities such as social classes tended to gravitate to the Liberal camp. Both parties had agreed on the Confederation project, but they viewed the venture differently: Conservatives projected the emergence of a new state-guided national economic empire; Liberals, as apostles of unfettered competitive free markets, envisioned private entrepreneurial opportunities in an expanding Canada. As fiscal conservatives, the Liberals consistently opposed the deficit financing and public indebtedness the Conservatives relied on to drive their nation-building agenda.[10] Leading politicians in both parties had close links to corporate interests, with the Liberals declaring in 1888 in favour of unrestricted free trade with the United States, and the Conservatives expressing fears it would jeopardize the possibility of free trade within the empire.[11]

The Conservatives respected and honoured traditional ways and were more apt than the Liberals to speak of moral values, self-sacrifice, and military spirit. Some conservative imperial federationists like Castell Hopkins were contemptuous of crass materialism, even expressing concern about social atomization.[12] They romanticized the past but accepted the popular idea of progress. Liberal continentalists were more tolerant of the ambitiousness of the self-made man and massive industrialization; they also exhibited less fondness for military training and service than the Conservatives. They believed with certitude that an innate possessive individualism motivates behaviour, that as the proprietor of his skills the individual owes nothing to society for them. Adam Smith's dictum that the "invisible hand" of the market produces the greatest happiness for the greatest number of people attracted Liberals. They championed the freedom of individuals to acquire and accumulate, to have, and to hold. Less than a century later, Liberals and Conservatives came to reverse their views of the individual, with Conservatives assigning a higher priority to the individual than the community, defining community as the sum of self-governing, equally free-willed individuals.

A version of the continentalist-imperialist debate among nationalists also played out in the discourse of French Canadians. The *rouge*-affiliated liberal Institut Canadien, founded in the 1840s by young liberal professionals, had folded in the 1870s, but its semi-republican nationalism lived on in the belief that Quebec was the homeland of all French Canadians. Quebec's Catholic hierarchy shared the view of Quebec as a French fortress but disdained republicanism because of its association with the materialism and anti-clericalism of liberalism. The church believed that the existing Canadian regime best served French Canadians both within and outside the province. Preferring consensus over conflict, the Liberals under both Wilfrid Laurier and his successor Mackenzie King proved more sensitive to French Canadian sensibilities than Macdonald's successors.

The 1890s

By the 1890s the transcontinental Canadian Pacific Railway had been completed, the worldwide depression of the 1870s had abated, and threat of invasion or annexation by the United States was effectively extinguished. Nevertheless American bravado undercut continentalist sentiments in Canada. For French sociologist André Siegfried little in the way of ideas and policies differentiated the Liberals and Conservatives,[13] but that was not the public's perception: in the prologue to the 1891 election the imperialist-continentalist debate took centre stage. The "question of the British Empire versus 'the Continent to which we belong' was the dominant and absorbing matter," according to Castell Hopkins. It was, in short, "the principles of British unity, British commerce, and British sympathy as against Continental unity, Continental trade, and Continental sympathy."[14]

American legislation in 1890 increased the tariff on cereals, Canada's primary export to the United States. This allowed Macdonald, who considered British and Canadian economic interests identical, to argue that the Liberal proposal in 1891 for free trade or "unrestricted reciprocity" with the Americans meant discriminating against Britain; it was "veiled treason."[15] A Conservative election campaign poster polemically depicted the sale of Canada into slavery to the United States. Laurier, who on another occasion proclaimed, "I hope to live my life a British subject and as a British subject die,"[16] countered that it was "folly to expect, that the interests of a Colony should always be identical with the interests of the Motherland." In a clash between them, he said, "much as I would regret the necessity, I would stand by my native land."[17] However, the Conservative party's refrain, "The Old Flag, the Old Policy, the Old Leader," played well with the public and they prevailed in the election. One historian contends that "the perpetuation and longevity of the British-Canadian view of Canada in the twentieth-century political arena are specifically the legacy of Sir John A. Macdonald and this election."[18]

The assertions that free trade meant inevitable annexation by the United States resonated with English Canadians. The chief advocate of unrestricted trade, renegade Tory and former Liberal finance minister Richard Cartwright, proposed that Canada serve as a linchpin between Britain and the United States in "An Alliance Between English-Speaking Nations."[19] This vision of an Anglosphere based on language and not on the British constitutional framework contrasted with the idea of empire envisioned by the imperial federationists whose ranks included some Liberals. Soon-to-be Conservative prime minister John Thompson suggested that Cartwright would become an American senator from the State of Ontario if free trade prevailed.[20]

Blake, who had sought to keep moderate protectionists within the Liberal party, undercut the party's free trade position the day after the 1891 election when an explosive letter he had penned earlier appeared in the press: it denounced free trade as subverting political independence and leading to unavoidable political union.[21] If the Liberals were to escape their status as perpetual opposition, their identification with free trade required moderation, so in 1893 they watered down their position by calling for "limited" free trade, accepting tariffs as strictly a revenue measure.

Undermining and sapping Canadian support for free trade, the platform of the Republicans in the United States issued a week before Canada's 1896 election called for imposing new tariffs on Canadian exports. In the election, language and religious schooling issues superseded the imperialist/continentalist question as primary but the question did not fade; the Conservatives led by Charles Tupper, who had endorsed the idea of Dominion cabinet ministers sitting in the Imperial Cabinet, proposed "the ultimate union of Britain and her colonies in one imperial whole."[22] With the shrewd Macdonald no longer at the Conservative helm, Laurier's Liberals prevailed even though they received fewer votes than the Conservatives; a Liberal landslide in Quebec made the difference.

Laurier acknowledged at a Liberal convention that there are "those of us who are attached to the Empire [and] those who are not" but he was keen "to avoid exciting subjects on which we [Liberals] may not be united."[23] He catered to imperialist feelings in 1897 by lowering the tariff on British goods and then, after admitting that in his view the Boers represented "no menace to Canada,"[24] acceded to the cacophonous demands in the English Canadian press in 1899 that volunteer Canadian troops be dispatched to the South African Boer War. It proved to be "the decisive event in the history of Canadian imperialism ... testimony to the growing strength of the imperial cause."[25] The Conservatives used the war to appeal to imperialist sentiments and "for high Tory loyalism ... with all guns blazing."[26] Anti-Americanism also fuelled the imperialist cause; in British Columbia, for example, legislation required miners, many of whom were Americans, to become British subjects.[27]

Given the imperial sentiments among English Canadians, whose numbers grew dramatically after 1896 with new waves of immigrants, Laurier's Boer War decision was politic. Although unpopular among French Canadians, the War hardly affected them; almost all the troops were English Canadians. Nevertheless, Laurier's decision stirred to action a protest movement led by the popular French Canadian nationalist Liberal MP Henri Bourassa who shunned closer imperial ties. One observer noted that refusing to aid the British, though tempting to Laurier, would have been "fatal" electorally "but he recovered his judgment in time."[28] Influential Liberal Israel Tarte of Quebec adopted the federationist notion that Canadian participation in an imperial war required representation in an imperial parliament.[29]

Lingering fear of American bellicosity bolstered the imperialist narrative of the Conservatives. At the same time, American belligerence on the world stage quieted talk among continentalist Liberals of Canada's destiny being tied more closely to that of the United States than to Britain; the increasingly truculent republic had intervened in the Cuban war of independence, declared war on Spain, took control of Puerto Rico and the Philippines, and annexed Hawaii. A pugnacious United States made it less attractive to Canadians as did violent outbreaks, many related to labour unrest, in the republic's small communities and cities. Lynching, a common phenomenon which peaked in the 1890s, was also alien to Canadian sensibilities.

The 1900s

Although the Boer War continued to hound the Liberals as the new century began, they won the 1900 election handily. French Canadian Conservatives criticized Laurier in Quebec for having sent troops while English Canadian Conservatives condemned him in Ontario for having hesitated to do so. The English-language media vilified him and the Québécois. In general, Laurier, who was powerless to do much about it, attributed these attacks to the Conservatives, accusing them of trading in imperialism and racial bigotry for partisan advantage.[30] Although the Liberal government had to defer to British foreign policy, it opposed attempts to establish a centralized imperial foreign policy; Laurier, for example, rebuffed Britain's pleas at the Colonial Conference of 1902 to establish a unified imperial defence scheme and an Imperial Council to act as a sort of quasi-Imperial Parliament. The Liberals also did what they could to limit the implications for Canada, especially for British Columbia, of the 1902 Anglo-Japanese Alliance prohibiting discrimination against Japanese immigrants.[31]

After Britain had once again sacrificed Canadian interests in the 1903 Alaska boundary dispute, Laurier concluded that British diplomacy had been untrustworthy. A Canadian official, quoted anonymously in the London Economist, compared Canada to "animals doomed to vivisection for the benefit of science ... operated on unsparingly for the good of the Empire."[32] Laurier told the Canadian Manufacturers Association that "in so far as Canada is concerned ... it is a repetition of sacrifices of Canadian interests."[33] Laurier also remonstrated against the conservative imperialist elevation of soldierly virtues and the Victorian manly ideal that emphasized character and Protestant virtue. His indictment of war and his fear of Canada being drawn into a maelstrom of militarism were consistent with the thinking in the robust international pacifist movement of the day. Laurier succeeded in keeping Quebec in the Liberal camp and because of that the Liberals retained office in the 1904 and 1908 elections.

Although the affection of English Canadians for their mother country drove political calculations, it did not override the differing orientations to Empire and continent of the political parties. The Dundonald affair exemplified the contrast, with the Conservatives looking to the British and Laurier looking to the United States. Britain had sent the Earl of Dundonald to command and reorganize the Canadian militia, but in their first meeting, Laurier told him not to "take the militia seriously for ... it will not be required for the defence of the country as the Monroe Doctrine protects us against enemy aggression."[34] After Dundonald criticized the minister of militia in 1904 for interfering for political purposes with the appointment of some officers to a new corps, and the Canadian and London press hotly debated the issue, the Liberal government dismissed Dundonald, describing his action as "an attack on the system of constitutional government in Canada."[35] This terminated the practice of Imperial officers commanding the militia. Meanwhile,

Dundonald's name was cheered whenever it was mentioned at Conservative meetings across the country.

Conservative imperialists persisted in envisioning a British Empire that harmonized the aspirations of its member colonies and Dominions in a larger political community. Edith Boulton Nordheimer for example, granddaughter of Family Compact Conservative D'Arcy Boulton, served as the founding president of the Imperial Order Daughters of the Empire, which adopted the motto "One Flag, One Throne, One Empire" upon its formation in 1901. Two years later, Brigadier General and future Conservative senator James Mason founded the Empire Club, whose cornerstone purpose, like that of the IODE, was to strengthen the imperial bond. Yet another ardent and particularly influential imperialist, "a Tory in the precapitalist sense [who] valued the community over the individual [and] organic growth over radical change," was the popular writer and political economist Stephen Leacock, who revelled in pillorying Liberal politicians.[36] An active Conservative, he criticized the hunger for wealth and the materialism pervading Canadian society.[37]

On the eve of the 1907 Imperial Conference – earlier gatherings of government leaders from the self-governing colonies and dominions of the empire had been termed Colonial Conferences – Leacock pleaded for "something other than independence, nobler than annexation, greater in purpose than a Little Canada."[38] Conference delegates, including Laurier, agreed to support and contribute to the Royal Navy, but they also decided that the dominions would enjoy autonomy in military matters.[39] This ambiguous formulation permitted Liberal procrastination until the 1909 "naval scare" – fear of Germany's navy overtaking Britain's – returning the imperial issue to the centre of the political stage. With war clouds forcing Laurier's hand, he responded by creating a Canadian navy controlled by Ottawa but with a provision for its transfer to the British Admiralty in a military emergency.

Because of the long-standing identification of the Liberals with freer trade, western farmers became a pillar of party support; with free trade, they would be able to buy cheaper American farm machinery and gain unfettered access to a large, easily accessible market. Agrarian pressure on the Liberals led to limited free trade negotiations but came to naught. Urged on by Liberal protectionists in the government like Tarte, and by Conservative leader Robert Borden's advocacy of a "constitutional means of ... mutual preferential trade within the Empire,"[40] the Liberals moved in the direction of economic nationalism, adopting an intermediate tariff that fell between the imperial preferential rate and the general rate.

The Liberals boasted of a booming economy, a fiscal budget in surplus, and spectacular gains in trade and population in a context of peace. For a brief period, 1903–4, Winnipeg's Union Bank building was the tallest in the empire, and Canada's own empire expanded with the creation in 1905 of Saskatchewan and Alberta – the population of the former growing by 439 per cent and of the latter by 413 per cent in the decade. Parliament reserved for itself, however, control of the natural resources of the Prairie provinces. Like a political emperor, Laurier appointed Liberal lieutenants governor in the new provinces who, in turn, called on Liberals to form the first provincial governments. With plans for another transcontinental railway, Laurier offered a grandiose view of Canada, suggesting it would become an economic transmission belt between Europe and Asia, with northern British Columbia's unlikely Port Simpson as a centre for exports and imports.[41]

As Empire Canada grew, ties to the British Empire loosened steadily. Simultaneously, American models, money, and movements increasingly influenced Canadian society. As one example, a Chicago millionaire soap-maker financed, and an Oregonian organized, the Direct Legislation League of Manitoba, "one more instance in the long series of American influences on political thought and custom in Canada."[42] On the agrarian and political fronts, American organizations such as the Society of Equity and the Non-Partisan League spread into Canada as had their forerunner, the Patrons of Industry, in the 1890s. American Progressivist reform causes such as proportional representation, empowering municipalities, abolishing property qualifications for voters, the scientific management of industry and government, and direct legislation – giving the public the power to participate directly in making laws – became particularly popular among western Liberals and other self-styled progressives.

Similarly, American unions extended their hold over the English Canadian labour movement. Many workers, however, especially recent British immigrants, rallied to the cause of nascent urban labour parties. Encouraged by British Labour party luminaries Keir Hardie and Ramsay MacDonald in their tours of Canada in 1906–7, these embryonic parties subscribed to British Labour's model of direct parliamentary action by labour parties rather than the non-partisan "reward your friends and punish your enemies" strategy of the American Federation of Labor.

The 1910s

As Laurier's Liberals had dominated the 1900s, Robert Borden's Conservatives dominated the 1910s. The landmark election of 1911, like that of 1891, revolved around freer continental trade in English Canada, while the main issue in French Quebec was perceived Canadian

servility to British imperialism. The popular Leacock's public addresses and well-crafted exhortations – he was the world's best-selling
humourist in the English language – contributed to the unanticipated
election defeat of the Liberals. As in 1891, the election featured contending identities: imperial, continental, and national, with Leacock hailing
the Conservative outcome in the British press as an "earnest wish for an
enduring union with the Empire."[43]

When Laurier toured western Canada in 1910, he received petitions in
favour of free trade at every stop, and nearly a thousand farmers came to
Parliament to demand it in a "Siege of Ottawa."[44] Changed sentiments
in the United States regarding free trade delighted the Liberals and led
to a quickly negotiated draft agreement between the two countries. In
a reprise of their opposition in the 1891 election, the federal Conservatives vigorously opposed the scheme; Borden declared that Canadians
"must decide whether the spirit of Canadianism or of Continentalism
shall prevail on the northern half of this continent."[45] The Conservative platform contended that the United States sought "to prevent [the]
consolidation of the British Empire,"[46] and the party issued campaign
posters once again implying free trade would lead to annexation.

In the campaign, central Canadian captains of finance and industry in
both parties fed a firestorm of anti-Americanism, blanketing the country
with pamphlets containing anti–free trade tracts and cartoons, bolstering
their argument with the club of empire. Liberal Sir Edmund Walker, president of the Bank of Commerce, a derider of the "extreme democracy"
of the United Sates, warned of the "evil ... of the giant American trusts."
Opponents of free trade framed the issue as Walker did, "between British
connection and what has been well called Continentalism ... between the
dangers of Americanization [and] ... the safe home of Empire."[47]

Quebec's Henri Bourassa supported free trade as a blow to the imperial idea.[48] However, he and Quebec's Conservative francophone
nationalists objected both to the creation of a Canadian navy and the
Liberal promise to transfer it to British command in an emergency.
Bourassa also rejected Borden's proposal in his Naval Aid Bill of 1912 to
contribute financially to the construction of three British battleships. In
light of Canada's development, however – the population had grown
by 26 per cent in the preceding decade and Canada was soon to have its
own minister of colonization – Borden had also proposed that Britain
share defence responsibilities with the dominions, since "the highest
future for this Dominion lies within this Empire upon conditions of
equal status."[49] Liberal senators, however, killed Borden's naval bill after he had used, for the first time in a Canadian parliament, closure – a
procedural device ending debate – to pass the bill in the Commons.

Both Conservative and Liberal governments moved Canada steadily in a more independent direction but framed greater independence differently. Borden argued Canada would gain greater autonomy by playing a larger role within the empire, and he presented the separate representation of Canada at international conferences in 1912 and in 1914 as strengthening the empire.[50] The Liberals, in contrast, regarded such representation positively as distancing Canada from the empire.

When war broke out in 1914, English Canadians rallied instinctively and faithfully to Britain's side. Many Conservatives believed that by "sharing in the burdens and responsibility of the Empire, Canadians could best develop and nurture their own nationalism."[51] The Liberals initially supported the Conservative war effort, with some Liberals like John Dafoe, the influential editor of the *Manitoba Free Press*, insisting that "Canada was in the war as a principal," not as a colony but as a state.[52] As the war dragged on, however, Laurier's Liberals opposed Borden's plans for conscription. His plans led to bloody riots, including some deaths, in Quebec and voter realignments within both parties.[53] Most of Laurier's English MPs deserted him and rallied in support of Borden's "Unionist" government, a coalition of Conservatives and defecting Liberals. The Conservatives won only three seats in Quebec in the 1917 election. The Québécois saw the war as Britain's, not Canada's. Insensitive recruitment practices and the poor treatment of French-Canadian volunteers in the war effort further alienated French Canada from the Conservatives. Estranged too were farmers; lifting their exemption from conscription led to another march on Ottawa and laid a foundation for the Progressive Party, which became the second-largest party in Parliament in the 1921 election.

The war imploded empires, numbering the days of the British Empire. One result of the war was Canada's exit from the cocoon of British colonialism but not its strong ties to Britain. Although Borden took the lead among the dominion prime ministers and played a considerable role in hammering out much of the Treaty of Versailles, Canada's signature, like those of the other dominions, appeared under the heading of the British delegation.[54] Tens of thousands of Canadian deaths frayed filial imperial ties and encouraged isolationism. Having imposed conscription, the Conservatives won no seats in Quebec in the 1921 election and came to hold office for only six years between then and 1957. The war also dispelled whatever rosy view some tory Conservatives may have had of French Quebec's conservatism; except for 1930, in the elections between 1917 and 1953, Quebec yielded the party no more than five seats.

English Canadians, including the labour-socialists, continued to value the British connection. Suspicion of the United States lingered among Conservatives. Many of them viewed Canada as a more stable and orderly society because loyalty under a common Crown did not require political conformity. They viewed America's republican society as weak, subject to popular impulse, riven by racial discord, and contemptuous of law and order, so they opposed what they deemed populist republican schemes. After western Liberals clamoured for direct legislation – allowing voters to introduce legislation through petition – Manitoba's Conservative premier, Sir Rodmond Roblin, dismissed it as an "Un-British Plan," a form of "degenerate republicanism."[55]

The 1920s

English Canada's cultural heritage and institutional infrastructure remained British, and Borden's successor, Arthur Meighen, considered Canada "an active partner in a great imperial enterprise."[56] Nevertheless Canada's economy became progressively tethered to that of the United States. Consistent with the Liberal vision of Canada as first and foremost a North American nation, continental economic integration proceeded rapidly. Americans replaced British capitalists in the 1920s as Canada's principal financiers.[57] Moreover, while British investment had been largely indirect in the form of portfolio investment – the purchase of Canadian government and corporate bonds – American corporations created subsidiaries; companies such General Motors and Westinghouse appeared on Canadian soil to avoid tariffs. Technological changes also spurred economic integration. Few branch lines of either Canadian or American railways crossed the forty-ninth parallel, for example, but the rise of the automobile in the 1920s led to many new north-south highways traversing the boundary.

The 1921 election ushered in the Age of Mackenzie King, someone much connected to the United States; his rebel grandfather William Lyon Mackenzie had escaped there, his mother was born there, he had studied at Harvard and the University of Chicago, and he had worked for American financier John D. Rockefeller Jr. King's research for Rockefeller became his book *Industry and Humanity*.[58] He and his trusted advisor, Laurier's biographer O.D. Skelton, were sceptical about tying Canada too closely to Britain and steered the country away from the remaining vestiges of colonial status to sovereign state.

King shifted Canada's foreign policy orientation from imperial cooperation and obligations to guarding Canadian autonomy. By now both political parties subscribed firmly to Canada's autonomy but they, like Canada, were torn between the pressure of American geography and British history. The Conservatives re-pledged their "firm adherence to British connection in full confidence that Canada will find its amplest scope for development, usefulness and influence as a member of the Britannic commonwealth," while the Liberals once again "resolved that we are strongly opposed to centralized Imperial control."[59] A military crisis involving Britain and Turkish forces threatening British rule in the Dardanelles in 1922 highlighted the differences of the Liberals and Conservatives in relation to British interests. Britain issued a call for military support in its standoff with Turkey and blithely assumed that Canada would respond. King, however, did not consider Canada tied to the dictates of imperial foreign policy. Meighen rebuked him: "Canada should have said: 'Ready, aye, ready; we stand by you.'"[60]

The Imperial Conference of 1923 endorsed Canada's negotiation and signing of the Halibut Treaty, concerning fishing rights in the northern Pacific Ocean, with the United States without British participation, and King broke with Britain, Australia, and New Zealand on issuing a common foreign policy statement. Emphasizing aloofness from the Old World – a sentiment shared by many Canadians in the 1920s – Liberal Senator Raoul Dandurand, King's delegate to the League of Nations, likened Canada to "a fire-proof house, far from inflammable materials. A vast ocean separates us from Europe."[61] King termed the league a "League of Notions"[62] and appointed Canada's first ever envoy with full diplomatic credentials to a foreign capital, Washington, in 1926. An Imperial Conference that year gave its imprimatur to King's vision of a non-imperial association of Britain's former colonies as self-governing equal members of a new British Commonwealth of Nations. In the 1926 election, the Liberals became a majority government by denouncing British Governor General Lord Byng; in their view, he acted as a colonial governor instead of a constitutional figurehead in appointing a Conservative government after having refused King's request for a fresh election.

Like Richard Cartwright in the 1890s, King styled Canada as a linchpin and "interpreter" between Britain and the United States. After his election as an MP in 1908, King sailed to London to express the concern of the American as well as the Canadian government about Japanese immigration to North America.[63] King catered to North American isolationism by telling American audiences that Canadians and Americans settled their differences amicably through arbitration, mediation, and conciliation, implicitly criticizing the Europeans, including the British, for having settled differences by waging war. At the same time, King ingratiated himself to British audiences by comparing the freedom of the dominions with the freedom of the city of London.[64]

The 1930s and Beyond

The imperial meme collapsed in the 1920s; by the 1930s, it was spent, acknowledged constitutionally by the Statute of Westminster. It established the legislative independence of the self-governing dominions. English-Canadian identification with Britain, however, persisted. As a telling indicator of continuing Conservative affinity, their campaign slogan in the 1930 election was "Canada first, then the Empire."[65] Prime Minster R.B. Bennett expressed his personal attraction for Britain by becoming the only prime minister to retire, die, and be buried there. During his term of office, however, Canada became even more economically dependent on trade with the United States after his attempted pivot towards more imperial trade failed.[66]

Under both Liberal and Conservative regimes, Canada became a military and economic partner to an American behemoth. On constitutional issues, Canada's Supreme Court became supreme in fact as well as name in 1949. Militarily, Canada pursued intimate links with its southern neighbour. They included a Permanent Joint Board on Defence, the Alaska Highway project, a Defence Production Sharing Agreement, the North American Aerospace Defence Command (NORAD), the stationing of American air force personnel at the high Arctic radar stations of the Distant Early Warning Line, and the testing of American cruise missiles on Canadian soil during the Cold War. By the early 1970s, 37 per cent of Canada's corporate non-financial assets and nearly 60 per cent of its manufacturing sector were foreign, largely American, owned. Parodying liberal nationalist historian Arthur Lower's *From Colony to Nation*, Harold Innis described Canada as having gone "from colony to nation to colony."[67]

Echoing Meighen, Conservative leader John Diefenbaker in 1956 criticized the Liberals for not standing with Britain in the Suez Crises, and his government, formed the following year, highlighted Canada's membership in the Commonwealth. He broke with the United States on the Cuban missile crisis and the stationing in Canada of their Bomarc missiles with nuclear-fitted warheads, which the Liberals supported. Diefenbaker charged that replacing the Red Ensign, featuring the Union Jack and used since 1868 as a Canadian flag, by the Liberal-sponsored Maple Leaf flag in 1965 denied Canada's British heritage. As a sign of the further distancing between Canada and Britain, Canadians lost their status as British subjects in the 1980s.

The trope of empire and continent resurfaced when Pierre Trudeau's Liberals proposed patriating Canada's Constitution and including in it a Charter of Rights. Manitoba's Conservative premier, Sterling Lyon, assaulted the proposal as a move to "a republican system ... an experiment with a concept foreign to our tradition."[68] It meant discarding the constitutional philosophy of 1867, he said, and embracing that of 1776. Alerted to Lyon's objections and the concerns of a number of provinces that a Charter of Rights would limit their powers, Britain's Foreign Affairs Committee hesitated to endorse Ottawa's proposed unilateral patriation of the Constitution. Trudeau responded by sarcastically referring to the title of the then popular film, *The Empire Strikes Back*.[69]

Conservative prime minister Brian Mulroney and Liberal leader John Turner reversed the historical positions of their parties vis-à-vis the United States in 1988. Mulroney had promised to be a "better ally, a super ally"[70] and negotiated a historic free trade agreement. Turner's Liberals condemned it as imperilling Canadian sovereignty; Liberal television ads showed a pencil erasing the forty-ninth parallel. Although he spurned the Commonwealth as a talking shop, Conservative prime minister Stephen Harper opened joint Canada-British diplomatic missions abroad. In contrast, former Liberal deputy prime minister John Manley called for an end to the monarchy, and over one-third of delegates at a Liberal convention in 2012 voted to study severing ties with the "British Crown."[71]

Between the 1890s and 1930s the British Empire dissolved, Canadian-American ties intensified, and a flood of non-British immigrants arrived; the population expanded from fewer than five to well over ten million, and Canada evolved from a rural to an urban nation. The uncertainties that followed the First World War and the onset of the Depression pricked the bubbles of political verities. In this context, new political parties appeared, and the duopoly of the Conservatives and Liberals, the "old-line parties," came to be challenged. The two-party system gave way to a multi-party system.

Chapter Three

Industrialization, Urbanization, and Depression: The Rise of Third Parties

The competitive system must be transformed into a cooperative system.[1]
United Church of Canada

The end of the First World War triggering inflation, high unemployment, and rising industrial unionism signalled the coming of a new era in party politics. The rise of third parties challenging the duopoly of the Liberals and Conservatives proved to be the most distinctive feature of party politics in the 1920s and 1930s.

The tumultuous 1920s and 1930s ushered in social, economic, and geopolitical conditions leading to voter realignments and new political parties more radical than the Liberals and Conservatives. In the 1921 election, for the first time since Confederation, neither of the older parties held a majority of the seats in the House of Commons. Since that watershed election in which the Progressive party became the second-largest party, the strength of third parties has led to more than a third of federal elections producing minority governments. The conduct and administration of elections has also changed; in 1920 Parliament created a chief electoral officer independent of the government and the political parties. Women also gained the right to vote. A decade later, the onset of the Depression following the stock market crash of 1929 set the stage for the rise of two third parties sturdier than the Progressives: the CCF and Social Credit.

The backdrop to these transformative events was Canada's full entry into the modern era. Most Canadians were rural residents in 1911; by 1921 most were urban. Elevators led to skyscrapers, and automobiles proliferated; registrations ballooned from 2,000 in 1907, to 276,000 in 1918, to 1.2 million in 1929. In the 1920s new industries in Ontario and Quebec produced home appliances such as vacuum cleaners, refrigerators, washing machines, and radios. Labour organizations increased in number as did the size of the non-agricultural paid workforce. The wheat economy, in contrast, experienced boom and bust. Canadian wheat exports, accounting for about half of world wheat exports in the late 1920s, were devastated during the Depression by drought, protected foreign markets, and depressed prices.[2]

Because of Canada's dependence on farm and raw material exports, the Depression affected it more severely than most countries. Between 1929 and 1933 gross domestic product deceased by over 40 per cent.[3] At the nadir of the Depression, a bushel of wheat fetched its lowest recorded price since the sixteenth century.[4] Both immigration and the birth rate plummeted. Despite grim rural conditions, however, the momentum of urbanization in the 1930s was retarded as many returned to rural areas to escape inadequate government relief in the cities. By and large the federal Liberal and Conservative governments considered the provinces and their municipalities responsible for the plight of the distressed and unemployed, driving the western provinces into bankruptcy. Poor conditions in federal relief work camps for the unemployed saw the communist-led Workers Unity League organize an On to Ottawa Trek of more than a thousand camp residents, during which a violent riot took place in Regina.[5]

In this setting, new political parties challenging the "old line" Liberal and Conservative parties broadened the ideological spectrum. The Progressives, the Cooperative Commonwealth Federation (CCF), and the Social Credit party all debuted in Parliament during the turbulent interwar years. The Progressives faded but the other two parties survived, becoming pivotal parliamentary players in subsequent decades. Another party that left a mark but failed to elect an MP – it elected one in the 1940s – was the Communist Party (CP). Three small ephemeral parties, appearing and departing like shooting stars, were the Reconstruction Party, the National Unity Party (originating in French Quebec as the Parti national social chrétien), and New Democracy.

Provincial politics also experienced turmoil; between 1919 and 1922, provincial counterparts of the federal Progressives came to power in Ontario, Alberta, and Manitoba as the United Farmers of Ontario (UFO), United Farmers of Alberta (UFA), and United Farmers of Manitoba (UFM) respectively. The first two disappeared like their federal kin, while Manitoba's Progressives coalesced with the Liberals in the early 1930s and carried on beyond the interwar years as Liberal-Progressives, although they were neither liberal nor progressive. Social Credit defeated the UFA in 1935, fielding federal Social Credit candidates that same year. No Farmers' government swept to power in

Saskatchewan because the dominant farm organization in the province, the Saskatchewan Grain Growers Association, and the governing Liberals had overlapping leadership in the person of future federal Liberal finance minister Charles Dunning. In Quebec a group of dissident Liberals joined a loose coalition with Conservatives led by Maurice Duplessis to form the nationalist, conservative Union Nationale, which favoured Quebec's autonomy and won office in 1936. English Canada's oldest regions, the Maritimes and Ontario, experienced no significant third party developments.

The new parties spoke to diverse concerns. The Progressives expressed farmers' anxieties about the emergence of an urbanizing, industrializing Canada. Launched in 1932 as a federation of provincial labour parties and some farmers' organizations, the CCF was energized by the movement of intellectuals from humanistic and religious orientations to a more scientific outlook advocating social and economic planning by government.[6] Social Credit criticized the financial system for serving the interests of an oligarchic elite at the expense of the common good and the common citizen. Subscribing to "scientific socialism" and the inevitable triumph of the working class, the Communists envisaged a revolutionary eradication of capitalism while the miniscule fascist National Unity Party offered as "its emblem, in place of the swastika, a flaming torch set off against a white background, surrounded by maple leaves."[7]

The Conservatives and Liberals had benefitted from being brokerage parties with few significant long-lasting policy differences. As brokerage parties they muffled and obscured the differences among conflicting societal and economic interests.[8] The disorderly interwar period severely tested this formula; "Each party represented a babel of mutually contradictory vested interests," noted J.R. Mallory, "and there was no coherent body of doctrine which could be an agreed basis of policy in either party."[9] Waning belief in laissez-faire during the Depression undermined the old parties' paradigm of *homo economicus*. Harsh conditions so shook the ideological moorings of the established parties that both Conservative prime minister R.B. Bennett and Liberal leader Mackenzie King agreed that preserving capitalism would require some redistribution of wealth.[10]

Drawing on American president Franklin Roosevelt's New Deal – a series of programs, public work projects, and financial reforms – and using radio as a tool of political marketing, Bennett took to the airwaves to promise unemployment insurance, health and accident insurance, a minimum wage, a maximum workweek, better pensions, and more progressive taxation. However, his proposals could not save his government from defeat in the 1935 election. Liberal party thinking had evolved earlier than Conservative thinking; in 1919 a party convention had endorsed a social welfare agenda including health, old age, and unemployment insurance programs. The Liberals won the election by discrediting the Conservative government rather than on policy differences. "The election merely demonstrated the wisdom of the Liberal Party to have no policy," observed Escott Reid. "The Liberals counted on the depression to defeat any government and it did."[11] In office the Liberals did little to deliver on their 1919 welfare agenda, and by referring Bennett's legislative proposals to the courts, which judged most as violating provincial jurisdiction, the Liberal government tied its own hands.

The Liberal majority in the 1935 election – 171 of the 245 seats (plus an additional 5 Independent Liberals) – was the most lopsided since Confederation, but not because of an upsurge in popular support; the vote for the party increased by a mere half percentage point. The Liberals triumphed easily because the new third parties attracted defecting Conservative voters whose government was saddled with the Depression.

The third parties of the 1920s and 1930s took many of their cues from foreign developments and were bolstered by some personnel from abroad. Influenced by populist movements in the United States and by American-cum-Canadian agrarians like veteran Missouri populist Henry Wise Wood, the Progressives proposed jettisoning many parliamentary conventions, including party discipline. The CCF and its forerunner Labour parties, many of whose followers and leaders were immigrant Britons like Harold Winch in British Columbia, M.J. Coldwell in Saskatchewan, and S.J. Farmer in Manitoba, pursued the parliamentary socialist path of the British Labour Party. Social Credit's federal leader, Idahoan John Blackmore, was spellbound by the monetary theories of Scottish engineer Major Douglas, who considered economic problems as engineering problems requiring remedies by economic engineers. Communist Party chairman Maurice Spector and party ideologue Sam Carr, both Ukraine-born, were loudspeakers for Moscow and its Comintern, while National Unity Party leader Adrien Arcand corresponded with and encouraged Sir Oswald Mosley, leader of the British Union of Fascists.

On international questions, the parties veered in different directions; the Conservatives continued to be the most keen to align Canadian policy with British policy; the Liberals continued to seek distancing from Britain and greater amity with the United States. The Progressives, like the Liberals, opposed centralized imperial control,[12] formally ended by Britain's Statute of Westminster in 1931. CCF campaign literature hailed the accomplishments of British, Australian, and New

Zealand Labour governments, while Social Credit criticized international financiers. Communists were prominent in the 1,200 Canadian Mackenzie-Papineau Battalion, fighting on the republican side
in Spain's Civil War, while Arcand's fiercely anti-communist fascists
cheered Francisco Franco's extreme nationalist and anti-liberal Falange,
which preached authoritarian conservatism.

Against a backdrop of economic turbulence, ethnic animosities persisted in the interwar era. Although European immigrants generally
supported the Liberals, many leading Liberals as well as Conservatives
were suspicious of them. Newspaper editor John Dafoe noted the opinions of Saskatchewan's Liberal premier Dunning:

> He is not friendly to immigration from Central Europe. He says the coun-
> try doesn't want any Poles at all. Ruthenians [Ukrainians] are a good deal
> better but he seems to think that they deteriorate in this country particu-
> larly if they are educated. He says they can be educated all right but that
> they cannot be civilized, at least not in one generation; and that the edu-
> cated Ruthenian is a menace to his own countrymen and to the commu-
> nity. He is also dubious about Swedes. Those who come to this country
> are, he says, almost without exception, just one remove from anarchists.[13]

Saskatchewan's Conservatives were little different; they prohibited
Catholics from holding executive positions in their party in the late
1920s. The anti-Catholic, anti-immigrant Ku Klux Klan boasted of having more than 125 locals in Saskatchewan alone. Disagreements about
Catholics and immigrants dominated the province's 1929 election.[14]

Mainstream ethnic media encouraged deference to the established
order and discouraged supporting third parties, disparaged as utopian
sorties that would draw rebuke and charges of disloyalty. "Affiliation
with small radical parties making strange and impossible promises will
bring us no advantage, only national dishonour," editorialized Manitoba's Ukrainian *Kanadiiskyi Farmer*. "All signs show that we have to elect
candidates put forward by the governing party."[15] Similarly, *Ukrainsky
Holos* (Ukrainian Voice) rebuffed Manitoba's sole Ukrainian CCF MLA.[16]

The Progressive Party

The meteoric appearance of the federal Progressives symbolized the
awakened reaction of agricultural rural Canada against the growing
power of urban-labour-industrial interests. Organized in accordance
with notions of bottom-up grass-roots governance, the western-pro-
pelled Progressives were at the peak of their popularity in the early

1920s. Composed overwhelmingly of erstwhile Liberals, the populist and undisciplined Progressives felt betrayed by their old party straying from their free trade principles, tolerating discriminatory transportation and tariff policies, making farm equipment and other goods unnecessarily expensive. Hostile to the banks and the railroads, resentful of the financial-industrial power of the barons of Montreal's St. James and Toronto's Bay Streets, and contemptuous of the patronage system, the Manitoba-led Progressives sought to redeem the Liberal party by striking out on independent political action. They were inspired by an American third party, Theodore Roosevelt's Progressives, and the success of North Dakota's left-wing populist Non-Partisan League. It had swept to power by contesting primaries – a system that narrows a field of candidates – to capture the nominating conventions of the old parties.[17]

Scornful of Parliament's conventional ways, the Progressives were standard-bearers for institutional reform. Some of Alberta's Progressives wanted to replace parties and parliamentary government altogether with "group government" in which delegates representing the interests of different economic classes would fashion public policy collectively. Also adopting the language of agrarians in the United States, they advocated citizen-initiated referendums and recall legislation, in which voters have an opportunity to remove an MP from office, as antidotes to the power of parties and party leaders. The courts, however, had already derailed efforts to institute legislation by referendum, ruling that they were constitutionally inconsistent with parliamentary government.[18] Unlike Manitoba's Progressives, Alberta's Progressives dismissed the Liberal and Conservative parties as unredeemable, steeped in iniquity. The unresolved conflict between those wanting the Liberals to atone for their errors and the more doctrinaire Albertans who had given up on the conventions of parliamentary government fractured the Progressives.[19]

Often characterized as a western Canadian protest party, the Progressives were more accurately an agrarian class party; twenty-four of their sixty-five MPs in 1921 were Ontarians representing largely rural constituencies. Most of the Ontario and Saskatchewan Progressives followed Progressive leader Thomas Crerar, a Manitoba free-trade Liberal who had resigned from Robert Borden's Unionist government over his tariff policies. Offered the premierships of both Ontario and Manitoba when the UFO and UFM won office in those provinces, Crerar exemplified the link between central and western Canadian farmers.[20]

Prairie Progressives resented federal control of their region's natural resources, evidence of the subordinate hinterland relationship of the Prairie provinces to imperial Ottawa. (Ottawa transferred control over resources to the Prairie provinces in 1930, but resentment related to federal resource policies continued.) The Progressives denounced the protectionist National Policy, the regime of tariffs introduced by the John A. Macdonald's Conservative government in 1879, and excoriated the first-past-the-post electoral system. They failed, however, to persuade Parliament to replace it with proportional representation, a system in which parties are allotted a percentage of seats equal to their percentage of the popular vote, or the alternative vote (AV) in which voters rank their choices, with the ultimate winner requiring majority support after ballots are transferred from less popular to more popular candidates. Nevertheless, the influence of Progressivism in Manitoba and Alberta had led Liberal governments in those provinces to adopt ranked ballots. During the tenure of the UFO government, backbenchers enjoyed their greatest freedom in Ontario's history, passing a record number of private members' bills.[21] The UFA championed local autonomy and control and had criticized cabinet government and parliament's conventions but, in office, the UFA's "group government" idea proved incompatible with the modus operandi of parliamentary government and was soon abandoned.

The irreconcilable differences between the Manitobans and Albertans, which collapsed the federal Progressive revolt, demonstrated that the party was in fact a fissiparous collection, its members sharing little beyond discontent with the status quo. The Progressives challenged but proved incapable of transforming the status quo by acting as a class. After Conservative leader Arthur Meighen mocked the Progressives as a "dilapidated annex to the Liberal party," most of their MPs returned to their Liberal roots by 1926.[22] Another reason for the Progressive party's implosion was the deftness of wily Mackenzie King, who exploited their restiveness and lack of discipline. Prepared to have Progressives in his cabinet if they rejoined his party, he described them as "an advanced Liberal group."[23] After the governor general dismissed King in 1926, King convinced Saskatchewan's premier Dunning, the former vice-president of the provincial Grain Growers Association, to run federally and King himself sought election in the province. With most of the Progressives swallowed by the Liberals under a blended Liberal-Progressive label, the federal Progressive movement was spent, effectively dead.

Post-war anxieties had fed the Progressive insurgency; subsequent prosperity undercut the movement: a dramatic rise in the price of wheat coincided with King's seduction of the insurgents. In the late 1920s Canada was the world's leading exporter of wheat, the world's second-largest producer of automobiles, and exporting record levels of minerals, pulp, and paper to a booming United States.[24]

The rise and demise of the Progressives spoke to both the success and transience of the reform movement, which had come to Canada from the United States. Reform ideas – the elimination of partisan patronage, electoral reforms, wheat pools, cooperatives, extending the right to vote to women – spread like wildfire in western Canada, often through the efforts of Americans; California marketing expert Aaron Shapiro, for example, sold prairie farmers on wheat pools, and George Bevington, a perennial nominee for the presidency of the UFA, campaigned conspicuously for monetary reform and promoted the Non-Partisan League.[25]

The Progressive party expired but its unrepentant UFA wing carried on as a gadfly in Parliament. Unlike the Manitoba Progressives, who had vigorously opposed the Winnipeg General Strike and ridiculed the demands of strikers, the UFA MPs looked favourably upon cooperation with labour organizations; cooperation was consistent with the group government philosophy of revered UFA president Henry Wise Wood. Cut from different ideological cloth than the more timid Progressives from the other provinces, the UFA MPs became the majority in the "ginger group" of MPs who believed the time had come to create an equivalent of the British Labour Party. They made common cause with two Labour MPs and provincial labour parties to form the CCF in 1932. Provincial UFAers, drawn primarily to the unorthodox banking and monetary theories circulating widely in their province, turned to Social Credit. Running as newly Christened federal CCFers, the former UFA MPs were defeated in the 1935 federal election and the provincial UFA regime gave way to Social Credit.

The CCF

Numerous political movements, sects, and parties served as forerunners to the CCF in the early part of the century: the Socialist Party of Canada, Social Democratic Party, Canadian Socialist League, Federated Labor Party, Dominion Labor Party, Socialist Labor Party, Canadian Labor Party, and the Independent Labor Party, among others. They failed to establish a national party, largely through their inability to agree on doctrine or politics. Once formed, the CCF, a federation of various parties and groups, considered itself both a movement and a party.[26] As a movement it sought to make people aware of the truth of their position in the capitalist social system; as a party it was set on winning office.

Labour candidates had garnered no more than 3 per cent of the votes, and no more than four Labour MPs had been elected in any of the three federal elections in the 1920s. Nevertheless they exerted some influence.

In 1927, for example, King's Liberal government created a rudimentary pension program in response to pressure by two Labour MPs, including the indomitable J.S. Woodsworth, the CCF's founding leader.[27] This set a pattern for the balance of the century: Liberals introducing welfare programs but only after being prodded by social democrats.

As a Methodist clergyman ministering to the poor and the working class for more than two decades, Woodsworth, a pacifist, left the church because of its support for the First World War effort. Charged with seditious libel during the 1919 Winnipeg General Strike, he became a hero to labour organizations. Inspired by Britain's labour-socialism and the Russian Revolution, 30,000 workers left their jobs in a matter of hours. After Methodists in the social gospel tradition – a tradition tied to disenchantment with the upheavals and inequalities that accompanied industrialization – inaugurated the United Church in 1925, the Church's humanitarian ethic promoted a socialist movement organically linked to the labour movement.

Driven primarily to improving worldly conditions and not just saving otherworldly souls, the church's highly trained pastorate, preaching social justice, adopted an anti-capitalist stance during the Depression. The Saskatchewan conference of the church, for example, resolved that "the competitive system must be transformed into a cooperative system and that production and distribution ... must be democratically controlled in the interests of human needs, rather than private profit."[28] This served as the credo of the CCF, which fared better among United Church members than those of any other denomination.[29] The CCF's social gospel pedigree contributed to the party's respectability; many thought Woodsworth a saintly prophet, despite some of his early writings reflecting a touch of racism.[30] Baptist preacher Tommy Douglas, another of the party's MPs following the British socialist tradition, spoke of creating a "New Jerusalem" in Canada, a society that included eugenics in Douglas's thesis as a graduate student.[31]

The CCF's founding Regina Manifesto, formulated as capitalist ideology floundered, had a hyperbolic ring: "No C.C.F. Government will rest content until it has eradicated capitalism."[32] The party's policies, however, were more restrained. CCFers affirmed their socialism by committing to redistribute income, wealth, and economic power, but at a time when both Germany's Nazis and Russia's Soviets styled themselves "socialists," the party's brain trust, a group of academics calling itself the League for Social Reconstruction (LSR), avoided the word in its book, *Social Planning for Canada*. The tome attracted substantial readership and commentary. Sir Stafford Cripps, who became British Labour's chancellor of the exchequer, assessed the LSR's program penned by academic supporters of the CCF as "essentially moderate and evolutionary."[33]

The CCF's British labour roots imparted a cultural legitimacy to the party, shielding it from charges of preaching an alien ideology, a charge to which the party's socialist competitor, the Communist Party, was vulnerable.[34] Britons enjoyed a social status that foreign-language-speaking continental Europeans did not. Winnipeg's Independent Labor Party (ILP), which boasted twenty-eight elected members at three levels of government in the early 1930s, reflected the party's British character. In the 1920s, 85 per cent of ILP aldermen were British immigrants; in the 1930s, 70 per cent.[35]

More a creature of the new, urban, and industrial than the old, rural, and agrarian Canada, the CCF brought together labour and socialist parties as well as some leftist farmers with roots in the Progressive movement. A robust cooperative movement helped mobilize support for the party.[36] However, no one from east of Montreal participated in the Regina meeting and the Montrealers were English speakers.[37] Deviating from the policy of Britain's Labour party, the CCF steered clear of insisting on land nationalization by acknowledging the nature of agricultural organization in the New World with its mainly freehold farmers. The creation of the CCF, therefore, represented a "broadening out" strategy designed to have the party appeal to others beyond its urban labour base. This strategy created some tensions. Manitoba's ILP, for example, of which Woodsworth had been a founding member, chafed at throwing their lot in with farmers; they had excluded UFM members from joining their party.[38] Bitter that every rural newspaper had condemned the Winnipeg General Strike, the crucible from which their party had emerged, ILP members felt "it was not that old country Scotch socialism that the farmers were talking about," recalled Beatrice Brigden, a leading member of the Brandon Labour Party and the CCF provincial secretary in the 1930s. "The old English or British working class viewpoint was entirely different from our farmers' viewpoint ... because the farmers' viewpoint and the people living in the city who hadn't come in with the British labour group were very, very, middle class in their outlook."[39]

With the exception of Saskatchewan, where the Farmer-Labour Party led by ex-Londoner M.J. Coldwell served as the forerunner to the CCF, the CCF was a marginal force in rural areas; the UFM shunned it, the UFA decayed and disaffiliated from it within a year, and the UFO gave it only a fleeting endorsement. But, unlike the provincial governments of those organizations and the Progressive party, the CCF survived the interwar era as an independent party.

Social Credit

Social Credit theory postulated that everything that is physically possible ought to be financially possible, that the existing financial system artificially limited society's real credit and misdirected many economic activities.[40] As a party, Social Credit was a successor rather than a continuation of the Progressives, but it had much more in common with them than did the CCF. Both the Progressives and Social Credit owed little to Canada's British heritage and much to the frontier spirit of the American West; both were voices and beneficiaries of sectional feelings of alienation. The party inherited the radical liberal populism of the Progressives, which prized individual initiative. Unlike the Progressives, however, Social Credit was not sanguine about the ability of "the people" to understand or determine policy; Alberta party leader William Aberhart told voters they did not have to understand Social Credit to vote for it because "we'll get experts to put the system in."[41]

As a reform-oriented economic doctrine, Social Credit proposed monetary reform to benefit consumers. Albertans elected the world's first Social Credit government in 1935 after the party promised a $25 monthly dividend to every adult in order to stimulate purchasing power. The CCF had been compromised in the province by its association with a discredited UFA regime, toppled in part because of a sex scandal involving its premier, John Brownlee.[42] The base of Social Credit support was southern Alberta, where American-born Mormons and other evangelical Christians, a "quite exceptional" 20 per cent of the province's Protestants, had settled in significant numbers.[43] Federal party leader John Blackmore, for example, lived in Cardston, founded by Brigham Young's son-in-law and one of seventeen Mormon settlements in the region.[44]

Social Credit proved to be much more of a provincial than a federal phenomenon. It won nine successive elections in Alberta and for all but three years came to govern British Columbia between 1952 and 1991 where, as essentially a coalition of federal Liberals and Conservatives, it detached itself from social credit theory. The party mustered only forty-six candidates in the 1935 federal election, all in western Canada. It benefitted, however, from its regional concentration of votes; with only 4 per cent of the national vote, it won seventeen seats – fifteen in Alberta and two in Saskatchewan constituencies adjacent to the Alberta border. However, the party did harbour national aspirations; in 1938 Social Credit study groups were formed in Nova Scotia, Ontario, and Quebec.[45] The following year, the party produced a French publication, *Vers Demain*.

Social Credit carried forward the monetary preoccupations of many UFAers such as J.W. Leedy, the former populist Kansas governor and former leader of Alberta's Non-Partisan League.[46] Although Social Credit's theoretical parentage was British, the Canadian version arguably owed more to the nineteenth-century agrarian American Greenback and Free Silver movements; the former wanted to increase the amount of money in circulation, the latter advocated the unlimited coinage of silver. In contrast to Social Credit in Britain, which was most robust in Catholic, urban, and cosmopolitan circles,[47] Social Credit in Canada was liveliest in evangelical rural districts and most suspect among Catholics and in cities. Mystified by their marriage of evangelical fundamentalism with monetary reform and convinced they were purblind, Social Credit's British founder, Major C.H. Douglas, disowned his Canadian acolytes.[48]

Indifference of the eastern banking community to the plight of devastated western farmers fed Social Credit's success. Fixated with monetary reform and the "money power," Blackmore alleged a plot to place Canada under the control of Wall Street.[49] The eastern Canadian press dismissed Social Credit's proposals for the banking system as "an effort at totalitarianism."[50] Monetary and banking reforms, however, were palliatives that appealed across party lines in the Dirty Thirties; the Conservatives, for example, had created the Bank of Canada partly in response to UFA premier Brownlee petitioning for a central bank to provide western farmers with government cost-regulated credit.[51]

Social Credit shared a certain kinship with western CCFers as critics of the capitalist system and central Canadian interests; some Social Crediters considered the Regina Manifesto "replete with Social Credit phraseology and ideas,"[52] and Aberhart's electrifying weekly *Back to the Bible Hour* radio broadcasts catapulted Social Credit into office in Alberta. William Irvine, a UFA MP and CCF founding member, was an example of someone drawn to both labour-socialism and monetary reform.[53] To Irvine's party, however, social credit ought to mean social control of the country's wealth. Some in the CCF wanted to join forces with Social Credit, others wanted a united front with the Communists, and a few wanted all three to band together in a common effort.[54] CCFer Tommy Douglas sought and accepted Social Credit's endorsement in the 1935 federal election.[55]

Social Credit and the CCF had very different visions of democracy. Like the UFA before it, many Social Crediters embraced the vision of democratic politics dominant in the United States: those elected ought to reflect the preferences of voters. CCFers in contrast were wedded to parliamentary politics: party candidates run on a shared common platform and act as a team. The Social Credit government in Alberta conveyed a republican view of democracy in 1938 when it refused to appear before the Royal Commission on Dominion-Provincial Relations, addressing its brief instead to "the Sovereign People of Canada,"[56] and an American-born Social Credit MLA protested his legislature's preoccupation with the 1937 coronation festivities rather than monetary reform. Social Credit theory prevailed in the party during the 1930s, but after the courts invalidated many of the Alberta party's initiatives, the party adopted conservative financial policies endorsed by the banking institutions that the party had previously vilified.

Communists, Fascists, Reconstructionists

In an era when the creeds of communist and fascist parties attained their zenith internationally, Communists in English Canada and fascists in Quebec offered polar alternatives to the failures of capitalism and liberal democracy. The RCMP estimated Communist Party membership in 1931 as 5,000: 3,000 Finns, 800 Ukrainians, 400 Jews, and only 200 Britons, including leader Tim Buck.[57] As an indicator of the vitality of the CP among some Ukrainians, at least eighteen Ukrainian communist newspapers and periodicals appeared in the interwar period.[58] Ukrainians helped elect North America's first Communist, a Ukrainian, to Winnipeg's city council in 1926. In contrast to the large immigrant and ethnic composition of the CP were the British character of the CCF and the exclusively French character of the Parti national social chrétien, which came out into the open in 1938.

Developments abroad prompted both the CP and the fascists; the CP barely disguised its allegiance to the Comintern, the international Communist organization founded in 1919 by Lenin in Moscow, proposing "Defence of the Soviet Union and Soviet China."[59] Arcand's fascist party and its short-lived pan-Canadian equivalent, the National Unity Party, which drew on Ontario's Swastika Clubs, hailed Italy's Benito Mussolini, Portugal's António Salazar, Germany's Adolf Hitler, and their authoritarian governments.[60] Describing himself as a Canadian führer, Arcand boasted he would march on Ottawa and take control of the country in the style of Mussolini.[61]

The CP and the CCF, representing different varieties of socialism, had a poisonous relationship. The CP spoke of revolutionary change and government by the working class; the CCF talked of economic and social transformation by the steady amelioration of inequitable conditions. The parties competed to attract organized labour, and although the CP was virtually outlawed during most of the 1930s, CP-affiliated groups organized effectively within and beyond the labour movement. By the end of the decade, the party was relatively larger than its counterparts in Britain and the United States.[62] In contrast, the CCF was small compared to Britain's Labour Party, but many more voters supported it than the CP. The CP's leaders were atheists but avoided God-punching and looked favourably upon the creation of the United Church, the praying arm of the CCF. A few Methodist-cum–United Church ministers joined the CP, most notably A.E. Smith, Brandon's Labour MLA in the 1920s.[63]

Fanatical, shrill-voiced, and demagogic, Arcand claimed his party had 80,000 members in Quebec and 100,000 nationally, certainly an exaggeration, although thousands crammed some of his Montreal rallies. Pressured by Arcand's blue-shirted followers, who threatened bloodshed, the mayor of Montreal cancelled a permit for a CP rally. Despite the intimidation, the mayor and the provincial police chief said they were "too busy stamping out the Communist menace to bother with the fascists."[64] Arcand considered half of Quebec's lower Catholic clergy as unconscious pawns of communism, but his party swore allegiance to the church; in Ontario, his short-lived National Unity Party declared loyalty to king and empire.

Some Social Credit MPs, such as Blackmore and Norman Jacques, shared anti-Semitism and anti-communism with Arcand's fascists, who accused Jews of running the government, plotting to rule the world through a communist revolution, and having planned the Depression. Arcand proposed establishing a "corporate state" in which members of various economic sectors are required to belong to an officially designated interest group that would participate in national policymaking.[65] Like the CP, his party was banned and he was jailed in 1940 for plotting to overthrow the state.

The Reconstruction Party proved to be very much a one-man party led by former Conservative finance minister H.H. Stevens. Many Conservative MPs looked kindly upon Stevens but had no desire to run under his party's banner. Influenced by New Deal thinking and anxieties about the banking sector – 60,000 farmers had lost their savings in the failure of the Home Bank in the 1920s – Stevens's biographer characterized Reconstruction as a "left-wing movement." The party's manifesto proposed public works programs, a commission to address monetary issues, ending "the oppression of secondary handlers" in the agricultural sector, and liquidating the national debt by exploiting Canada's oil and mineral resources.[66]

Fielding 174 candidates in the 1935 election, the Reconstruction party fell victim to the geographic diffusion of its support; it outpolled both the CCF and Social Credit but its 9 per cent of the national vote resulted in only one seat. The Conservatives were the major victim of the Reconstructionists. The UFO endorsed Stevens's party, but it fared better in urban than rural Ontario. The party ended in 1938 when Stevens, its sole MP, crossed the floor and rejoined his old party.

W.D. Herridge, a former speech-writer for Bennett and his envoy to Washington, launched New Democracy in 1939, imagining it as a trans-partisan alliance of CCFers, Social Crediters, and disaffected Conservatives. Herridge referred to New Democracy as a movement rather than a party. Like Stevens, he was frustrated by his old party's resistance to his left-leaning ideas, which included a more equitable distribution of wealth, government economic planning, and extensive regulation of business. These ideas dovetailed with those of the CCF but the CCF rejected Herridge's overtures. His speeches about the need for increased purchasing power and monetary reform attracted Alberta premier Aberhart, who thought New Democracy could serve as a vehicle for Social Credit becoming a truly national party. This led in 1939 to Social Credit's MPs referring to themselves as New Democracy MPs, but after Herridge failed to get elected in the 1940 election and differed with Aberhart on conscription, they repudiated him and resumed using their original name.[67]

"No other country has produced so many electorally effective minor parties," wrote Seymour Martin Lipset, "provincial as well as federal."[68] Canada's experience is unusual because the first-past-the-post electoral system weighs heavily against the success of third parties. Geography, a unique ethno-cultural mix, the parliamentary system, federalism, as well as the logic of the single-member plurality electoral system in which successful candidates do not require majority support at the polls help to explain the Canadian case.

Support for the three most successful third parties, the Progressives, the CCF, and Social Credit, was concentrated largely in the West, where the unkindness of nature and the perceived malevolence of eastern interests fed intense discontent. The West had been rapidly populated in the century's first two decades by large numbers of settlers bringing with them ideological baggage from their older societies – in the case of the Progressives, Ontario's Grit tradition that runs back to the radical agrarian populists of the 1850s. In the case of the CCF, transplanted working-class Britons brought a labour-socialist ideological orientation from the Old World, while Americans and their Great Plains' populist politics provided a support base for Social Credit.[69]

These third parties pricked the established Liberal and Conservative parties, but unlike the United States where third parties were like bees – "once they have stung, they die"[70] – Social Credit and the CCF persisted as political forces. Social Crediters continued in Parliament until the late 1970s and some still sat in British Columbia's legislature in the 1990s. Over time, Liberal and Conservative governments adopted many policies of the CCF and of its successor, the New Democratic Party (NDP).

Unlike the case of political parties in the United States, Canada's political parties are grounded in a parliamentary system of government. Unlike Britain's unitary system of government in which the national government is supreme, Canada's federal system contributes to the rise of provincial as well as national parties. In the United States, primary elections permitted third parties like North Dakota's Non-Partisan League to capture the machinery of the Republican Party and led to Minnesota's Farmer-Labor party redefining the Democratic Party. Unlike the United States, where bipartisan congressional blocs of Republicans and Democrats can shape policy, the conventions or unwritten rules of Canada's parliamentary system impede policymaking by coalitions across party lines.

Canada's third parties did not gain national power in the 1920s and 1930s, but they struck deep roots in many provinces and continued as national political forces well beyond the interwar years: Farmers' parties formed governments in three provinces, Social Credit triumphed in Alberta, and the CCF won power in Saskatchewan in 1944, holding power there in every decade for the rest of the century. The successor party of the Manitoba CCF, the NDP, has held power in every decade since the 1960s and the NDP also came to hold office in British Columbia, Ontario, Nova Scotia, and Alberta. Third parties have also flourished in Quebec, where the oldest party, the Conservatives, disappeared.

The signal event that ended the Dirty Thirties was the Second World War, accompanied by political parties adopting Keynesianism as the new economic paradigm. Developed during the Depression, Keynesian theory called for increased government spending to stimulate overall economic activity and growth.[71] Unprecedented spending on armaments during the war was followed by unprecedented spending on social welfare programs.

Chapter Four

Parties of Warfare and Welfare

A New Social Order for Canada[1]

Liberal party leaflet

The outbreak of the Second World War prompted the growing size and web of government. The exigencies of war were followed by programs to construct a welfare state. Emblematic of party politics during the 1940s and well into the 1950s, the Liberal party successfully presented itself as a centrist party, ideologically positioning itself between influential enemies on the right, the Conservatives, and the left, the CCF.[2]

Unlike the First World War, which many considered to be a war of empires, the Second World War against Hitler and Nazism was considered a "good war" – a crusade for democracy. Overwhelming pressure in English Canada to rally to Britain's side led the Ontario legislature to pass a resolution in favour of conscripting both wealth and manpower months before hostilities broke out.[3] With only minimal opposition, notably the redoubtable CCF leader J.S. Woodsworth and a few Quebec MPs, Parliament declared war on Germany. It did so a week after Britain had declared war, unlike the First World War when Britain's declaration of war obligated the whole British Empire. And unlike the First World War, Canadians did not sing "Rule Britannia" as they entered the conflict. French Canadians and some ethnic minorities were much less enthused than English Canadians about Canada's engagement in the war and the possibility of mandatory military service.

Prime minister Mackenzie King's cunning snap election call in 1940 left the opposition parties unprepared, and the Liberals won 55 per cent of the popular vote.[4] Before the election, Conservative leader R.J. Manion, who had become his party's leader in 1938, had called for a "national government," a government of national unity along the lines of the government that came to be formed in Britain. King dismissed Manion's call, and the election results obviated pressure on the Liberals for such a government; Canada, unlike Britain, was not being attacked directly.

In contrast to the denouement of the First World War – rising unemployment and declining incomes – the economy expanded impressively during and after the Second World War. The size of the civil service and the gross national product more than doubled, putting paid to the Depression. Ottawa's budget, less than $700 million in 1939, grew to over $5 billion in 1945. Favouring the governing Liberals during the war were a recovering United States economy, growing demand and higher export prices for Canada's resources and goods, frantic activity in communities with naval and air bases, and plummeting unemployment as many enlisted. Full employment in 1941 was followed by labour shortages in 1942. The 1940 Unemployment Insurance Act, the first Canada-wide social-insurance program, which all the provinces supported, had linked the mobilization of labour to the war effort. Over a million men served overseas before war's end. The Liberal government, in spreading the state's regulatory net, simultaneously organized production and waged all-out war. Corporate executives were co-opted to manage production, blurring the line between the public and private sectors.[5]

The spirit of resignation among many Canadians during the Depression faded as victory came into view; thoughts turned to a bright new social order. Wartime and post-war demand stimulated manufacturing industries while federal and provincial legislation led to an explosion in union membership; non-agricultural union members, 359,000 at the beginning of 1940, increased to over one million by the end of the decade, accounting for 30 per cent of all non-agricultural workers.[6] The growth of organized labour initially boosted the prospects of both the CCF and the much smaller Communist Party (CP), but trade unionism also aided the Liberals, who had sponsored hundreds of joint labour-management committees during the war, giving unions a voice in management.[7] It was something that even collective bargaining, the negotiation of wages, and other conditions of employment by unions had not ensured. Candidates calling themselves Liberal-Labour appeared in northwestern Ontario, and in the provincial election of 1945 the communist Labour Progressive Party (LPP) nominated some candidates jointly with the Liberals in an attempt to foil the CCF.

War and its resolution raised expectations about the post-war order. As the state's net swelled, suffusing the everyday lives of Canadians as never before, all political parties proposed transforming the warfare state into the welfare state. The war had built faith in the wisdom of government; centralized planning had proven efficacious, and government came to be seen as having more responsibility for the public's health and welfare, for alleviating illiteracy, malnourishment, and homelessness. Canadians had accepted an expanded role for the state during the war and expected it to continue. For many Canadians, the receipt of social welfare was no longer equated with loss of one's personal dignity.

As the temper of the times changed, the political parties embarked on modernizing their programs. In the context of a more capable state, they offered social policy agendas that promised unemployment insurance, family allowances, day nurseries, improved labour conditions, and stable agricultural prices. King had expressed support for a cautious welfare state in his book *Industry and Humanity*.[8]

Views varied, however, about the post-war world order. In contrast to their pre-war posture, the Liberals became increasingly willing to engage internationally. The government articulated the "functional principle"[9] – that a country should exercise influence commensurate with its capability – and they defined Canada as a "middle power," not a great power but large enough to influence international affairs. In the new world order of 1945, the Liberals signed on to the United Nations with more commitment than they had shown to the League of Nations. The Conservative party also supported the establishment of the UN, but not without qualms of a few of their MPs; fearing the "dissolution" of the "British Empire" – which had actually dissolved some time earlier – MP Tommy Church, Toronto's former mayor, disapproved of the creation of both the UN and the International Monetary Fund (IMF), even as Britain favoured both.[10]

The smaller parties were sharply divided on Canada's role in the post-war international order. The CCF was especially supportive of international organizations; party leader M.J. Coldwell had participated as a member of Canada's delegation at the UN's founding meeting in San Francisco. Some Social Credit MPs, in contrast, were inclined "to smell a rat." They predicted the UN would be "unworkable," possibly "highly dangerous," and argued that the IMF would control Canada's currency and potentially grab control of the Canadian Pacific Railroad.[11] Social Credit suspected the UN was part of a plot for "world government" under socialist-banker control. Party leader Solon Low also criticized the Soviet Union's veto in the Security Council, while the lone Communist MP, Fred Rose, defended it as a provision of the Yalta agreement in which Franklin Roosevelt, Winston Churchill, and Joseph Stalin – the heads of government of the United States, the United

Kingdom, and the Soviet Union – reorganized post-war Europe.[12] Soon after, Soviet embassy clerk Igor Gouzenko defected, revealed a Soviet espionage ring operating in Canada since 1924, and exposed Rose as a spy. With the Soviet Red Army occupying Eastern Europe, popular fear and loathing of Nazi Germany was transferred to detestation of the Soviet Union. In the emerging Cold War between West and East, peace became seen as a left-wing issue, with many identifying peace activism by groups such as the Canadian section of the Women's International League for Peace and Freedom as a front for Soviet power.

Liberal Dominance

The King Liberals appeared stable, competent, and attuned to the urgent currents of politics. Before the war, King had hesitated to engage with European matters, suggesting as war clouds appeared in 1937 and 1938 that Canada might remain neutral in a conflict involving Britain: "It was made clear in the [Imperial] conference [of 1937]," he told Parliament, "that Canada was not committed to joining in any Imperial or league [sic: League of Nations] military undertakings, and equally, that there was no commitment against such participation."[13] King met Hitler and, delusional, concluded, "The world will yet come to see a very great man."[14] Although he harboured a long-held distrust of the military, King had a particularly strong cabinet, which benefitted his party when war came: men like Minister of Munitions C.D. Howe, First World War battalion commander and Minister of National Defence J.L. Ralston, former Nova Scotia premier and army veteran Angus Macdonald as naval minister, and former Saskatchewan premier Jimmy Gardiner, who commanded a formidable political machine in that province.[15]

Media coverage also advantaged the Liberals. In the 1940 election, for example, many traditionally Conservative newspapers, including the *Montreal Star* and *Hamilton Spectator*, adopted a more neutral political stance, effectively benefitting the Liberals. The Liberals profited from the noticeable, unprecedented plethora of government press releases issued during the war. This set a pattern for future administrations. The prorated allocation of free radio time on the CBC to political parties, introduced in 1940, benefitted the Liberals as well. King devoted great attention to crafting his broadcast messages.[16] Although radio did not replace the whistle-stop train tours by party leaders, it did transform campaigning, and King's Liberals made the most of it. In the 1949 election campaign, for example, the Liberals were apportioned seven half-hours and seven quarter-hours of free broadcast time, compared to just half an hour for Social Credit.[17]

King's Liberals, historically classical laissez-faire liberals in the British mould as advocates of private property, an unhampered market economy, and free trade, conveyed an image of themselves as non-doctrinaire and the natural governing party. Prescient and intuitive, King floated in a syrup of abstruseness during and after the war, intoning most famously "not necessarily conscription, but conscription if necessary."[18] Similarly the Liberals promised welfare if necessary, but not necessarily welfare. F.R. Scott, the CCF's national chairman, sized up King sarcastically:

> Truly he will be remembered
> Wherever men honour ingenuity,
> Ambiguity, inactivity, and political longevity.[19]

The Liberal idiom became to style their party as the middle way between its major adversaries: the allegedly backward-looking Conservatives and the radical CCF bent on socialism. The Liberals characterized the Conservative party as a torpid backwater of snobbish elitists, and they countered the CCF's promise of social security with their own welfare agenda. The Liberals presented their government as an impartial referee encouraging harmony among competing economic interests, mediating between employers and employees in the service of the broader community.

The Liberal stranglehold on Quebec explains a large part of the party's success. King, who did not learn French, was no crusader trying to change French Canadians, but he intuitively recognized that they shared a durable sense of themselves as a collectivity; they possessed a "mentality," he wrote, "wholly diff't from the Anglo-Saxon."[20] Adroitly navigating the shoals of biculturalism, his obsession before, during, and after the war was that the differences between French and English Canada not threaten political stability or his party's fortunes. Zealously concerned with maintaining national unity, King appreciated the importance of having a French-Canadian lieutenant: Ernest Lapointe, his top adviser on Quebec and the party's *chef* there. He recruited Louis St. Laurent to replace Lapointe after Lapointe's death in 1941. Even though the Liberals had introduced conscription and, despite the opposing votes of many of their Quebec MPs, the party won over half the vote in the province in the 1945 election. French Canadians recognized the Liberals as their only alternative.

The Liberals commissioned CCFer Leonard Marsh, a League for Social Reconstruction member, to author a *Report on Social Security for Canada* – "the most important single document in the history of the development of the welfare state in Canada,"[21] – but they initially cast it aside. Responding to public opinion, they then poached the popular welfare policies of the CCF, diluting its ideological profile as the avatar of the welfare state. The Liberal platform at war's end, "A New Social Order for Canada," proposed radical welfare measures: comprehensive social security through contributory social insurance schemes and universal public health insurance. However, Ontario's Conservative premier George Drew and his conservative Quebec counterpart, Union Nationale leader Maurice Duplessis, stymied the plans of the Liberals. In a policy area where provincial agreement was not necessary, the Liberals created a federal Crown corporation, the Central Mortgage and Housing Corporation, to help returning soldiers purchase homes. They also took up the proposal in the Marsh report to introduce family allowances. Although they dismantled much of the apparatus of state intervention that had been constructed during the war, the Liberals adopted the technocratic Keynesian welfare state model that came to define the post-war years: assisting private enterprise to produce jobs rather than engaging directly in the economy, as the CCF had proposed.

King's Liberals had a firm grip on federal power, but their relations with some of their provincial kin were often strained. King had a notoriously bad relationship with Ontario Liberal premier Mitchell Hepburn. He also differed with Nova Scotia Liberal premier Angus Macdonald over a post-war tax rental agreement in which some provinces vacated the fields of personal and corporate income taxes, and succession duties in exchange for funds transferred from Ottawa. "Macdonald is in his way just as bad as Hepburn was," reads King's diary, "and may succeed in doing for Nova Scotia Liberalism what Hepburn did for Liberalism in Ontario. Pretty effectively destroy it."[22] Although not particularly popular, King was a shrewd tactician, consistently outsmarting his adversaries. His Machiavellian cunning led the widely read journalist Bruce Hutchison to depict him as *The Incredible Canadian*.[23]

Under King and his successor, St. Laurent, the outlooks of the Liberal party and Ottawa's senior bureaucrats seemed to merge; together state and party became "an instrument for the depoliticization," paradoxically, of political life.[24] Senior state officials like Mitchell Sharp and Walter Gordon, who laboured in the King and St. Laurent administrations, went on to become prominent Liberal cabinet ministers in later decades. Under St. Laurent, the Liberals unsurprisingly kept their grip on Quebec. To English Canadians, St. Laurent's avuncular comportment proved reassuring at a time when the economy was growing and no scandal scarred the government's record. For many voters, many more than for any other party, the Liberals represented a paragon of steadiness and tested experience. They were the only party that demonstrated substantial support in every region of the country. In the 1949 election they captured about three-quarters of the seats in the House of Commons with about one-half the popular vote.

Conservative Turmoil

Reflecting commotion in Conservative thinking as well as their failure at the polls, the Conservatives had four leaders in the 1940s while the Liberals had a single leader between 1919 and 1948. The Conservatives appeared mired in a chronic crisis of leadership and identity. Manion, a decorated soldier and pro-conscription Liberal MP who had supported Conservative Robert Borden's Unionist government during the First World War, called for Canada to do "her bit" when the Second World War began, but he opposed conscription.[25] This turned many Ontario Conservatives, the party's traditional base, against him.

The other side of Liberal dominance in Quebec was Conservative failure there. Roman Catholic Manion had a French-Canadian wife, and the province's political culture was conservative – the province had no Department of Education and women were denied the right to vote in provincial elections until the 1940s – but French Canadians continued to perceive the Conservatives as overly attached to Britain. Premier Duplessis, the former Quebec Conservative party leader, had promised to support Manion in a future election, but King's dissolution of Parliament and an earlier than expected election in 1940 caught the Conservatives off-guard. They were organizationally weak in the provinces and had little in their coffers. Traditional corporate supporters were taken aback at Manion's musings that "reactionary rich men" threatened democracy and that the country's options were "reform or revolution."[26]

Manion lost his seat in the 1940 election and died soon after. An influential figure from the past, Arthur Meighen, the two-time Conservative prime minister in the 1920s, stepped in to helm the party, which dispensed with a leadership convention. Unlike Manion, Meighen was part of the conscriptionist wing of the party. However, with his defeat by a CCF upstart in a 1942 by-election, the party's drive for a national government and conscription fizzled. A plebiscite on conscription that year, in which the majority of French Canadians voted "No," reinforced the image of the Conservatives as the party of Anglo-Saxon Protestants.

The party was in an existential crisis, "as close as it had yet been to extinction."[27] Courted by Meighen and Conservative delegates from every province,[28] Manitoba's John Bracken, the Commonwealth's longest-governing prime minister or premier, became the party's new hope. Seen as a winner who could deliver western Canadian voters, Bracken had skilfully co-opted Manitoba's opposition parties to join him in a wartime coalition government. In taking leadership of the federal Conservatives, Bracken insisted the party change its name by adding "Progressive" to the Conservative tag. "Progressive" was the name his provincial party, formerly the Bracken Party and before that the United Farmers of Manitoba, had adopted in the 1930s when it merged with the provincial Liberals to form the Liberal-Progressive party. He had a reputation nationally as a progressive but had governed his province as a fiscal conservative, keeping a tight rein on education, health, and welfare expenditures reducing, for example, allowances for widowed and deserted mothers in the 1920s.[29]

In the run-up to the 1942 convention that selected Bracken, over a hundred Conservative delegates from across the country met unofficially in Port Hope, adopting a charter interpreted as "tending toward 'left wing conservatism' or a 'middle way' course between the left and right extremes of political thought."[30] W.D. Herridge's earlier proposals had presaged the ideas of the Port Hope delegates for rebranding the Conservative image: "Let us do those things necessary," he had written, "so that reformed progressivism may become a sort of cadet branch of the Conservative Party, and in due course lose itself in the New Toryism."[31] Senior party sources acknowledged that the charter "caught unquestionably the imagination of the rank and file of the party,"[32] but the cautious Bracken countered, commissioning social conservative and future Ottawa mayor Charlotte Whitton to critique the Marsh report. She decried it and the social welfare vision proffered by the CCF for emphasizing income security, dismissing them as inapplicable to Canadian circumstances.[33]

The influences of the Port Hope Charter and the CCF's strength were apparent in 1943 when Ontario's Conservatives ran on a radical platform promising "economic and social security from the cradle to the grave," pensions, mothers' allowances, and "the fairest and most advanced labour laws."[34] Not to be outflanked on welfare policy by the Liberals, the federal Conservatives offered a "People's Charter," which recognized "the right of every worker to a fair day's pay ... [and] of every citizen to security against loss of income arising from accident, sickness, loss of employment, old-age or other disability."[35] The Conservative message in the 1945 election campaign confirmed that the social welfare state had become part of the popular zeitgeist.

Reflecting the Conservative credo of promoting personal achievement and limiting the orbit of government, the party platform adopted at the convention that had selected Bracken also included "relaxing bureaucratic controls, and regimentation" after the war, and "maintenance of the basic Canadian tradition of free enterprise and personal initiative in economic and political life."[36] Consistent with its history, the party also committed to "holding fast to the British connection" and "all-out mobilization of ... manpower resources" in the war effort. These planks did not go over well in Quebec; the Conservatives managed to field only twenty-nine candidates to contest the province's sixty-four seats in the 1945 federal election, and their 8 per cent of the popular vote came mostly from ridings with English-speaking majorities.

Bracken's failure nationally and George Drew's success provincially in Ontario, where he converted a narrow Conservative minority government into a commanding majority in 1945, led to Drew's easy accession to the party's federal leadership in 1948. However, he failed to mount an effective challenge to the Liberals in the following year's election, although it was not for lack of effort; he allied himself with Duplessis and with Montreal mayor Camillien Houde, the anti-conscriptionist wartime internee and sympathizer of Mussolini's fascist Italy and the French Vichy regime collaborating with Nazi Germany. A photograph on the front page of the *Toronto Daily Star* showing Drew and Houde sharing a stage appeared under an eight-column headline, "Keep Canada British, Destroy Drew's Houde, God Save the King,"[37] proved devastating: Conservative seats in Ontario shrank from forty-eight in 1945 to twenty-five in 1949. Although the party's vote in Quebec increased, the Conservatives managed to win only two seats in the province, where Drew's military background – the press often referred to him as Colonel Drew – did not help.

CCF Ascent and Decline

The CCF was ambivalent initially about the war. The party's position in the 1930s had been that fascism and war were twin evils of capitalism and that war had an unavoidable imperial character.[38] Once war came, however, the party's leadership, of two minds, faced a dilemma. Many leading members had criticized war as a method of solving international problems; J.S. Woodsworth, the undeviating pacifist party leader, and party intellectual Frank Underhill had advocated Canadian neutrality in the event of war.[39] But the overwhelming sentiment among party activists was, as it had been among activists of Labour parties during the First World War, to stand shoulder to shoulder with Britain. The party abandoned Woodsworth's position as his health abandoned him, and M.J. Coldwell took the party's reins barely a month after the war began.

Many party members, especially in British Columbia but also elsewhere, continued to oppose going to war, but what had been rigid opposition by the federal party's leadership gave way. The party supported sending an expeditionary force and later supported a "Yes" vote in the conscription plebiscite. Nevertheless, party leaders argued that conscripting and nationalizing war industries was more vital than conscripting workers.[40] Defeating Hitler, creating a new post-war economic and social order, and protecting civil liberties soon became the three thrusts in the CCF's position.[41] Efficacious centralized wartime planning gave credence to the party's call for extended state planning, a case made by CCF officials David Lewis and Frank Scott in their national best-seller *Make This Your Canada*, and in Coldwell's *Left Turn, Canada*.[42] The latter cited and echoed Sweden's social democratic welfare model.Both books also carved out space for small private enterprise in a way that the Regina Manifesto, drafted by Underhill, had not.

Reflecting the growing popularity of the CCF, the party gained votes or seats in all nine provincial elections between 1941 and 1944, holding 109 provincial seats in seven of the nine provinces. Meighen's defeat by a CCFer in a Toronto by-election particularly buoyed the party. At one point in 1943, the only time in the history of the federal party, the Gallup poll put it ahead of both the Liberals and Conservatives.[43] Fearful that the first-past-the-post electoral system would bring the CCF to power in British Columbia, the province's Liberal and Conservative parties formed a coalition government in 1941 that endured until 1952. In Ontario the party came within a whisker of gaining office in 1943. In Saskatchewan, the party prevailed in 1944 after muting or abandoning some of its more militant positions such as land nationalization. Against the pleas of federal party secretary Lewis and CCF leaders in the other provinces, the Manitoba CCF had entered Bracken's coalition government in 1940, but when Bracken left to lead the federal Conservatives, the CCF extricated itself. It then performed well in the 1945 provincial election but ran third because of a rurally skewed electoral map. In the 1945 federal election, CCF candidates outnumbered Conservative candidates. However, the party was chronically weak in the Maritimes – it never won more than one seat there – and in Quebec, where its only victory came in a by-election.

A smear campaign associating the party with Bolshevism and atheism was a significant factor in dashing the CCF's prospects in the 1945 federal election. A prominent advertisement in the *Globe and Mail*, for example, disparaged the CCF as rejecting the "Christian way of life" and of being "tied hand and foot" to the Communist party.[44] A Conservative poster similarly asserted, "Religious Socialism and Christian Socialism are expressions implying a contradiction in terms."[45] Cartoons in the

Globe and Mail depicted CCFers as either cap-and-gown academics or nasty looking foreigners, and a twenty-four-page tabloid titled *Social Suicide* mailed to millions of Canadians claimed the CCF's objective was total regimentation of everyday life.[46]

The CCF's success in Saskatchewan led to a common mischaracterization of the CCF as essentially an agrarian party.[47] The 1945 federal election contributed to this image when the party captured eighteen of Saskatchewan's twenty-eight seats but none of Ontario's eighty-two. However, almost a third of the CCF's voters were in Ontario and only a fifth were in Saskatchewan, concealing the party's urban-industrial base of support. Indeed, Saskatchewan too demonstrated the CCF's urban strength; all seven urban provincial constituencies returned CCFers continuously between 1944 and 1960, and by 1952 the party's urban votes exceeded its rural votes, even though the four largest cities constituted only 19 per cent of the population.[48]

The CCF took pride in itself as an educational movement as well as a party competing for power, but when the party after the Second World War repeatedly predicted a reprise of post–First World War conditions of unemployment and recession, the prognosis proved faulty. By 1947 there was full employment, and the gross domestic product increased by over 30 per cent between 1945 and 1948. Economic security as the party's totemic message proved insufficient and a revised message was not forthcoming; "Time is short," forecast the Manitoba party's director of education. "This spell of industrial activity will not last much longer, and then will come the day of depression."[49] "Beat the Depression Now" headlined a 1949 election pamphlet. Although intimate relations developed with trade union leaders and the party became increasingly dependent on their support,[50] union members did not seem to consider their condition as hopeless or stagnant.

The CCF suffered from being associated with communism as the Cold War took hold, even though the party forbade association with the communist Labour Progressive Party. The expulsion of some CCF MLAs in British Columbia and Manitoba for flirting with the LPP only reinforced adverse publicity. Determined to dissociate itself from communists, the party attacked the Soviet Union at every opportunity, endorsed Canadian membership in NATO, refrained from criticizing the Liberal government's foreign policy, and expelled some communist dissenters.

Social Credit Makeover

John Blackmore led ten Social Credit MPs in the early 1940s when the party sometimes referred to itself as the New Democracy Party. Alberta premiers William Aberhart and Ernest Manning, however, were the primary faces of the party. Aberhart described partyism as "a vicious and alarming negation of democracy in its true essence."[51] As president of the Democratic Monetary Reform Organization of Canada (DMRO), formed in 1941, he pledged to have the party's MPs use that name in the next federal election. A joint caucus meeting of the party's MPs and MLAs demonstrated the intimate link between the federal and Alberta wings of the movement. Promoting Social Credit guru Major Douglas's ideas about monetary reform and parliamentary democracy, they issued a manifesto advocating social dividends to "provide the individual citizen with a basic minimum standard of living" and a "reconstituted democracy" under a new monetary system.[52] Party MPs voted for conscription in 1942, but when the conscription plebiscite took place, some Albertans thought the party "took a non-committal attitude ... which many interpreted as a whisper campaign against a Yes vote."[53]

Social Credit created a party organization outside of Parliament in 1944 after Aberhart's death and the demise of the DMRO. Solon Low, Aberhart's former finance minister, was acclaimed as leader. As in the 1930s, when the party cooperated sometimes with CCFers and even Communists, during the war some associated Social Credit with socialism; in 1941 the Calgary Board of Trade described the party's theories as promoting "autocratic state socialism."[54] The party pledged to increase the purchasing power of consumers, but unlike the CCF, it opposed wealth redistribution. Nevertheless Ernest Manning's government looked kindly upon some social programs, including day nurseries for young children of mothers engaged in the war industry.[55]

Under Manning, Social Credit broke with Douglas's denunciation of parliamentary government, gave up on his monetary ideas, and disavowed many forms of government intervention that it had promoted in the 1930s. The party took a decisive turn to the right, becoming a staunch opponent of socialism and contending that socialists were conspiring with finance capital. However, the party eventually made peace with the banks. At times Social Credit exhibited policy schizophrenia: in the 1943 budget debate, for example, one of its MPs proposed nationalizing the banks while Blackmore insisted they remain private.[56] Similarly, after a 1942 party conference proposed liquidating the Bank of Canada and instituting a privately controlled monetary system, Manning proposed expanding credit through the Bank of Canada.[57]

The party's federal organ, the *Canadian Social Crediter*, depicted marketing boards, trade unions, and cooperatives as "collectivist" and "dictatorial."[58] The paper featured many anti-Semitic diatribes, and although Manning rejected anti-Semitism and purged some Alberta provincial party members, anti-Semitic sentiments persisted, voiced by many, including MP Norman Jacques. Conspiracy theories were a staple of Social Credit thinking from its very origins. In the 1940s, talk of a Jewish communist conspiracy complemented the talk in the 1930s of a Jewish financial conspiracy. When accused of anti-Semitism, Low responded "that if he condemned Jews for supporting the communists, he did so because they were communists and not because they were Jews."[59] Manning claimed elements in the news media and universities as well as socialists, labour leaders, and communists were co-conspirators, and Jacques asserted that communists had infiltrated the CBC.[60]

Rebuffed by the courts for entering fields under federal jurisdiction, Alberta's Social Credit government shifted to calling on Ottawa to fund programs such as old age pensions, mothers' allowances, and medical and health services by transferring money to the provinces. Meanwhile the federal party sharpened its strident opposition to socialism, comparing the CCF to Nazism because both allegedly believed in a supreme totalitarian state; Low pronounced that "communism, fascism, and socialism were all in the same bag."[61]

Impeding Social Credit was opposition by the Catholic Church, whose Canadian primate forbade its clergy to support the party or attend its meetings.[62] Unlike Britain's Social Credit movement, however, Social Credit in Canada frequently used religious references to underscore the worthiness of its proposals. In the 1949 election campaign, for example, Low compared the Liberal government's budgeting policy unfavourably to the biblical Joseph's grain storage plan: "Joseph," he intoned, "would stick closely to the Social Credit platform if the drafting of Canada's economic future were in his hands."[63]

Communists: Toeing Stalin's Line

After denouncing the CCF as "social fascists" traitorous to the working class,[64] the CP presented itself after 1935 as the vanguard of a Popular Front in the fight against fascism. However, once Germany and the Soviet Union signed a non-aggression pact in 1939, the party characterized the war as an imperialist struggle and labelled the other parties warmongers; Hitler, in this narrative, was no worse than Mackenzie King. Some ethnic organizations affiliated with the party initially supported the war effort perhaps to demonstrate their allegiance to Canada, which many mainstream Canadians suspected. Alberta's communist-affiliated United Labour Farmer Temple Association, a Ukrainian organization boasting 3,000 members, declared that they "would take their place with the people of Canada and the British Commonwealth of Nations to defeat German aggression."[65] In 1940 the CP was banned, its leaders incarcerated and forced underground. After Germany attacked the Soviet Union in 1941, the Communists toed Stalin's line again: Canada was in a holy war in which the Liberal government deserved unquestioned support, and the CCF's campaign for socialism only undermined the effort.

In 1943 the CP emerged from the shadows as the Labour Progressive Party. In the interim, some Communists like Manitoba MLA William Kardash ran under the Workers Party label, the original party name used in the early 1920s. Others, like future Ontario MPP A.A. MacLeod, ran under the "People's Movement" banner in Alberta.[66] In 1945 the CP denounced the CCF for facilitating "Tory reaction" by splitting the "progressive" vote and elevated Mackenzie King to the leadership of the country's "progressive" forces. The revelations of Soviet espionage by Gouzenko, the Soviet embassy clerk, led the CP to pivot once again, endorsing CCF candidates in 1949. For a while, CCF and CP fortunes rose and declined in tandem. Partisan opponents and media outlets lumped the two socialist parties together, and the public rewarded and penalized them together; support for both, relatively high during the war, plummeted afterwards. However, there was never much love lost between the parties throughout the 1940s, and they engaged in strenuous competition for trade union leadership positions.

Bloc populaire canadien

Shortly after the conscription plebiscite, the anti-war, nationalist Bloc populaire canadien was born when Liberal MP Maxime Raymond crossed the floor along with a couple of other disgruntled Quebec Liberals. Raymond described the Bloc's philosophy as equally opposed to "the economic dictatorship which now exists," and to "state monopoly which socialism would create."[67] Led provincially by André Laurendeau, the future editor of Le Devoir and future co-chair of the Royal Commission on Bilingualism and Biculturalism, the Bloc captured 15 per cent of the vote in Quebec's 1944 election and elected four MLAs. In the 1945 federal election, the party elected two MPs. The Bloc disappeared federally shortly after its two MPs voted against Canada's participation in NATO in 1949. Riven by ideological quarrels and personality clashes, the provincial Bloc had withered earlier, in 1947. One side – pan-Canadian, socially conservative, and anti-imperialist – had envisaged a messianic role for French Canada's Catholic culture in North America; the other side, more committed to defeating the Union

Nationale, accepted that French Canada would become an increasingly secular, state-centred, urban-industrial society.[68] The Bloc was in some ways a harbinger of the Quiet Revolution and a forerunner to the Bloc Québécois of the 1990s.

The 1940s began with well over half a million Canadians unemployed and Canada not fully recovered from the Depression. The rigours and uncertainties of war also challenged the country. The decade ended with the economy booming, the public largely content, and a Liberal-legislated but still limited welfare state luring penurious Newfoundland into Confederation. Ottawa's revenues in 1939 had barely exceeded a half billion dollars; by 1950, they exceeded three billion.[69] That year all the federal political parties and provincial governments supported extending the social security of Canadians, agreeing to transfer constitutional authority for old age pensions to a Liberal-dominated Parliament.

The Conservative party began the 1940s off-balance, with little support in the business community and led by R.J. Manion, whose "Hibernian temper got the better of him,"[70] making him appear to many unsuitable as a wartime leader. At the end of the decade, the federal Conservatives and their provincial counterparts in Ontario and Quebec divided on policy: the federal party proposed adding hundreds of millions of dollars to government expenditures for old age pensions and family allowances while conservative provincial governments in Ontario and Quebec resisted federal Liberal government initiatives in the name of provincial rights.[71]

When the war began, the Liberals and Conservatives were in accord on full cooperation with Britain, but with no conscription of manpower. In contrast, the CCF was divided between its pacifist leader and most of the party's followers. When the war ended, the Liberal and CCF positions were in accord on expanding the welfare state. All the parties claimed to voice the interests of common folk against those of big business, but the Conservatives, while speaking of social security, implicitly shied away from it by focusing on fiscal issues, tax cuts, warning against statism, and cautioning that a vote for the Liberals was a vote for "an alliance of Liberals and Socialists."[72] By the 1950s, however, even conservative business circles accepted the welfare state as "a first charge on the nation's wealth." The *Globe and Mail*, as the voice of the financiers of Bay Street, editorialized that "only when the majority of people have been assured a comparatively high standard of living, with security against unemployment, old age and sickness is a surplus available for any other purpose."[73]

English and French Canada, divided when the war began, were no less divided when it ended. However, relations between the two solitudes had not shattered under the Liberals as they might have under a Conservative administration. When the decade ended, the Conservatives held a lower percentage of seats in Parliament than when the war began. The CCF began the decade as a weak third party and, after advancing in popularity during the war, ended the decade on another weak note as a victim of the Cold War. Social Credit's popularity did not fluctuate despite the party's ideological metamorphosis from champion of monetary reform to antagonist of socialism; it captured no more than 4 per cent of the vote in any of the three elections in the decade.

The Liberal government of Louis St. Laurent, who in 1949 described the CCF as "Liberals in a hurry,"[74] continued constructing the welfare state in the next decade with legislation creating a national hospital insurance program in 1957. A month later, the Conservative party returned to office after more than two decades in opposition, forming a minority government.

Chapter Five

Minority Governments:
The Diefenbaker-Pearson Years

What is the difference between a cactus and the Conservative caucus? On a cactus, the pricks are on the outside.[1]

George Hees

The election of John Diefenbaker's Conservative minority government in 1957 began a new era in Canadian party politics: an unprecedented string of minority governments. The election was the first of five between 1957 and 1965, four of which produced minority governments, an unparalleled number in such a short period. Diefenbaker led the Conservatives in all five contests and Lester Pearson headed the Liberals in four. Two of the three elections in the 1970s also produced minority governments. A striking development in this distinct period in the history of the political parties was the emergence of competing Conservative, Liberal, and social democratic visions of Canadian nationalism.

A reputed benefit of the first-past-the-post single member plurality electoral system is the likely election of stable majority governments.[2] Since 1921, however, when Canada's two-party system fractured, thirteen of the thirty federal elections have produced minority governments. The Conservatives claimed in 1958 that they needed a majority to govern effectively and the Liberals made the same case in 1965.[3] Diefenbaker and Pearson occupied centre stage in the 1950s and 1960s, but secondary actors, the CCF-NDP and Social Credit – the latter splitting into two parties – influenced public policy and determined whether a minority government would survive or be undone.

With the Liberals still in office at mid-century, Canadian politics were soporific; voter turnout in the 1953 election was lower than in any election between 1925 and 1997. In the context of the Cold War, the

Liberals presented themselves as reliable guardians of national security, boasting of having introduced "drastic legislation" to protect "our institutions, our defence establishments and essential industries from subversion and sabotage." The Conservatives proposed going further by criminalizing "Communist or other subversive activities,"a proposal the CCF associated with developments in the United States, terming it "'McCarthyism' and witch-hunting."[4]

Neither Diefenbaker nor Pearson was his party's leader when the 1950s began or when the 1960s ended. However, during their terms as leaders the social bases of support for their parties changed dramatically. The political realignment of voters brought on by the Diefenbaker phenomenon – in 1958 his Conservatives formed the largest majority government in Canadian history up until that time – still resonates. No longer identified with established central Canadian corporate interests, the Conservatives became the dominant party on the formerly uncongenial prairies and in small-town and rural English Canada. For their part, the Liberals became the principal party of metropolitan English Canada – they had long held sway in Montreal – in a dramatic shift, given that the Conservatives won seventeen of the eighteen seats in Toronto in 1957.

Diefenbaker had been remarkably unsuccessful in the 1930s as the leader of the Saskatchewan Conservative party; under his leadership the party won no seats. A failed candidate for the mayoralty of Prince Albert and a twice-failed candidate for both Parliament and the national Conservative leadership, he nevertheless gained a national reputation as a formidable criminal lawyer and eloquent parliamentarian. His populist style contrasted with the patrician demeanour of George Drew, his uninspiring predecessor who came from Ontario. Within months of gaining his party's leadership in 1956, Diefenbaker became the first Conservative prime minister elected since 1935. After twenty-two uninterrupted years of Liberal government, the Conservative minority government underscored the hitherto spasmodic and episodic success of the party.

Pearson had a greater policy impact than Diefenbaker as prime minister. A diplomat whose distinguished career included serving as president of the United Nations General Assembly, Pearson brought honour to himself and Canada by being awarded the Nobel Peace Prize in 1957 for his peace-keeping initiative in the 1956 Suez crisis, when a military and political confrontation in Egypt threatened to divide the United States and Britain and harm the Western military alliance. "Three wise men" from Montreal whom Pearson recruited to his government in 1965 – Jean Marchand, Gérard Pelletier, and Pierre Trudeau – fundamentally changed Ottawa's relationship to Quebec; Quebecers, whose role in government had long been to interpret federal policy to their province, now actively shaped it.

Influential journalists like Peter Newman assessed Diefenbaker's government more critically than Pearson's. Newman judged both regimes disparagingly, but his appraisal of the Conservatives as incompetent and of Diefenbaker as an eccentric, autocratic, and paranoid loner was much more severe than his evaluation of the Liberal government and Pearson. The titles of Newman's books reveal the contrast: Diefenbaker was a *Renegade in Power* while Pearson's failings reflect *The Distemper of Our Times*.[5] Charles Lynch, "the most widely read and probably the most influential political columnist," called Diefenbaker's defence minister, George Pearkes, "a Colonel Blimp" and held that "Diefenbaker will go to his grave believing to the end that the press helped to dig that grave."[6]

Much changed between the 1950s and 1960s in the method of selecting and deposing leaders. Ex officio delegates – delegates by virtue of the party positions they held – dominated the leadership conventions that chose Diefenbaker and Pearson in the 1950s; a decade later, grass-roots delegates exerted more authority than party officials in selecting the new leaders, Robert Stanfield and Pierre Trudeau. By the 1960s, the election of party presidents and other party officials became, according to Conservative president Dalton Camp, "a proxy war between elements within the party and over issues larger than the candidates themselves."[7] Television, a marginal political force when Diefenbaker and Pearson became leaders – indeed party leaders had unanimously declined free-time telecasts in the 1953 election[8] – was the dominant medium when they departed. The leadership conventions of the 1960s were broadcast live, unlike those of the 1950s. Convention speeches were scheduled for prime time exposure, and the Liberals strategically timed their convention to be least affected by the popular Stanley Cup hockey broadcasts.

Provincial governments were relatively weak and passive in the 1950s but asserted a much more prominent role vis-à-vis Ottawa in the period following the leaderships of Diefenbaker and Pearson. With provinces more assertive in their policy and resource capacities, provincialism began to supersede regionalism. Quebec led the way; Liberal party leader Jean Lesage severed formal ties with the federal Liberals during the Quiet Revolution. As a consequence of the Quiet Revolution and Quebec's growing ambitions, Ontario's Conservative premier John Robarts convened a meeting of the premiers at a Confederation of Tomorrow Conference,[9] which involved neither the federal Conservative party nor Pearson's Liberal government.

Campaign management also changed between the 1950s and 1960s, becoming more "scientific," more poll-driven, and increasingly reliant on practitioners from the worlds of advertising (the Conservatives' Dalton Camp) and media (the Liberals' Keith Davey).

Diefenbaker's sweeping triumph in 1958 had a particularly strong impact on the minor parties. It led the CCF to refurbish itself as the New Democratic Party, and Social Credit temporarily disappeared from Parliament. After Social Credit returned in the 1960s, it ruptured, its leader Robert Thompson resigned and was elected as a Conservative MP. Social Credit's Quebec members, calling themselves the Ralliement des créditistes, survived the 1960s but disappeared by 1980. By turns, the minor parties propped up the Conservative and Liberal minority governments, with the NDP leveraging its position to impose its social welfare agenda on the Liberals. At times the two major parties joined forces to beat back non-confidence motions supported by the minor parties.

The Conservatives: Ascent and Decline

Throughout the 1950s and 1960s, the Conservatives continued to place a premium on the British connection and British institutional traditions. During the Suez crisis they called on prime minister Louis St. Laurent to "repent in sackcloth and ashes" for his "gratuitous condemnation" of Britain, but their motion to censure the Liberal government was defeated by the three other parties.[10]

After they lost power in 1963, the Conservatives demonstrated a lingering and increasingly anachronistic attachment to Canada's British heritage by castigating every Liberal act to Canadianize institutions as an attempt to subvert that heritage. As Canada's imperial past was being symbolically discarded they objected vigorously, opposing the push for a new Canadian flag to replace the Red Ensign and its Union Jack, remonstrating against the rebranding of the Royal Mail as Canada Post, and protesting the amalgamation of the Royal Canadian Navy and Royal Canadian Air Force with the Army to become the Canadian Armed Forces, with no hint in the title of the royal connection.

In the four federal elections leading up to 1957, the Conservatives won only 239 to the Liberals' 1,017 seats. After the 1953 election, they were weaker than they had been in 1945 when they fielded only twenty-nine candidates to contest Quebec's 75 seats.[11] Against this backdrop of failure, the 1956 convention that elected Diefenbaker as leader began with a motion to drop "Progressive" from the party's name, returning it to what it had been between 1922 and 1940. This motion failed, however, with only 36 of the 1,324 delegates voting in favour.

In a well-received convention speech, Diefenbaker promised that the party's caucus would decide the composition of his shadow cabinet.[12] However, given the opposition to him in Quebec, it seemed unlikely that the party could win office in the near future; the province's 300-plus delegates, whose preferred candidate was Donald Fleming, considered a unanimous push against Diefenbaker. An influential Quebec delegate opined that he would "be out in two years," and a Liberal organizer concluded, "This means we don't even have a fight on our hands in Quebec."[13]

This made the Conservative victory and Diefenbaker's role as a giant killer less than six months later all the more remarkable. Lambasting the Liberals for disregarding the rights of Parliament and aligning their policies too closely with those of the United States, the Conservatives used "It's time for a change" as their campaign slogan in 1957. A growing nationalist current, tinged with anti-Americanism in a setting of unease over penetration of the Canadian economy by the United States, aided the party. So too did newfound support in populous Ontario. Premier Leslie Frost stumped for Diefenbaker "as he had never done" for Drew, and dispatched a cabinet minister to woo the Social Credit premiers of Alberta and British Columbia, Ernest Manning and W.A.C. Bennett, "to line up a coalition of the Conservative and Social Credit" parties behind Diefenbaker.[14] The Conservative vote leapt by 8 per cent in Ontario and was greater still in six other provinces.[15]

Although they won fewer votes than the Liberals, the Conservatives won more seats, placing them at the head of a minority government. Momentum led some prominent Conservative voices, including the *Globe and Mail*, to urge Diefenbaker to call an immediate election in search of a majority mandate.[16] When the election came nine months later, Diefenbaker drew large enthusiastic crowds on the hustings, party posters urging voters to "Follow John." One observer noted that Diefenbaker's "appeal to the emotions of the voters seems to have had an almost hypnotic effect upon them."[17]

The departure of Quebec native son St. Laurent, and the organizational efforts of Maurice Duplessis's Union Nationale government, helped the Conservatives in the 1957–8 elections. In the West, Social Credit's complete collapse was an advantage as well; the Conservatives took all nineteen Social Credit seats in Alberta and British Columbia in 1958 and, for only the second time since 1921, a party won a majority of the popular vote, 54 per cent.

A key to Conservative success was that many Canadians of neither British nor French origins who had never voted for the Conservatives switched to them in something of an ethnic revolt. Termed a "third force" in politics,[18] these minority groups rallied to Diefenbaker, whose name and heritage personified this force: he described his ancestors as "dispossessed Scottish Highlanders and discontented Palatine Germans."[19] In this respect he was unlike Robert Borden, Arthur Meighen, R.J. Manion, John Bracken, and George Drew. Hugh Segal, a Jew and future candidate for the party's leadership, recalled being a young student and how Diefenbaker's message of opportunity for people of all ethnic backgrounds "grabbed me by the throat."[20]

Diefenbaker shunned the notion of hyphenated Canadians, the reference to Canadians as British- or French-Canadians, as many MPs referred to themselves in the 1940s.[21] Paradoxically, Diefenbaker's "unhyphenated Canadian" formulation attracted many such as Ukrainian, Polish, and German Canadians who identified with their ancestral homelands, something Diefenbaker played to, telling a Ukrainian organization, for example, that "those behind the Iron Curtain would not be forgotten" by his party.[22]

Diefenbaker's 1960 Bill of Rights, his appointment of the first female and Ukrainian cabinet ministers (Ellen Fairclough and Michael Starr), the relaxation of some discriminatory immigration provisions, the extension of the federal franchise to First Nations peoples, and his stand against South African apartheid, a system of segregation based on race, at the 1961 Commonwealth Conference reflected his broader interest in human rights.[23]

An economic downturn, high unemployment, a sagging Canadian dollar, a very public spat with the governor of the Bank of Canada, and the cancellation of the Avro Arrow, an interceptor aircraft designed and built in Canada, badly damaged Diefenbaker, and his party suffered in the 1962 election. A surprising upsurge by Social Credit in Quebec hurt both major parties, with each capturing 37 per cent of the national vote. Reduced to a minority, Diefenbaker's government limped along, propped up by Social Credit on most parliamentary votes.

However, Diefenbaker soon lost control of his cabinet and then of Parliament itself. He alienated the United States during the Cuban missile crisis – a political and military standoff over the installation of nuclear-armed Soviet missiles – by delaying its requested state of readiness for Canada's NORAD units; he implied that Canada's military position could be untethered from that of its neighbour.[24] Journalists such as Peter Newman, who had been "buoyed up by the great expectations the Conservative leader had roused," came to see him as self-deluded.[25] George Hees, Diefenbaker's campaign manager when he won the party's leadership, resigned in 1963 along with two other cabinet ministers over Diefenbaker's opposition to the stationing of nuclear weapons on Canadian soil. One media report suggested that at least six ministers were at odds with Diefenbaker,[26] and for the first time in almost four decades a Canadian government fell, toppled by the other three parties.

A Conservative minority government gave way to a Liberal minority government in the 1963 election, but Diefenbaker continued to capture national attention as no other politician in Canada had before. In his best-selling *Lament for a Nation*, philosopher George Grant famously characterized Diefenbaker's defeat as the dying breath of Canada's distinct conservative values: "The impossibility of conservatism in our era is the impossibility of Canada."[27] According to Grant, American liberalism promoted technology and world domination directed by American multinational corporations.[28] Diefenbaker's undoing, in Grant's eyes, was his refusal to cede to the will of the United States.

Red toryism, as championed by Grant, still flavoured Conservative thinking in the Diefenbaker era. Tory W.L. Morton, one of Canada's leading twentieth-century historians, stressed the centrality to conservativism of respect for tradition, authority, and loyalty.[29] To Morton, a generation shares a bond or social contract with the generations that came before it and those that follow. Unlike liberals, he observed, conservatives believe "the individual man is weak, imperfect and limited."[30] Discomforted by American notions of the general will, popular sovereignty, and majoritarian democracy, Morton, like Diefenbaker, considered monarchy a crucial salutary feature of Canadian parliamentary government.[31] At the invitation of Diefenbaker's Conservatives, in 1957 the Queen opened Parliament for the first time ever.

Conservatives came to both love and loathe Diefenbaker in equal measure. He lost control of his party's extra-parliamentary apparatus – the party organization outside of Parliament – to media-savvy party president Dalton Camp, who had helped the Conservatives win the 1957 and 1958 elections. Fratricidal fighting and bitter enmity followed the party's 1963 defeat over whether and how to remove Diefenbaker. He insisted that he would not retire until a successor of whom he approved was available. Diefenbaker, booed at the party's 1966 annual meeting, witnessed Camp's re-election as party president and delegates voted overwhelmingly in favour of a leadership convention.[32]

With Diefenbaker refusing to indicate whether he would be a candidate, the field of prospective successors grew to include a number of his former cabinet colleagues as well as Conservative premiers Duff Roblin of Manitoba and Robert Stanfield of Nova Scotia. A surprising feature of the convention was last-minute candidate Mary Walker-Sawka, a movie producer and the first woman to seek the leadership of a major party. Stanfield won the leadership despite lukewarm caucus support and Diefenbaker remained in the caucus. He captured media attention as a fierce opponent of the "two nations" (*deux nations*) formulation – recognition of Quebec as a nation – adopted by most of the leadership contenders. Under Stanfield, the Conservatives offered greater acceptance of bilingualism than they had under Diefenbaker, who vocally criticized Pierre Trudeau's policies of bilingualism and multiculturalism.

Diefenbaker became a hero to future Conservative leaders Brian Mulroney, Joe Clark, and Stephen Harper. As a teenager, Mulroney worked for Diefenbaker's leadership bid in 1956 and received friendly telephone calls from him after he became prime minister.[33] Harper opined, "If ever there was a Conservative prime minister whose reputation needs to be reclaimed from Liberal slander it is the Chief, 'Honest John.' No other prime minister of any stripe did more for the cause of fairness and equality and inclusion."[34] Harper's government named an icebreaker and a government building after Diefenbaker, and announced during the 2015 election that Diefenbaker's birthplace would be designated a national historic site. Harper also restored "Royal" to the titles of the navy and the air force forty-three years after the Liberals had discarded the practice, against Diefenbaker's protestation.

The Liberals: Weakened and Leashed

More than any other event, the 1956 "pipeline debate" undermined the Liberal government of Louis St. Laurent. The Conservatives opposed the level of American investment in a proposed trans-Canada pipeline, the CCF argued for public ownership, and both parties accused the United States ambassador of intruding on the rights of Parliament by criticizing the views of Conservative leader George Drew on the issue. Social Credit supported the pipeline, but after the Liberals curtailed debate on the project, all the opposition parties accused the government of being contemptuous of parliamentary democracy.[35] The issue resonated strongly with the public, whose growing perception was that, after over twenty years in power, the Liberals had become arrogant and gotten too comfortable.

Defeated in the 1957 election, St. Laurent stepped down as party leader and was replaced by Lester Pearson. The outcome, like the outcome of the convention that had selected St. Laurent a decade earlier, was a foregone conclusion, given that most of the constituency delegates voted as their MP preferred.[36] Pearson's political inexperience showed almost immediately. Diefenbaker ridiculed him on his first day as party leader in Parliament for demanding that the government resign and turn power back to the Liberals without an election.[37]

The 1957–8 elections demonstrated that the Liberals were neither as indispensable nor as infallible as they presented themselves and as many believed. They had not fared so poorly in Quebec since the 1880s, and the only seat they won in the West was the Northwest Territories. Essentially a federation of provincial Liberal parties, the National Liberal Federation was shell-shocked and humiliated in the Conservative landslide of 1958. A public session of the federation's advisory council, not held since the 1930 election after the party had also been rebuffed, met to plot the party's future.[38]

In the introduction to a book by Jack Pickersgill, a Pearson cabinet minister who had assisted Mackenzie King and St. Laurent on virtually all aspects of policy, Pearson articulated his vision of liberalism: the state was "the creation of man to protect and serve him, and not the reverse." Pearson wrote of liberalism seeking "the removal of privilege, discrimination, and class distinctions,"[39] distinctions that the tory Morton highlighted by noting that a conservative "instinctively wants to know who your people are and where you come from."

During Pearson's leadership, there was much talk of democratizing the party. A group of Toronto-centred, upper-middle-class professionals nationalized the party's regionalized structures, reducing the influence of the party's regional chieftains. In Quebec, future cabinet minister Maurice Lamontagne led a purge of the corrupt Montreal party machine known as "la poubelle – the garbage can."[40] Quebecers began returning to the Liberal fold as Pearson promoted the political role of French Canadians and the equality of the French and English languages.

Weak provincial Liberal parties hurt the federal Liberals – the only Liberal government in 1959 was in Newfoundland. The federal party struggled to overcome the realigned partisan attachments wrought by the Diefenbaker phenomenon. Keith Davey, the party's national campaign director in the 1960s, noted, "Today in Canada we really have two majorities. One in Eastern Canada which is predominantly Liberal and one on the Prairies which is predominantly Conservative. I think I understand why this has happened but I really must confess I don't know what we can do about it. Particularly since attempting to build a base in the West could easily jeopardize our base in the East."[41]

Strong regional identities contributed to declining comity between the federal Liberal party and the provincial Liberal parties; in Saskatchewan, for example, party finance issues resulted in persistent estrangement.[42] Another challenge was countering Conservative gains among Canadians of neither British- nor French-Canadian heritage. Pearson acknowledged to a Polish-language newspaper that unlike an earlier time when "relations between the Liberal Party and the New Canadians were very lively ... [they] became a little dull."[43]

This was a period of soul searching for the Liberals. St. Laurent and his American-born "minister of everything," C.D. Howe, had espoused a continentalist economic vision.[44] Pearson took a different tack; at what came to be known as the "thinkers' conference," he warned of a growing threat to Canadian independence in the form of capital from the United States, an issue his future finance minister Walter Gordon took up by commissioning a task force on foreign ownership.[45] At the conference Pearson proposed (and Gordon opposed) an Atlantic free trade area. Various speakers suggested military conscription, devaluing the dollar – something the Conservatives were to do and which the Liberals criticized – and stationing missile bases on Canadian soil, the pivotal issue in the 1963 election that returned the Liberals to power. Lampooning Pearson's "over-intellectualism," the *Globe and Mail* dismissed his "egghead Conference."[46]

Tom Kent, who became a key advisor to Pearson and a deputy minister, proposed a wide-ranging social welfare agenda that the *Globe* mocked because he proposed to pay for it with a 50 per cent tax on advertising. However, a half century later, the paper described his ideas as having "caught the imagination of the press and the public" and the conference as a turning point in Liberal fortunes, providing a policy blueprint for a Liberal government.[47]

The Liberals capitalized on the economic challenges faced by the Conservatives; unemployment more than doubled between 1956 and 1961, and Ottawa sought temporary lines of credit from Britain, the United States, and the International Monetary Fund.[48] With the Canadian dollar devalued and pegged at 92.5 US cents, the Liberals characterized the Conservatives as poor economic stewards. They printed widely distributed "Diefenbucks," phony scrip resembling banknotes with a caricature of Diefenbaker in the place of the Queen's image.[49] These developments seem to have had an impact; the election of 1962 reduced the Conservative government to a minority.

After 1963 Pearson's government divided, as Diefenbaker's government had done, on many issues, but there was no cabinet revolt. Gordon, an economic nationalist, clashed with Mitchell Sharp, his successor as finance minister, who shelved Gordon's task force report. As a fiscal liberal, Gordon also had disagreements with fiscally conservative trade and commerce minister Robert Winters, the future runner-up to Pierre Trudeau as Pearson's successor.[50]

The American administration of John F. Kennedy was happy to see the back of Diefenbaker. On the eve of the 1963 election, an American general had openly contradicted him regarding Canada's defence commitments.[51] However, as prime minister, Pearson did not always please the Americans. A scathing speech he gave in Philadelphia regarding their role in Vietnam led to President Lyndon Johnson reportedly upbraiding him for violating what he considered an inviolable precept: "You don't piss on your neighbour's rug."[52]

Unlike the charismatic Diefenbaker, Pearson had little appeal as a retail politician, someone who likes direct contact with voters: meeting, talking, and appealing personally for their support. Diefenbaker revelled in political jousting; Pearson did so only "in spots" and ironically recognized his limitations: "I was never able to make a platitude sound like a pronouncement or an indiscretion sound like a platitude."[53] However, Pearson's government left its policy mark by introducing national universal medicare and pension systems, originating interest-free loans to university students, extending eligibility for the family allowance, and concluding the Canada–United States Auto Pact that integrated the Canadian and American auto industries in a shared North American market. It served as the building block for the free trade agreement the Conservatives were to negotiate with the United States two decades later. Pearson's government also contributed to refashioning national identity: proposing the Maple Leaf flag, creating the Order of Canada, and establishing a royal commission that pointed the way to bilingualism in government operations. Although in office for a shorter period than Diefenbaker, Pearson came to be judged one of the country's most transformative prime ministers.[54]

Flirtation between the Liberals and the NDP, federally and in Ontario, paralleled the dalliance of the Conservatives and Social Credit. Senior Liberals and NDPers met in Toronto in 1964 to discuss potential cooperation and a possible alliance. An Ontario Liberal MLA envisaged a two-party system with some left-wing Conservatives joining a united left party and some right-wing Liberals joining the Conservative party.[55] A short-lived organization known as EPIC (Exchange for Political Ideas in Canada), co-chaired by Liberal MP Pauline Jewitt and NDP MP Douglas Fisher, brought together 170 left-leaning thinkers in both parties, but rapprochement came to naught.[56] NDP MP Ed Schreyer, the future premier of Manitoba and governor general, was the only respondent in a 1965 survey of journalists, intellectuals, and politicians who viewed the idea of a Liberal-NDP merger with equanimity.[57]

The Liberals and the NDP developed an antagonistic-symbiotic relationship wherein the Liberals relied on the NDP for innovative policy ideas (such as medicare) and the NDP depended on the Liberals to implement them. To the CCF-NDP, the Liberals were opportunists susceptible to pressure; by responding to the welfare agenda of the NDP, the Liberals effectively pre-empted the NDP's appeal.

The CCF-NDP: Socialists Take Stock

Post-war prosperity and the Cold War devastated the CCF, compelling party leaders to take stock. Economic growth and a more fluid social structure blurred the class basis of the party's original appeal. On foreign policy, the party supported NATO, but its socialist lineage led many to associate it with communism and its main international champion, the Soviet Union. Disassociation proved challenging, despite the party's secretary, Lorne Ingle, making it clear that "there is no question but that socialists would stand with the Western powers because only if the Western powers succeed in defeating communism in such a conflict would the ideals which we stand for have any chance of survival."[58]

Re-articulating the egalitarian and liberal elements of the CCF's socialist credo, party luminary David Lewis attacked the Soviet system, pointed to Roosevelt's New Deal policies, and lauded the Scandinavian states for demonstrating that the "tools of control and planning [can] be effectively applied without actually replacing private with public ownership."[59] The party's 1956 Winnipeg Declaration made a kind of peace with capitalism, asserting the "need for private enterprise which can make a useful contribution to the development of our economy."[60] However, modifying the CCF's economic message did not go far enough for a few, such as former party MP Ross Thatcher, who left the party over the issue of corporate taxation and eventually became the Liberal premier of Saskatchewan.

After the Trades and Labour Congress and the Canadian Congress of Labour merged to become the Canadian Labour Congress in 1956 and the CCF was badly bruised in the 1958 election (winning only eight seats on less than 10 per cent of the popular vote), CLC leaders approached the CCF about merging their political efforts and forming a new party. That new party became the NDP, which cultivated stronger organizational and financial links than the CCF had done with the union movement. Unionists became more influential at party forums and in fashioning the NDP's labour policies.[61]

The CCF's transformation into the NDP in 1961 confirmed the party's ideological reorientation; where the CCF's original name included "farmer-labour-socialist," the NDP described itself as appealing also to "liberally minded Canadians."[62] To capitalize on the unpopularity of the Liberal and Conservative leaders, an NDP campaign leaflet offered a cartoon of them wrestling and the NDP acronym spelled as "Neither Diefenbaker nor Pearson."[63]

Not all CCFers, however, embraced the rebrand. Opposition came from three future Manitoba NDP cabinet ministers, including eventual premier Howard Pawley, who had voted against the Winnipeg Declaration. His concern was the forsaking of socialist content: "This tendency to want to become similar, wanting to become respectable, wanting to become no different from the two old-line parties. I didn't think [the NDP] would work. Philosophically, I thought it was wrong."[64] A notable defector from the new party was Hazen Argue, who had become the CCF leader after the defeat of M.J. Coldwell in the Diefenbaker sweep of 1958. Months after Tommy Douglas defeated Argue for the leadership of the fledgling NDP, Argue joined the Liberals and was elected as a Liberal MP and then appointed as a Liberal senator.

In common with Western Europe's post-war social democratic parties, the NDP argued for a mixed economy, Keynesian economics, a welfare state, political liberalism, and greater economic equality.[65] Rather than treat post-war prosperity as a prelude to depression, as some party spokesmen had done in the late 1940s, the party presented a more affluent society as an opportunity to further social reform. Welfare liberalism and social democracy appeared to converge, although the NDP found that pursuing welfare reforms from the governing Liberals was akin to pulling teeth. The success of the party in finally winning the Liberals over to universal medical care and pension schemes led one NDP MP to assert that hers was *The Party That Changed Canada*, and future party leaders Lewis and Ed Broadbent claimed Canada's welfare state as the party's signal achievement.[66]

More purposefully bilingual in its operations, more supportive of official bilingualism, and more accommodative of Quebec's national aspirations than the CCF, the NDP attracted Robert Cliché, who became its leader in Quebec, well-known broadcast journalist Laurier LaPierre, and philosopher Charles Taylor, who became a party vice-president. All three ran but failed as candidates for Parliament; Taylor did so in all four elections between 1962 and 1968, including a loss to Liberal Pierre Trudeau. Quebec proved as barren for the party as it had been for the CCF. To be sure, the NDP in the 1960s garnered a higher percentage of the vote nationally than the CCF had in the 1950s but it remained, along with Social Credit, one of two weak sisters in a Parliament with four and sometimes five parties.

Social Credit: Fractured and Fading

Like the CCF, Social Credit referred to the Liberals and Conservatives as the "old-line parties."[67] The party's modest support rose between 1949 and 1957; it more than doubled its percentage of the vote, to over 5 per cent in 1953 and over 6 per cent in 1957. It jumped from ten to fifteen to nineteen parliamentary seats with its votes concentrated in the far west, unable to win any seats east of Alberta. In Quebec the Union des électeurs voiced Social Credit thinking, but after the Union allied itself with the provincial Liberals in 1956, party leader Solon Low accused it of anti-Semitism, denounced the alliance with the Liberals as perfidious, and termed the Union an embarrassment.[68]

Echoing the monetary theories of Major Douglas, the first plank of Social Credit's 1958 platform promised a national dividend for consumers with money printed by the Bank of Canada.[69] However, the party failed to retain any seats in that year's election. Defeated, Low became a high school teacher; later, Alberta premier Ernest Manning appointed him a provincial judge.

After a fifteen-year public service career in Africa, Robert Thompson returned to Canada and, handpicked by Manning, succeeded Low as the party's federal leader. Thompson defeated the fiery orator Réal Caouette, who was captivated by Major Douglas's theories long after Manning's government had discarded them. Caouette promised, as had Alberta premier William Aberhart, a cash dividend to every man, woman, and child.[70] A Union des électeurs MP in the 1940s and a defeated provincial Liberal candidate in 1956, Caouette sparred with Thompson after Social Credit elected thirty MPs, twenty-six of them from Quebec, in the 1962 election. After the western wing of the party failed to improve on its four seats in the 1963 election, Caouette led the Quebecers out of the caucus and formed the Ralliement des créditistes.

Frustrated by Social Credit's federal failure in English Canada, Manning proposed a realignment of the federal parties: Social Crediters ought to throw in their lot with the Conservatives to confront a merged "leftist" party of Liberals and NDPers.[71] Manning had strongly opposed the Liberals' national hospital insurance scheme in the 1950s and the national medicare program of the 1960s as "socialistic," entailing compulsion and "welfare state-ism."[72] Critical of the "big banks" and the monetary system when he had been Aberhart's finance minister, Manning stepped down as premier in 1968 and, having made peace with the banks, became a director of the Canadian Imperial Bank of Commerce.

Social Credit succeeded electorally in 1952 as a provincial party in British Columbia. The BC party benefitted from the party's image in Alberta, where Manning's government used oil royalties to spend liberally on health, education, welfare, and highway programs.[73] Led by streetcar operator Lyle Wicks, the BC party raised its profile in rural areas, ignoring the large cities. It was a shrewd strategy; it took only 900 and 1,600 votes respectively to elect an MLA in Grand Forks–Greenwood and Kaslo-Slocan but 36,000 votes to elect an MLA in Vancouver Point Grey.[74] Social Credit also benefitted from the preferential ballot system introduced by the provincial Liberal-Conservative coalition government when their coalition dissolved in 1952. Seeking to foil the CCF, the Liberals and Conservatives miscalculated, assuming that Liberal and Conservative voters would opt for candidates of each other's party as their second choice rather than CCF candidates. However, many Liberal, Conservative, and CCF voters selected Social Credit candidates as their second choice and Social Credit became the government, defeating the CCF by one seat.

The newly minted Social Credit MLAs selected hardware merchant W.A.C. Bennett as their premier.[75] A former Conservative MLA, Bennett had defected to Social Credit after voting against some of his party's bills and challenging its leader in 1950. He rode to power on Social Credit's name rather than its monetary theories, to which he did not subscribe. Bennett's government survived until 1972, when it was defeated by the NDP – whom he described as "barbarians at the gates" preaching "Marxian socialism."[76]

The years 1956 and 1968 were particularly pivotal in Canada's political history. In 1956 a debate related to a pipeline mortally wounded the long-governing Liberals, and Diefenbaker became the Conservative leader. In 1968, Pearson departed as the Liberal leader, and a majority Liberal government led by Pierre Trudeau came into office after three elections in less than four years had produced consecutive minority governments.

As Canada celebrated the centenary of Confederation, the power and prestige of Britain in the world continued to decline. The opening of the Conservative party by Diefenbaker to voters who were of neither British or French ethnic origin, and the efforts of Pearson to highlight Canada's distinctiveness at home and abroad contributed to the rapid evaporation of Britishness as the core identity of English Canada. Together with the continued isolation of English Canadians and the Québécois ("Two Solitudes" in the words of novelist Hugh

MacLennan),[77] new challenges appeared to the concept of Canadian identity. The challenges persist to this day.

During the Diefenbaker-Pearson era, some academics presumed that the new importance of technical and managerial expertise in the developed world would soon render ideological differences among political parties obsolete: technology and technocrats would engineer the "good society."[78] However, like others in the West, Canadians continued to believe that ideological differences mattered as much as, if not more than, ever. For Pierre Trudeau, the new prime minister, the good society meant a "just society," the slogan he used in his ride to power.

Chapter Six

Economy, Language, Unity

Just watch me.[1]

Pierre Trudeau

Trudeaumania, the excitement generated by Pierre Trudeau's entry into the race for the leadership of the Liberal Party and his performance in the 1968 election, signalled the beginning of another era in federal party politics. The irrepressible power of Québécois nationalism against a background of stagflation – a stagnating economy in the midst of raging inflation – became the motif characterizing his time as prime minister.

"It's the economy, stupid" served as the de facto slogan for Bill Clinton's successful presidential election campaign in 1992. Canadians thought so too: the economy was the most critical election issue, according to public opinion surveys in the 1970s and 1980s.[2] This may have led the governing Liberals to use "The Land Is Strong" as their 1972 election campaign slogan when the economy was booming: the value of agricultural sales abroad and labour force participation rates set records, average wages increased substantially, and Canada led the world in mineral exports.[3]

However, the economy proved less critical to the election outcome than the Liberals assumed it would. Another minority government, the fourth in a decade, resulted. It was a dramatic comedown for the Liberals after the Trudeaumania phenomenon of 1968, which had come on the heels of the self-confidence generated by Canada's centennial celebrations and Expo 67, the world's fair held in Montreal. The promise of 1967–8 gave way to significant disenchantment by 1972, and the Liberals came within two seats of losing power.

Other elections in the 1970s and early 1980s also provided evidence that the economy was not the main axis around which the public's choices fell. Flourishing Alberta, for example, led the country in growth, enjoying a tremendous construction boom and previously unimaginable wealth generated by its petroleum resources, yet the province did not elect any Liberals in any of the federal elections they won. Indeed, the Liberals did better after the economy declined in 1973 with an oil price shock fuelling pervasive inflation and rising unemployment nationally; they returned to majority power in the 1974 election.

Although the Liberals lost power in the 1979 election after unemployment reached a modern record, another oil price shock, and historically high interest rates,[4] their popular vote exceeded the vote for the Conservatives. The Conservatives prevailed in 1979 only because the votes for them were more efficiently distributed; they won more seats than the Liberals with fewer votes, as they had in the Diefenbaker victory of 1957.

The Liberal loss of power in 1984, coming after a banner year of brisk economic growth of almost 5 per cent, inflation at a ten-year low, and a declining although still high unemployment rate, cast further doubt on the connection between the economy and electoral performance.[5] The Conservatives won the 1984 election decisively, but it is doubtful that their promises – closer economic ties with the United States, increased defence spending, tax reform, and deregulation – were particularly significant issues in the calculations of voters. More noteworthy was Conservative leader Brian Mulroney's performance in a televised leaders' debate: he effectively castigated new Liberal leader John Turner for his compliance with the unpopular outgoing prime minister Trudeau's wholesale awarding of patronage positions to Liberal stalwarts.[6] Turner's pratfalls hurt his party; the press lampooned him for patting the backsides of women after a party leaders' debate devoted to women's issues – the only such debate ever held.[7]

Women proved critical in contributing to Canada's economic growth between the 1960s and 1980s; their participation in the labour force increased by 58 per cent between 1963 and 1972, as opposed to 22 per cent for men.[8] Fewer children per family, changing social norms regarding gender roles, an expanding service sector, and the proliferation of home electrical appliances afforded women more employment opportunities. However, the political participation of women lagged dramatically. Of the thirty-six female candidates in the 1968 election, only one was a Liberal. The majority of female candidates, NDPers, contested constituencies in which their party was not competitive. Although the number of female candidates ballooned to 195 by 1979, a plurality ran for the tiny Marxist-Leninist Party. Together with the NDP, they fielded nearly half the female candidates. The Conservatives nominated only fourteen women in the 282 constituencies, fewer than the feeble Communist Party, which ran nineteen women in 71 constituencies.[9]

Despite the affluence of the 1970s, many Canadians doubted that their economic well-being would continue to increase or that labour would benefit from the fruits of ever-expanding production. Stagflation – a sustained slowdown in economic growth occurring simultaneously with high rates of inflation and unemployment – undermined the Keynesian thinking that had taken hold after the Second World War. Keynesian economics proposed adjusting fiscal policy as the solution to market failures, but the remedy of deficit spending during recessionary times fell short in the 1970s.

Public pessimism spawned by double-digit inflation led the Conservatives in 1974 to promise a ninety-day freeze of prices and incomes.[10] The Liberals countered by running television ads using Trudeau's response to a taunting heckler: "Zap. You're frozen!"[11] The Liberals, however, delivered on the Conservative promise a year later and went even further, imposing wage and price controls for three years. Supported by the business community, the controls on wages incensed the labour movement, which called a one-day national general strike in 1976.

The rise to power that year of the separatist Parti Québécois (PQ) propelled the issue of national unity, which eventually overtook the economy as the primary political concern of the Liberal government. Although scandals tarnished the Liberals, the PQ's election worked in the Liberals' favour because Canadians as a whole perceived the Liberals, led by Quebecer Trudeau, as best equipped to handle the separatist challenge.

The Liberals had dealt with the intractable national unity issue by extending bilingualism in the federal government and rejecting special status for Quebec. The Conservatives, on the other hand, shifted the position they had under Diefenbaker and adopted a bi-nationalist position, recognizing the special status of the French language. Nevertheless, seventeen Conservative MPs had defied leader Robert Stanfield and voted against the 1969 Official Languages Act.[12] For its part, the NDP recognized Quebec's special status in 1968, underlining its right to control "social security, education, town planning and community development," while "Canadians elsewhere can seek federal action in these fields."[13] However, Conservative and NDP outreach to Quebec failed to win over its nationalists.

Quebec's status had been brought into sharp focus by the Quiet Revolution of the 1960s, a period of profound political and social change, including the secularization of government, and by the kidnappings of a British diplomat and Quebec cabinet minister Pierre Laporte by the then little-known Front de libération du Québec (FLQ) in 1970. Reacting to the FLQ threat, the Liberals imposed the War Measures Act, a 1914 law giving the government broad powers to maintain security and order during times of war or insurrection. It was an action supported by public opinion in and outside of Quebec (although 3,000 Université de Montréal students initially demonstrated support for the FLQ).[14] After Laporte was murdered, the Conservatives voted unanimously in favour of the government's action. Creditiste leader Réal Caouette went further, proposing that FLQ leaders be shot by a firing squad.[15] Only the NDP, with the exception of four of its MPs, opposed the War Measures Act.[16]

Repeated efforts at constitutional reform through the 1970s floundered until the Liberals returned to office after the defeat of Joe Clark's short-lived 1979 Conservative government. After all the provinces but Quebec agreed to patriate the Constitution with an amending formula and a charter of rights, seventeen Conservatives, five Liberals, and two NDPers defied the positions of their parties and voted against the Liberals' constitutional resolution. Quebecers constituted the majority of the Liberal caucus, but only three of them voted against the resolution, with Quebec MP Warren Allmand, a former Trudeau minister, alleging it would mean second-class standing for Quebec's English minority.[17]

The Constitution's new Charter of Rights and Freedoms in 1982 was a formative act like the British North America Act had been in 1867. The PQ and most of French Quebec's intellectuals and media opposed the constitutional resolution, characterizing the failure to gain the Quebec government's agreement as the "night of long knives,"[18] a reference to a Nazi purge in the 1930s in which many were executed for political reasons. Quebec's status in the Constitution remained uncertain.

The Liberals: Trudeau's Time and Thinking

The witty intellectual Pierre Trudeau was an unlikely Liberal leader; a year before becoming party leader, a lengthy inventory of Lester Pearson's potential successors did not include him.[19] However, once Trudeau became a candidate, his magnetism and audacity enchanted much of the press and the public. Asked which political figure he most admired, he provocatively replied, "Machiavelli."[20] Shod in sandals and wearing a scarf, his raffish image was consistent with the countercultural zeitgeist of the day. Trudeau broke the mould of conventional politics; treated like a "rock" star, he kissed girls and women as well as babies.

Trudeau dissolved Parliament three days after becoming prime minister. In the ensuing election, his Liberals ended a string of minority governments. Simultaneously elusive and vividly present, Trudeau brought Canada unprecedented international attention. Soon wary of the media, he began to avoid them, developing a reputation as a "peekaboo" prime minister refusing to participate in a leaders' debate in 1974.[21] In 1976 he spent almost as much time travelling abroad as on business in Canada. Many considered Trudeau's self-assurance and contempt for opponents as bordering on arrogance. He told parliamentarians, "When they are 50 yards from Parliament Hill, they are no longer honourable members – they are just nobodies," and to a Saskatchewan heckler he responded impolitically, "Why should I sell your wheat?"[22]

Trudeau was not as much a party man as his own man. In contrast, his opponents – Conservatives Stanfield and Clark, NDPers Tommy Douglas, David Lewis, and Ed Broadbent – were life-long partisans who had always conscientiously conformed to the positions of their parties. Enigmatic, paradoxical, contradictory, and at turns socialist and liberal, Trudeau noted, "The only constant to be found in my thinking over the years has been my opposition to accepted opinion."[23] He underwent a remarkable transmutation from his youth to adulthood; initially reflecting the education and conservative culture of old Quebec, his studies at Harvard in the 1940s liberalized his thinking.[24]

In challenging the clerics and educators of Quebec's corrupt, discredited conservative regime, Trudeau's *Cité Libre* journal, which he founded in 1950, had voiced what others only dared whisper. A passionate exponent of individual rights, he debunked Quebec's increasingly assertive and aggressive nationalism, labelling it the "New Treason of the Intellectuals."[25] Contemptuous of nationalism as breeding intolerance, totalitarianism, and discrimination, he castigated the separatist quest of Quebec's nationalists as a self-deluding passion, dismissing them as intellectually indulgent sorcerers and spiritual escapists. In turn, they dismissed Trudeau; historian Michel Brunet termed him "un fumiste."[26] Trudeau's anti-nationalism contributed indirectly to hardening other nationalisms among Indigenous peoples, whose assimilation a Liberal White Paper proposed, as well as among the Québécois.[27]

Prodding the Québécois to break out from their ethnically nationalist "wigwam" complex to spur Canada's redefinition as a multinational, polyethnic, federal state,[28] Trudeau believed Quebec possessed all the necessary constitutional powers to achieve its legitimate aspirations, breaking with Pearson's conciliatory posture towards the province. Former CCF chairman Frank Scott, an intellectual father figure to

Trudeau, influenced his attitude to both Québécois nationalism and the virtues of a bill of rights, which Saskatchewan's CCF government had introduced on Scott's advice in 1947. Trudeau revealed his indebtedness to Scott when the Queen signed the Constitution Act, 1982: "If we have a charter of rights in this country," he told her, "we owe it to this one man."[29]

Trudeau's liberalism may have been deeply rooted, but his Liberalism was late in coming; he had damned Pearson's Liberals for their defence policies and flirted with the NDP, which courted him. He penned a chapter in *Social Purpose for Canada*, which styled itself a successor to *Social Planning for Canada*, authored by the CCF's brain trust in the 1930s. Trudeau argued that the route to building socialism was through the provinces, not "vastly increased centralization" in Ottawa.[30] Nevertheless, when he was prime minister he did not hesitate to run roughshod over the premiers, damning them for viewing Canada as "a confederation of shopping centers" and declaring that he would not be a "head waiter" at a table for them.[31] Still, Trudeau eventually offered to negotiate jurisdictional areas with them, including immigration, communications, agriculture, and social services, a list of fields remarkably similar to one Clark's Conservatives had presented.

If the Liberals' 1960 "thinkers' conference" had signalled a turn to the left, the party's 1977 convention seemed to turn to the right. In fact both conferences revealed the party's ideological abstruseness. One delegate summarized the mood of the 1977 meeting: "Get government back to the people; get the bureaucracy under control.... We want no new institutions that immediately become new bureaucracies and new centralized programs." Another delegate, Trudeau's minister of Indian affairs, Warren Allmand, castigated the party for tunnel vision, for being a smug "inner Canadian" party made up of white middle-class technocrats insensitive to those with low incomes and few opportunities.[32] Another minister, James Richardson, demonstrated his discomfort with Trudeau's push to constitutionalize official bilingualism by resigning from his cabinet.[33]

Trudeau's policies, a tug of war between freedom and authority, defined him and his Liberals. On the one hand, they partially legalized abortion, homosexual acts between consenting adults ("There's no place for the state in the bedrooms of the nation," he famously said[34]), and entrenched a charter of rights. On the other hand, they resorted to the War Measures Act, placed limits on gun ownership, and limited parliamentary debate and scrutiny by resorting to omnibus bills consisting of several diverse unrelated subjects subject to a single vote. Some judged Trudeau's threat of unilateral action during his standoff with the premiers over constitutional patriation as a "constitutional coup d'état." After British lawmakers hesitated to act on his unilateral request, he referred to their action as "The Empire Strikes Back," the title of the then popular science fiction film.[35]

Under Trudeau, unprecedented power gravitated to the prime minister's office (PMO). As one example, he blindsided his finance minister, Jean Chrétien, by announcing a cut of two billion dollars in expenditures without informing him.[36] Regional desks in the PMO supplanted the previously unchallenged power of regional ministers to offer advice on policy and patronage. Limiting their independence, Trudeau downgraded the influence of designated regional ministers, although some ministers demonstrated a continuing ability to mobilize their department's resources to fund projects in their own regions.[37] Taking direct responsibility for conducting relations with the provinces against the backdrop of the PQ's victory, Trudeau required that his office assess all proposals made by his ministers.[38] The influence of the extra-parliamentary Liberal party, which had waxed during the 1972–4 minority government period, waned as the decade wore on.[39]

When he became prime minister in 1968, Trudeau was younger and more physically energetic than Stanfield or the NDP's Douglas. A decade later, at fifty-nine, he had become the old man in the leaders' arena: Clark was thirty-nine and NDP leader Broadbent was forty-two. The fifteen-year-old Liberal regime appeared sclerotic, neither vital nor innovative. Trudeau resigned as party leader after his party's election loss in 1979, but he soon returned to lead the party to power after the Clark Conservative interregnum of that year. The 1980 election result was not so much a vote for Trudeau or his Liberals as it was a consequence of the erroneous assumption by the Conservatives that their minority Parliament would pass and the public would accept an austere budget.

The Conservatives: Syndrome of Opposition

If the Trudeau years confirmed that the Liberals were the natural governing party, the corollary was that the Conservatives were the natural opposition party. Chronic weakness in Quebec, home to a quarter of the population, helps to explain their secondary status. Also contributing to their lesser status was the self-lacerating factionalism wracking the party. Persistent internal conflict revolved around the party's leadership.[40] Conservatives quarrelled about what they stood for, and leaders Stanfield and especially Clark faced snide attacks by fellow colleagues.

A plodding speaker, the calm, unassuming, and modest Stanfield lacked Trudeau's colour and flair. Peeling and eating a banana was the strongest image of Stanfield at the 1967 leadership convention that selected him; the strongest image at the Liberal convention was that of the nattily dressed Trudeau, a rose in his lapel. A visual metaphor that appeared on most of the country's front pages for Stanfield losing election campaign in 1974 was a photograph of him fumbling a football.[41] Stanfield encountered a national media a lot less docile than the Nova Scotia media he had dealt with as a premier.[42] The grandson of the underwear company's founder, he was often drawn by cartoonists as wearing his ancestor's underwear. The media also belittled Clark; many outlets labelled him "Joe Who" when he became the party leader, ridiculed him when an airline lost his luggage on a foreign trip, and some mocked him because his wife retained her maiden name.[43]

Stanfield adopted positions unpopular with many party activists: outreach to Quebec, official bilingualism, price controls, and a guaranteed annual income, making him the first major party leader to propose it. Like Trudeau, Stanfield considered official bilingualism part of the country's fabric. However, Trudeau's Liberals were better suited to confront the divisive issues of language and national unity, given Trudeau's background and the histories of the parties. Stanfield's gambit to overcome his party's weakness in Quebec was to recruit Marcel Faribault, a Union Nationale supporter, and then high-profile provincial Liberal Claude Wagner as his Quebec lieutenants to challenge Trudeau's contempt for Québécois nationalism. Nevertheless, Quebecers continued to vote for parties led by native sons: Trudeau, and Caouette whose Social Credit party in 1972 captured considerably more of the conservative vote in Quebec than the Conservatives did.

Stanfield curated his image of the party in an address to his caucus. He defined its bedrock principle as pursuit of a stable yet dynamic progressive conservative social order. He harked back to the party's connection to British conservatism and its emphasis on social order as an essential condition for securing individual freedom. Stanfield rejected "the supreme importance of private enterprise and the undesirability of government initiative and interference [as] ... Liberal nineteenth century doctrine." He opposed "enshrining private enterprise as the most fundamental principle of our party" because, he said, "Conservatism does not place private enterprise in a central position around which everything else revolves." Citing Edmund Burke, Stanfield described "the world as a very imperfect place," "man as an imperfect being," and the obligation to assist the less fortunate and vulnerable classes.[44]

After three losing campaigns, Stanfield resigned and the thirty-seven-year old Clark, who had worked in Stanfield's office, and whose only career had been in politics, emerged the victor in the subsequent leadership race. Clark was a surprise winner, having placed a distant third on the first ballot behind Wagner and Mulroney; in the end, with more than 2,300 ballots cast, Clark won by a narrow sixty-five-vote margin. Ideological divisions were apparent to those voting, with Clark seen as on the party's left and Wagner on its right.[45]

Coming out of the convention, the Conservatives continued to be poorly organized and divided. Candidate James Gillies, later a senior advisor to Clark during his prime ministership, summarized the conflict at the convention: "Red Tory. Blue Tory. Nobody has to tell you about these divisions ... this is a contest for control of the party being waged between different groups."[46] The party's blue tories were business liberals seeking to limit government restraints on individual freedom. Sceptical of state intrusions in the marketplace, they touted free markets and low taxes as economic elixirs. Red tories looked more favourably at a muscular and authoritative, if small, state. In a party whose ethos has always been more liberal than tory, the business liberal perspective grew stronger during the Stanfield and Clark years.

Regional factionalism contributed to party disunity; western delegates, who had a more populist temperament, preferred Clark to the French-Canadian Wagner. Clark's most memorable assertion, the communitarian formulation that Canada was a "community of communities,"[47] was consistent with the Trudeau Liberals' multiculturalism policy of 1971, which recognized the cultural contributions of diverse ethnic groups to society. Both articulations proved to be more popular in Ontario than in western Conservative circles.

Clark faced constant sniping after becoming leader. A feud between him and MP Jack Horner, who had been unsuccessful in his own bid for the leadership, led to Horner's defection to the Liberals. Horner, also critical of Stanfield as "a very, very sad choice," said of Clark, "I didn't like him. More important, I didn't respect him."[48] One of the party's few Quebec Conservative MPs, Jacques Lavoie, deserted the caucus, complaining that it had "a lack of interest and understanding of the problems of my region."[49] Like Horner, Wagner also did not get along with Clark,[50] and Mulroney displayed his aloofness by not running for Parliament under Clark's leadership in the 1979 election.

Clark appeared politically immature and inexperienced as prime minister. His short-lived Conservative government fell over a budget measure imposing an additional eighteen-cent per gallon gasoline tax. To mollify his detractors, Clark resigned as party leader and ran to succeed himself, losing to Mulroney at a 1983 convention. Delegates thought of the businessman Mulroney as an accomplished business liberal who was ideologically "centre to slightly right-of-centre" in the party.[51]

The fluently bilingual Mulroney had roots in Quebec and became the first Conservative leader from that province since John Abbott in 1891. The major impediment to John Crosbie's leadership bid at the 1983 convention was his inability to speak French; he ran third. Bilingualism had become obligatory in the selection of major party leaders, something Crosbie had denied when he entered the race but eventually conceded in his memoirs.[52]

The NDP: The Good Fight, Continued

With its agenda for social welfare and concern for the less privileged, many considered the NDP as the social conscience of Parliament. In the late 1960s the party became concerned with swelling American influence in Canada. Foreign, primarily American ownership of Canada's economy peaked at about 60 per cent of manufacturing industries and 37 per cent of corporate non-financial assets in the early 1970s.[53] The Liberals had commissioned a study of the issue during the Pearson years,[54] but its lead author, academic Mel Watkins, became disillusioned with Liberal inaction and joined the NDP, eventually becoming a party vice-president and candidate.

With Watkins in its vanguard, a left-wing NDP faction known as the Waffle drafted a Manifesto for an Independent Socialist Canada in 1969. Influenced by the New Left in the United States, a broad political movement of activists opposed to America's role in the Vietnam War, the manifesto's authors advocated economic nationalism. The Waffle faction argued, "Capitalism must be replaced by socialism ... by the public ownership of the means of production." Future party leader Ed Broadbent, among others, initially signed the document but subsequently withdrew his support.

The manifesto contended, "The major threat to Canadian survival today is American control of the Canadian economy. The major issue of our times is not national unity but national survival." Depicting the United States as a bully abroad and racist at home, the Waffle manifesto described "the American empire [as] the central reality for Canadians."[55] To party veteran David Lewis, the manifesto represented "ill-digested and not well understood Marxism."[56] He and the party's favourite intellectual, philosopher Charles Taylor, penned an alternative document that prevailed over the Waffle manifesto at a party convention.

Intra-party feuding persisted, however. Tommy Douglas's defeat as an MP in the 1968 election and his subsequent resignation as party leader led to a leadership convention pitting the party's elder statesman Lewis, who had served as the CCF's national secretary in the 1930s, 1940s, and 1950s, against thirty-year-old Waffle leader James Laxer. After Lewis triumphed, the Ontario NDP, led by Lewis's son Stephen, expelled the Waffle, which soon faded. Nevertheless its nationalism, if not its socialism, accorded with new nationalist stirrings in the public and the older parties.

Lewis's forceful campaign against "corporate welfare bums" in the 1972 election led to NDP gains. Holding the balance of power in Parliament, the NDP influenced government policy as it had in the 1960s; it claimed credit for increases in pensions, the creation of a government-owned petroleum company (Petro-Canada) and a foreign investment review agency (FIRA), landmark election and party finance reforms, and the establishment of a prices-review board.[57] However, in the 1974 election the NDP's popular vote declined in all the provinces west of Quebec, and its parliamentary representation shrank from a record high thirty-one to sixteen seats. In British Columbia the party lost nine of its eleven seats, possibly because of the growing unpopularity of the province's NDP government.

Lewis's defeat in his own constituency in the 1974 election led to Ed Broadbent's election as party leader in a contest in which a Black Jamaican-born MLA from British Columbia, Rosemary Brown, ran second. Her strong performance symbolized the party's growing affinity for adding concern with dimensions of exclusion and exploitation such as race, gender, and ethnicity to the older socialist concern with the condition of the working class. Moderating the party's image, Broadbent spoke of taxing, not nationalizing, natural resource industries; he dismissed nationalization as "flying in the face of political reality."[58]

Saluting the NDP's more moderate comportment, the *Toronto Star*, Canada's largest newspaper, endorsed the party in the 1979 election, something no large media outlet had ever done.[59] The equal treatment accorded Broadbent in the 1979 leaders' debate – in the first televised debate, in 1968, Douglas had been allotted less air time than Trudeau and Stanfield – confirmed the NDP's advance into the mainstream of Canadian politics. So too did Trudeau's standing offer to NDP premier Ed Schreyer to join his cabinet and, more dramatically, his offer of a coalition government in 1980, which Broadbent rejected.[60]

The CCF had advocated centralizing public policy in Ottawa, but the NDP reconciled itself to provincial state power. Party successes in the provinces contributed to the shift; by the mid-1970s the NDP had held power in Manitoba, Saskatchewan, and British Columbia, and served as the official opposition in Ontario. This led to some policy differences between the party's federal and provincial wings; for example, the federal party vigorously opposed wage controls, but the Prairie NDP governments, without complaining, worked within the Liberal guidelines. Nevertheless the federal and provincial wings of the party were more in harmony ideologically and in policy than the federal and provincial wings of the other parties.[61]

Quebec continued to be barren terrain for the NDP. Only 13 of the 517 delegates at the party's 1979 convention were from the province; in 1983, only three of 402.[62] The party found it challenging to recruit candidates to contest Quebec's seventy-five seats. Although the NDP performed somewhat better in Quebec than had the CCF, its popular vote averaged no more than 7 per cent in any of the elections between 1968 and 1984.

Organized labour, an integral constituency of the NDP, was changing in character. Union membership was still increasing, by over 7 per cent in 1971 alone, but two of the three largest unions were now public sector unions.[63] This was a result of the Liberals, with NDP encouragement, having extended collective bargaining rights to the public service in 1965. Public sector unions grew as the percentage of workers belonging to unions began to decline in the 1980s. The decline of unions eventually contributed to a weakening of the union movement's influence in the party.

Social Credit: Decline and Demise

Social Credit's English and French wings expressed opposition to bureaucratized and centralized power in government, business, and labour organizations.[64] The two wings, reunited at a 1971 convention of almost a thousand delegates of whom over two-thirds were Quebecers, elected Réal Caouette leader. The reconstituted party promised "periodic payments of credits to all Canadians," and almost every speech by the party's MPs – known as *créditistes* in Quebec – urged implementation of Major Douglas's economic theories. Silent on Quebec's status in Canada, the party endorsed Ottawa's bilingualism policy.[65]

Under Caouette's leadership, internal divisions continued to tear the party asunder, and it continued to fade; western Social Crediters shifted en masse to the Conservatives, and in Quebec the party declined steadily, mustering only 6 per cent of the vote in the 1980 election. Failure to make inroads among younger and urban voters was the party's Achilles heel. After Caouette resigned as leader in 1976, André Fortin became the first of a series of party leaders, including Caouette's son Gilles. Fabien Roy, the former leader of the provincial *créditistes*, took the helm in 1979 but, divided between the party's separatist and federalist elements in Quebec, the party collapsed after failing to win any seats in 1980.

The Social Credit story unfolded differently in its two western provincial bastions. In both, sons of party leaders played pivotal roles. Supported by a young group around Preston Manning, son of Alberta premier Ernest Manning, agriculture minister Harry Strom, a dour evangelical Bible teacher, became the premier after the elder Manning, also an evangelical Bible teacher, resigned in 1968.[66] The party's defeat in 1971, after thirty-six years of uninterrupted rule, reflected Alberta's increasingly urban-driven economy and its more secular political culture. Social Credit dwindled, dropping to four seats in Parliament in each of the next two elections and less than 1 per cent of the vote after that.

In British Columbia the provincial Social Credit party captured most of the urban federal Liberal supporters. The party's drive in 1975 to unseat the provincial NDP government "forced a real coalition of the two major federal parties."[67] This "renewed" the provincial Social Credit party, now led by Bill Bennett, the son of long-time premier W.A.C. Bennett.

The Parti Québécois: The Disruptor Party

As modernization of the Quebec state lost momentum, nationalists complained after 1966 that the federal government was refusing any substantial transfer of resources.[68] Former provincial Liberal cabinet minister René Lévesque quit the party after their defeat that year and soon formed the Mouvement souveraineté-association. Within months the MSA merged with two small parties, the anti-capitalist Rassemblement pour l'indépendance nationale (RIN) and the anti-statist, populist Ralliement national (RN) led by former Créditiste MP Gilles Grégoire, to form the Parti Québécois.

A by-product of the Quiet Revolution, the PQ was unlike any previous significant provincial party in Quebec, a nationalist party dedicated to Quebec's independence. After winning office in 1976, the PQ extended the role of the state in the economy, enlarged the scope of the province's French-language regime, and directly threatened the unity of Canada. More than any other provincial or federal party, the PQ operated as a mass party, relying on a large number of small contributors and constitutionally empowering the membership to determine party policy; for its 1976 campaign, over 50,000 individuals contributed $1.2 million.[69]

Committed to expanding the welfare state, the PQ established North America's highest minimum wage, outlawed the use of replacement workers by strike-bound firms, and supplemented the incomes of the working poor. However, the party's zeal for increasing state intervention and creating new state enterprises cooled before the end of its first term in office. Styling itself a social democratic party and pointing to Sweden as a model for Quebec's development, it applied to join the Socialist International.[70] Opposed by the NDP, a member party of the SI whose membership included only national parties, the PQ application was unsuccessful.

Unlike the NDP, which subscribed to the North American model of competitive labour-management relations, the PQ convened economic summits of leaders of Quebec's peak economic associations of capital and labour. They, along with the premier and senior cabinet ministers, met to formulate a collective agenda for the economy.[71] The PQ and the NDP also differed in their relationship to the labour movement; it was a constituent part of the NDP, but to the PQ it was "just one of the various sets of representatives of 'the population.'"[72]

The PQ had promised but soon abandoned electoral reform. The logic for the promise lay in the upshots of the first two elections in which the party competed. In 1970 it ran second to the Liberals, winning 24 per cent of the vote but finishing as the fourth-largest party in the National Assembly with only seven seats. In 1973 the PQ captured 30 per cent of the vote but its representation dropped; averaging 148,000 votes per MNA, the PQ won 6 seats; averaging 16,000 votes per MNA, the Liberals won 102 seats. In government, the PQ begged off electoral reform, alleging public opinion was not keen; "The electorate can only absorb so many reforms and then it balks," a minister asserted.[73] A more plausible reason, not articulated publicly, was that proportional representation would almost certainly have meant the PQ would not be able form another majority government after an election.

Language policy was the PQ government's major legacy. Although courts struck down some of its provisions, the 1977 Charter of the French Language, popularly known as Bill 101, posited a unilingual regime for Quebec to counterpose Ottawa's bilingual regime. Bill 101 incrementally extended and strengthened the status of the French language in schooling, public administration, municipal affairs, commercial signage, and in the workplace. Premier Lévesque's inaugural address in the National Assembly, the equivalent of the Speech from the Throne in Parliament and the other provincial legislatures, was delivered for the first time entirely in French.[74]

The PQ's posture vis-à-vis Canada was subtle: political independence twinned with economic association. In practice this was reflected in its discussions with the other provinces "for constitutional change *within* the existing federal system, in spite of its own formal commitment to separatism and constitutional change only *outside* Confederation."[75] After losing a 1981 referendum proposing sovereignty-association – an independent Quebec state in a political and economic association with the rest of Canada – talk of independence declined in government circles but not amongst party militants.[76]

Contested by an increasing number of candidates, the outcomes of leadership conventions between the late 1960s and early 1980s became less predictable. Only three candidates had run for their party's leadership when Diefenbaker and Pearson won their positions in the 1950s. In the history of the Conservatives, no more than six candidates had ever participated in a leadership race, but in 1967 there were eleven contenders, in 1976 twelve, in 1983 eight. Nine Liberal candidates ran in 1968, seven in 1984. No more than two candidates had ever contested the leadership of the CCF-NDP until 1971. Leaders of the two older parties had reasonable prospects of becoming the prime minister; leaders of the CCF-NDP did not.

Paul Hellyer, who served in the Pearson and Trudeau cabinets, ran for the Liberal leadership in 1968 and the Conservative leadership in 1976. In between, as he was appearing as the star attraction at a Social Credit convention, he tried to form a new political party.[77] In the 1990s he formed the economically nationalist and electorally irrelevant Canadian Action Party; it failed to gain more than .02 per cent of the vote in any of the seven general elections it contested.

In 1983 Brian Mulroney's successful bid for the Conservative leadership demonstrated that parliamentary experience was no longer a sine qua non. It also confirmed that party caucuses counted for less and the extra-parliamentary party counted for more than they had in the past in the selection of party leaders. Mobilizing support outside of a party's caucus became the key to success for aspirants in leadership races. This contributed to further distancing the leader from his caucus and reinforced his status as its undisputed master. Not having selected the leader, the caucus lost some of its ability to dislodge him. To be sure, party caucuses can still dismiss him or her as their leader in Parliament, but none have done so.

The status of political parties, which are voluntary organizations, changed fundamentally in 1974. Parties had previously operated like private clubs outside the orbit of the law. What they did and how they did it was largely their own business. The introduction of the Election Expenses Act required them to register and disclose the details of their election campaign financing.[78] The Act empowered party leaders by adding party names to ballots: the law required that candidates gain their leader's formal endorsement if their party's name was to appear next to theirs on the ballot. Stanfield alienated some Conservatives in 1974 when he disqualified Moncton mayor Leonard Jones as a party candidate because of his outspoken criticism of official bilingualism.[79] Leaders have come to use this power on occasion to parachute their preferred candidates into ridings over the objections of local party riding associations.

With the election of new Conservative and Liberal leaders within the space of one year, in 1983–4, something that had not occurred since 1967–8, a new era of party politics began: the major parties traded places on the government benches and in their historical orientations to the United States.

Chapter Seven

Trading Places

Continentalism is treason.[1]

S.M. Crean

The election of Brian Mulroney's Conservatives in 1984 signalled the beginning of another era in party politics: the rise of neoconservativism and a reprised battle over free trade with the United States against the backdrop of a continuing struggle over the Constitution.

Some long-held tenets undergirding the Liberal and Conservative parties gave way. The parties traded places on a number of issues, most markedly on Canada's relationship to the United States. These attitudes, however, did not change overnight; positions evolved, taking a more definite form during Mulroney's prime ministership. The Liberals and Conservatives no longer abided by many past standards. During the 1984 election campaign, Mulroney and Liberal leader John Turner had given insubstantial speeches, articulating similarly bland economic nostrums.[2] By 1988, in contrast, a heated debate between them over free trade evoked passionate fears and hopes. To many, Canada's very sovereignty was at stake. The clash between Mulroney and Turner on free trade demonstrated the ability of leaders to redefine their party, sometimes abruptly.

Canada's British connection had been the leitmotif of nineteenth-century conservatism and the Conservative party. Particularly leery of republicanism, Conservatives looked askance at the institutional architecture of the United States. The Liberals, more amenable to the gravitational pull of economic continentalism, campaigned for freer trade with the United States in the 1891 and 1911 elections, while the Conservatives campaigned against it. After the Liberals became the leading party in the twentieth century, they demonstrated more wariness than the

Conservatives of the imperial link to London, favouring closer political, military, and economic links with the United States. More acutely sensitive and deferential to Westminster's requests in foreign affairs than the Liberals, Conservatives were keener to say, "Ready, aye, ready" to British causes, as they had in 1922 when Mackenzie King did not respond to a request to dispatch soldiers in aid of British troops in Turkey.[3]

Like the Americans before the Second World War, Mackenzie King's Liberals displayed a more detached disposition towards Europe, the League of Nations, and international engagement. In contrast, King's Liberals established a Permanent Joint Board on Defence with the United States in 1940, and Louis St. Laurent's Liberals agreed to share defence production with the Americans in 1956. In between these points in time, the Liberals and the Americans committed to building the St. Lawrence Seaway as a bi-national project while the Conservatives bewailed the Liberals' refusal – a refusal shared with the United States – to rally to Britain's side in the Suez crisis.

These long-standing inclinations of the two parties changed notably after John Diefenbaker's departure as the Conservative leader and during Lester Pearson's leadership of the Liberals. Diefenbaker had disappointed the Americans by selling wheat to China and refusing their request to raise the alert status of Canadian forces during the Cuban missile crisis. He and John Kennedy cared little for each other; there were some "vicious disagreements" between Ottawa and Washington.[4] For their part, the Liberals began to look sceptically at American investment in Canada and at the war the United States was waging in Vietnam. Pearson, in contrast to King, was a multilateralist, believing isolationism had been disastrous and immoral, contributing to war.[5]

The British-tinged conservatism of the Conservatives, reflected in Robert Stanfield's references to Edmund Burke and the concern of British conservatism for social order,[6] diminished steadily among his MPs and party activists. Market or business liberalism increasingly drove the party, as it did Margaret Thatcher's British Conservatives and Ronald Reagan's Republicans in the 1980s. The 1988 debate over free trade crystallized the reversal of Liberal and Conservative attitudes towards the United States by re-enacting the long-ago campaigns at the turn of the century but with the parties trading places on the issue. During Mulroney's first term as prime minister, Conservative opposition to free trade melted after the United States imposed a tax on Canadian softwood lumber exports and threatened duties on Canadian potash. Hoping to exempt such commodities from the vagaries of US trade laws, the Conservatives led Parliament in passing a motion supporting free trade negotiations in 1987.

Centralized policymaking had also differentiated the two major parties. John A. Macdonald's Conservatives had imposed federal authority and overrode provincial ambitions in a wide range of fields. Using Ottawa's constitutional powers of reservation and disallowance – instituted throughout the British Empire as a mechanism to delay or overrule legislation – the Conservatives had struck down provincial legislation over a hundred times.[7] The Liberals, in contrast, championed provincial rights. Ontario Liberal premier Oliver Mowat chaired the first interprovincial conference in 1887, which resolved to do away with the federal powers of reservation and disallowance. For their part, Wilfrid Laurier's Liberal caucus, whose Catholic MPs outnumbered Catholic Conservative MPs, ferociously opposed a federal Conservative bill that would have undone Manitoba provincial legislation removing funding for Catholic schools.

King's Liberals, opposed to centralizing power in Ottawa, struck a devolutionist posture. The rudimentary old-age pension program they had introduced in the 1920s in response to constant pressure by two Labour MPs made the program contingent on provincial participation.[8] As a lawyer, St. Laurent argued the Quebec Liberal government's position that the program was a violation of provincial jurisdiction.[9] King's Liberals similarly questioned the constitutionality of labour legislation introduced by the federal Conservatives in the 1930s to alleviate the effects of the Depression.

After the Second World War, Liberal and Conservative attitudes to Ottawa's public policy role shifted; King's Liberals introduced a national family allowance program, St. Laurent's Liberals wielded the federal spending power to cajole provinces into a shared-cost hospital insurance program, and Pearson's Liberals did the same in launching a national medicare scheme over the loud objections of some Conservative MPs and conservative premiers. The Conservative and Social Credit parties became the new defenders of provincial rights. In the medicare debate, former Conservative finance minister Davie Futon condemned the Liberals for "dictatorial federalism of the worst sort ... [and their] heavy-handed and ruthless" ways.[10] Ontario Conservative premier John Robarts decried medicare as a "Machiavellian scheme," one of Canada's "greatest political frauds."[11] Alberta Social Credit premier Ernest Manning, who at the time advocated the alignment of his federal party with the federal Conservatives, also objected to compulsory "socialistic" public health insurance.[12] In contrast to the estrangement of Pierre Trudeau's Liberals from the provinces in the 1970s over issues such as tax-sharing and patriation of the Constitution, Brian Mulroney's Conservatives accommodated them in the 1980s. In response to western Canadian objections, he discarded the Liberals' National Energy Program, which attempted to gain greater control over the petroleum industry, secure oil supplies, and redistribute some of Alberta's oil wealth to other parts of the country. Mulroney's government also signed accords with Newfoundland and Nova Scotia to share in the management and theretofore exclusive federal revenues from the oil and gas reserves off their coasts.

In the 1980s the Conservatives also reversed themselves on social programs. Before becoming party leader, Mulroney had decried welfare programs as contributing to "the tragic process of Swedenizing Canada,"[13] his byword for high taxes, high fees, and a heavy-handed welfare state. Once on the hustings, however, he spoke of Canada's social programs as a "sacred trust" not to be violated. He rejected means tests – investigating people's financial circumstances to determine whether they are eligible for a social program – and claimed such programs were "a cornerstone of our party's philosophy."[14]

Public enterprise was another example of the two major parties trading places. In the past, federal and provincial Conservative parties had created a number of significant Crown corporations spanning banking, broadcasting, grain marketing, transportation, and hydroelectric power. Conservative governments had embedded the ethos of a "public enterprise country" in the fabric of society.[15] To be sure, the Conservatives also underwrote private enterprise, often at significant public expense – most famously in the construction of the Canadian Pacific Railway in the 1870s and 1880s, with the objective of nation-building, or "national purpose."[16] Macdonald's National Policy, which protected nascent Canadian industries, exemplified the political intent of the Conservatives to ward off the allure of continental economic integration.

The Liberals kept the Conservative-created Crown corporations and created some of their own after the Second World War. In an about-face, the Conservatives turned their backs on government enterprise. Their platform in the 1979 election promised to privatize Petro-Canada, which, proposed by the NDP, had been created by the Liberals. As opposition leader, Mulroney made it clear that he wanted less government intervention in the economy.[17] Departing from his party's legacy of nation-building via public ownership, his government strengthened private markets at the state's expense. During Mulroney's first term in office, the Conservatives preached market liberalism, wholly or partially privatizing a dozen Crown corporations.[18] Hallmarks of their market orientation included increased contracting out of government services, promoting user-pay methods for public services, and economic deregulation.

Mulroney also reversed the testy relationships that Pearson and Trudeau had with American presidents. Pearson's criticism of the American role in Vietnam had upset Lyndon Johnson; Richard Nixon thought Trudeau was a "clever son of a bitch" and an "asshole"; Reagan reportedly dressed down Trudeau during his 1983 peace initiative world tour at a time when US-Soviet relations were particularly tense.[19] Mulroney, in contrast, had a particularly convivial relationship with Reagan and George H.W. Bush; he and Reagan, both of Irish background, sang to each other at their so-called Shamrock Summit in Quebec City, and Bush recalled Mulroney as "my most trusted friend, confidant and adviser."[20] By invitation, Mulroney spoke at his funeral, something no other prime minister had ever done. Mulroney admired Margaret Thatcher and, like her and Reagan, believed that the civil service was bloated, the government inefficient, and its activities too wide ranging.[21]

The French-Canadian question was yet another locus of historical difference between the Liberals and Conservatives. The public had perceived the Liberals as defenders of Quebec and the French language, while the Conservatives appeared less sympathetic. These perceptions changed in the 1980s when Mulroney and Turner led their parties. Quebecers no longer saw the Liberals as defending their interests, after Trudeau proceeded to patriate the Constitution without Quebec's approval.

The Conservatives: Transforming the State

Historically favourable to Britain, the Conservative party became a close friend of the United States during Mulroney's prime ministership. The fourth prime minister in sixteen years, he was the last in a cavalcade of three in one year, 1984, and became the most durable Conservative prime minister since Robert Borden. Winning half the votes cast in the election – only the third time that had happened since the two-party system had fractured in 1921 – the Conservatives commanded the largest parliamentary majority in federal history. Their elephantine victory was strikingly similar to the magnitude of their 1958 triumph under Diefenbaker.

Arguing that "democracy requires alternation,"[22] Mulroney's Conservatives obtained a strong mandate from every region of the country. He successfully constructed and brokered a "grand coalition" of often conflicting bases of support: social conservatives, fiscal conservatives, westerners, and Québécois nationalists. Avoiding divisive issues, Mulroney built an "internal party coalition," bridging the diverse interests of his party's factions.[23] Dwelling on economic issues about which there was party consensus, he abstained from engaging with issues such as abortion and capital punishment. Mulroney responded to Liberal characterizations of his party as a right-wing force by vowing to penalize provinces that undermined the universality of medicare. Such positions led his ideological soulmate Margaret Thatcher to opine, "As Leader of the Progressive Conservatives, I thought he put too much stress on the adjective as opposed to the noun."[24] Driven by polls, Mulroney seemed to seek "power less for the sake of achieving great things with it, than for the sake of wielding it."[25]

Mulroney's highly evocative language exploited the patronage appointments made by Trudeau and Turner in the weeks leading to the 1984 election. The appointment of outgoing Liberal cabinet minister Bryce Mackasey as an ambassador led Mulroney to refer to him as "no whore like an old whore." Mulroney later acknowledged with equally descriptive clarity, "If I'd been in [his] position, I'd have been right in there with my nose in the public trough like the rest of them."[26] True to that backhanded endorsement of rewarding friends and allies, his government engaged in Canada's deeply engrained culture of partisan patronage. As had happened to the Liberals, it came back to haunt the Conservatives.

In turning to the fluently bilingual Quebecer Mulroney as their leader, the Conservatives opened the door to Quebec. His street vernacular played well after the Liberals had won seventy-four of its seventy-five ridings in 1980. In the 1984 election campaign, lawyer Mulroney presented himself as le "p'tit gars de Baie Comeau," a simple hardworking boy with a hardscrabble background with whom the Québécois could identify.[27] To counter his party's anti-French image, he supported constitutionally entrenching French-language rights in Manitoba. The play of forces in Quebec politics also changed in favour of the Conservatives; Parti Québécois premier René Lévesque effectively endorsed Mulroney, bringing him the support of many Québécois nationalists.[28] In English Canada, Mulroney's folksy Irish blarney helped to render irrelevant the fact that only a few months earlier he had been a corporate titan, the president of the Iron Ore Company.

Quebec's refusal to accept the 1982 Constitution offered Mulroney an opportunity to exploit that refusal to his party's advantage. His opening came with the election of Robert Bourassa's Quebec Liberals in 1985. Calculating that he could succeed where Trudeau's Liberals had failed, Mulroney vowed to persuade Quebec's new government to sign on to the Constitution "with honour and dignity."[29] He and Bourassa formed an alliance; Bourassa listed conditions for signing, Mulroney accommodated him, and the other premiers agreed to the conditions in the ill-fated 1987 Meech Lake Accord. Its most controversial element directed the courts to interpret the Constitution in a manner consistent with the recognition that Quebec constituted a "distinct society."

Unlike 1984, when the vague Conservative platform refrained from making significant specific policy commitments and both Mulroney and Turner offered a bushel of banalities, the 1988 election revolved around a signature issue: free trade with the United States. The issue did not come totally out of the blue; John Crosbie had campaigned in favour of free trade in the 1983 Conservative leadership race, contending that "any government with any guts will start looking at the question,"[30] while recognizing that it would unnerve the public. After the Liberal-dominated Senate refused to accept the free trade agreement negotiated by the Conservative government unless an election were held, the 1988 contest became a de facto referendum on the issue. The Meech Lake Accord received barely any attention because all three federal parties supported it. Both the Liberals and the NDP opposed the free trade proposal, but the Conservatives won the election as the opposition parties divided the anti-free trade vote amongst themselves.

Mulroney found himself alienating as he accommodated the various components of the Conservative coalition. To pacify the party's social conservative wing his government attempted, unsuccessfully, to recriminalize abortion. However, the government's 1986 Employment Equity Act further institutionalizing affirmative action programs and a proposed amendment to the Canadian Human Rights Act related to sexual orientation made those same social conservatives uneasy.[31] Mulroney reluctantly promised a free vote on the death penalty.[32] For the party's Quebec wing, he introduced a new Official Languages Act, unpopular among western Conservatives. For the party's more polyethnic Ontario base he created a Department of Multiculturalism, unpopular among the Québécois. Despite discarding the West's bugaboo, the Liberals' National Energy Program, western Conservative voters formed the impression that central Canadian interests were given priority over their own concerns. Disenchanting fiscal conservatives in his party by reversing his position on cutting social spending, which accounted for 40 per cent of Ottawa's spending when the Conservatives came into power, Mulroney regained their confidence by endorsing free trade, which he had long opposed.[33]

The Meech Lake Accord came back to dominate the national political agenda after the election of Liberal governments in New Brunswick and Newfoundland and the defeat of the NDP government in Manitoba. Opposition to the accord crossed party lines, and the new premiers demonstrated they were not satraps. Claiming he could improve the accord, New Brunswick premier Frank McKenna postponed ratification by his legislature. Newfoundland's premier Clyde Wells had his legislature reverse its previous ratification. Manitoba's Conservatives nominally supported the accord, but Manitoba's legislature had not given its imprimatur.

The accord died in 1990 but the constitutional issue did not. The lesson the Mulroney Conservatives took from the accord's demise was that a more inclusive process, eventually including a referendum, was necessary. This led in 1992 to the Charlottetown Accord, agreed to by the premiers and Aboriginal leaders. Among many other provisions, it included the "distinct society" clause for Quebec. Public rejection of the accord – denounced in Quebec for its shortcomings and in the rest of Canada for ceding too much to Quebec – demonstrated that the pursuit of mega-constitutional reform was impolitic for its advocates and disintegrative for the polity. Constitution-making proved to be an injudicious undertaking. Governing parties that supported the Charlottetown Accord, notably the federal Conservatives as well as the Quebec and Ontario Liberals, were defeated in ensuing elections. In the end, Mulroney's attempts at reconstructing the constitutional system failed disastrously and his popularity suffered badly.

The widely hated Goods and Services Tax, a visible value added tax that replaced an invisible manufacturers' sales tax in 1991, disillusioned the broader public as well as many fiscal conservatives. The imposition of party discipline revealed strains in Conservative ranks; the caucus expelled two MPs who voted against the GST. To overcome Liberal opposition in the Senate to the new tax, Mulroney resorted to a long-forgotten and never exercised constitutional provision that permitted the appointment of eight additional Senators to give the Conservatives a majority in the upper chamber.[34]

The Conservatives were saddled with an unpopular prime minister, and the public seemed happy to see Mulroney's back when he resigned. Hoping to revamp their image, party grandees turned to defence minister Kim Campbell, a former Social Credit MLA, a westerner, a woman, and a one-term MP, to lead the party. It seemed a successful tack; a poll indicated that 50 per cent of the electorate would vote for the party if she became leader.[35] However, a bungled election campaign led to a humiliating and astonishing defeat, spelling the end of the Progressive Conservatives as a major party. The Conservative coalition Mulroney had built proved brittle, breaking with the rise of the Reform party and the Bloc Québécois.

The Conservative policy legacy included free trade, closer ties with the United States, strengthening the capacity of the provinces, the GST, reinforcing bilingualism and multiculturalism, and the failed effort to accommodate Quebec. All were examples of the party reversing former positions it had held. Many were unpopular. Nevertheless a panel of thirty leading historians, political scientists, economists, former senior government officials, and journalists came to rank Mulroney as Canada's second-best prime minister, after Pearson and ahead of Trudeau.[36]

The Liberals: Falling from and Returning to Grace

If the 1980s exposed the vincibility of the Liberals, the 1990s demonstrated their resilience. The Conservatives led the Liberals by 23 per cent in a Gallup poll a month before the abrasive Trudeau resigned as party leader in 1984.[37] Turner, who had left Trudeau's government in 1975, was widely presumed to be his heir apparent, but his relations with Trudeau – they had not met in eight years[38] – were cool, unlike Trudeau's relations with Jean Chrétien, his preferred successor. Turner, like Mulroney, was more business-oriented than were their predecessors, Trudeau and Joe Clark. A majority of Liberal riding association presidents categorized Turner as "right wing," while over 70 per cent labelled Chrétien "left wing."[39] Turner, for example, while opposing Mulroney's proposal to privatize Petro-Canada, insisted it had to be a profit-making enterprise.

The Liberals bounced up in the polls immediately after Turner took over as leader, but redemption from Trudeau's political sins did not follow. To refurbish their image, the Liberals curated an image of Turner as a man with corporate expertise, competent to run a huge bureaucracy in both private and public sectors; he had been finance minister and chairman of the IMF Executive Committee.[40] In turning to Turner, the Liberals turned their backs on French Canada and Quebec. Breaking with a position Trudeau and Mulroney shared, Turner was indecisive on the issue of constitutionalizing French-language rights in Manitoba. The Société franco-manitobaine bewailed his "surprising naivety."[41] Turner's posture was surprising since he had piloted the Official Languages Act through Parliament as justice minister. The Manitoba language issue divided the Conservatives, but Mulroney imposed his position on prospective party candidates.[42]

Turner's rusty political skills and poor performance in the 1984 televised leaders' debates undid the Liberal campaign. His propensity for strategic miscalculation and ineptitude resulted in a rout, the Liberals' worst-ever defeat. His decision to contest a constituency in Vancouver rather than in Montreal, his birthplace, suggested the Liberals were taking Quebec for granted. They paid dearly; the record-low seventeen seats they had won there in 1984 was followed by a new record-low twelve seats in 1988, as Quebec's provincial Liberals allied with the federal Conservatives on the free trade issue. In both elections, the Liberals' National Energy Program hampered the party in the West.

Paradoxically, provincial Liberal victories in New Brunswick and Newfoundland and the skyrocketing performance of the Liberals in Manitoba's 1988 election, which resulted in a minority Conservative government, weakened the federal Liberals. All three provincial Liberal parties opposed the Meech Lake Accord, which Turner supported. The opposition of Trudeau, Chrétien, and the majority of Liberal senators to the accord also undercut his position. The divisions put paid to the observation of Trudeau cabinet secretary Michael Pitfield that "the Liberal Party has no creed. Its creed is unity – national unity and party unity."[43] Amidst low expectations of Turner, bitter public infighting handicapped the Liberals from the beginning of the 1988 election campaign. Two fumbled attempts to replace him as leader suggested a party in disarray. Disorder picked at the fibre of the party as an entourage of Chrétienites continuously attacked Turner.

During Pearson's prime ministership a nationalist wing of the party had grown with the encouragement of his finance minister, Walter Gordon. In a context of public anxieties about American influence in Canada's economy and culture, Turner's 1988 campaign appealed to the party's nationalists and others appalled by the idea of free trade with the United States. It was a reversal of an earlier Liberal position; Trudeau's government had engaged in tentative free trade talks in his last year as prime minister. But the Liberals subsequently held back, concerned that those talks would upset the party's nationalist flank and, like the Conservatives at the time, they preferred multilateral negotiations and limited sectoral trade arrangements with the United States.[44]

After public opinion surveys confirmed that Turner had decisively won the 1988 English-language televised debates,[45] the Conservatives decided on a strategy of "bombing the bridges,"using negative advertising to undermine his credibility.[46] Liberals expect their leaders to win, so although the party more than doubled its parliamentary representation in the election, from forty to eighty-three MPs, dissatisfaction with Turner grew. Chrétien's supporters in Parliament began disrupting the party's weekly caucus meetings, and Turner soon resigned.[47] Appropriately the party anointed Meech Lake opponent Chrétien as party leader on the same day that the accord died. Chrétien's team of organizers had proven much more successful at recruiting members for constituency meetings that selected delegates than the team of freshman MP Paul Martin. Chrétien's people signed up many members of ethno-cultural communities, most of whom "thought Trudeau was a god, and if he didn't like it [Meech], neither did they."[48]

Referring to Chrétien's thirty years of service in the party, most of it in Parliament, his opponents and the punditocracy dubbed him "yesterday's man."[49] He was not particularly popular, but Kim Campbell and her perceived goofs and gaffes in the 1993 election campaign proved godsends for the Liberals.[50] The public did not so much embrace them as reject the Conservatives. The media pilloried Campbell for opining, "You can't have a debate on such a key issue as the modernization of social programs in 47 days."[51] In an effort to reverse a commanding Liberal lead in the polls, Conservative campaign manager John Tory approved and defended running a negative TV advertisement, featuring images of Chrétien's facial disfigurement, asking, "Is this a prime minister?" Chrétien's retort, "God gave me a physical defect and I've accepted that since I was a kid," elicited public sympathy and undercut the Conservative campaign message that, under Campbell, the party was "doing politics differently."[52] Even conservative journalists derided the advertisement, one of them describing it as "the face that sank a thousand Tories."[53]

Chrétien lacked Trudeau's intellectual agility but was a superior retail politician. Where Trudeau had spoken of a "just society" and of constitution-making, esoteric subjects for most voters, Chrétien simply promised "jobs, jobs, jobs."[54] The Liberal platform, in a document labelled the *Red Book*, proved to be a brilliant prop in the economic context of the election: an unpopular GST, unemployment over 11 per cent, and record high budgetary deficits and debt at a time of economic recession. Facing a conservative movement divided between the Reform party and the Conservatives, the Liberals returned in the 1993 election as the hegemon among the parties.

The NDP: From Apogee to Irrelevance

If the Mulroney-Campbell era represented the best and worst years for the Conservatives, it was no less so for the NDP. With only ten fewer MPs than the Liberals in 1984, the NDP was in striking distance of overtaking them. Despite the Conservative landslide, it had gained a record-high percentage of the vote and captured more seats than ever before. Although the NDP had long ceased promising to use state power to discipline capitalism, leader Ed Broadbent was effective in branding Mulroney and Turner as the "Bobbsey Twins of Bay Street."[55] Still, the social democratic ideal of a more egalitarian society lived on in the party as it was becoming tied ever more closely to the reality of a more culturally diverse society.

The NDP conveyed an image of Broadbent, an academic with working-class roots, as a man of the people. Hopes were high that the party would soon displace the Liberals, becoming one of two major parties. Polls in 1987 only heightened optimism; for the first time, the party was leading the other parties by a comfortable margin.[56] By-election victories soon followed in Yukon, Newfoundland, and Ontario. Broadbent was also the most popular party leader, perceived as honest, principled, sincere, and intelligent.[57] There was no questioning of his political skills, unlike what Turner faced. This led the NDP to make Broadbent the centrepiece of its 1988 campaign.

Disappointment followed. Support proved flaccid after the Liberals capitalized on the public's anti-free sentiments at the NDP's expense. The NDP argument against free trade was that harmonizing economies threatened social programs; one television ad raised the misleading spectre of American corporations running Canada's hospitals. The Liberal tack proved more effective: the appeal to visceral nationalist concerns about Canada's sovereignty and cultural identity. Despite the setback in the election, NDP spirits were buoyed once again by the election of the party's namesake provincial parties in Ontario, British Columbia, and Saskatchewan in 1990–1. As provincial NDP parties became electorally more successful, the federal party, which once had favoured federal centralization and nationalization, extended a shift it began in the 1970s, looking more positively at the role of provinces as their fiscal capacities and technical and policy expertise grew.

Neophyte MP Audrey McLaughlin, the first female federal party leader, the first leader representing a territory, and something of an enigma, took over from Broadbent after he resigned. In the economic context of the times, choosing McLaughlin, a social worker – a group disproportionately supportive of the NDP[58] – proved disastrous. Women viewers of the 1993 televised leaders' debates rated neither her nor Campbell particularly well.[59] Nor were they well received in Quebec: after the NDP's modest but best performance ever in the province in 1988, winning just under 15 per cent of the vote, the party sank to less than 2 per cent under McLaughlin, who was barely bilingual. She and the party's support for the Charlottetown Accord also alienated many of the party's traditional western supporters, where opposition to the accord was highest. NDP support for the accord fed the narrative of Preston Manning, leader of the upstart Reform party, that the NDP had become one of the "old-line parties," a favourite descriptor the CCF-NDP had used for decades to characterize the Liberals and Conservatives.[60]

The upshot in 1993 was the worst-ever setback for the NDP. For the first time it lost official party status in Parliament. Shut out in Ontario and with only nine seats, all in the West, the devastating result led the leading historian of the party to compare the NDP to the Progressives and the CCF; the party "may be coming to the end of its role" and "may no longer be the best vehicle for Canadian social democracy."[61] The party no longer seemed like an alternative vehicle for channelling dissent. That role fell to the Reform party and the Bloc Québécois. Nevertheless the NDP remained the nominal custodian of Canadian social democracy.

Reform: Western Revolt

The revanchist Reform party emerged in response to a perceived betrayal of conservative principles by the Conservatives, the party most Reform activists had previously supported. Their departure from the Conservative tent was not so much a case of ideological conversion as it was of greater politicization; they felt the Conservative party had left them.[62] Western Reformers subscribed to principles of market liberalism, invoked traditional western grievances, and bridled at what they felt was parliamentary dysfunction. Sparking the party's creation was a military aircraft maintenance contract awarded by the Conservative government to a Montreal firm despite a cheaper, technologically superior bid by a Winnipeg competitor firm recommended by the non-partisan civil service.

Reformers considered Mulroney an ideological apostate. Some referred derogatorily to Pierre Elliott Mulroney;[63] he had backtracked on his promise to use business criteria, not political calculations, in awarding government contracts. In the eyes of Reformers, he had acted like the Liberals, favouring interests in central Canada, a politician mollifying Quebec because it had many more MPs than Manitoba. This led to Reform's original slogan, "The West Wants In," and it ran candidates exclusively in western Canada in 1988.

Reform preyed on the frustration of many with government. Party leader Preston Manning associated the roots of his party with the populism of the Progressives, Social Credit, and the CCF. He contrasted the "old Canada" – the provinces east of the Ottawa River – with the new Canada. Reform's first platform reflected early twentieth-century plebiscitarian populism, the belief that plebiscites are closer to the democratic ideal than parliamentary democracy. In addition to referendums, the party proposed popular ratification of constitutional changes, greater accountability by MPs, an effective, elected Senate with equal representation for each province, and free votes in the House of Commons.[64] Reform regarded politicians as corrupted by the privileges of power and viewed government as a problem, not a solution. The party contended that state intervention and the welfare state had failed, that attempts to improve the position of the less well-to-do by altering the redistribution of wealth or opportunity produced objectionable and unnatural results.[65]

The consuming free trade debate overwhelmed Reform's hope of defeating western Conservative MPs in 1988. A few months later, however, Reformer Deborah Grey won a by-election, raised the party's profile in Parliament, and hired future Conservative prime minister Stephen Harper, who had been a young Liberal in high school, as her assistant. Like Manning and his father Ernest, Grey was a Bible school graduate and all three practised an evangelical politics.

Reform benefitted after the Conservatives discredited themselves on both fiscal issues and the constitutional file. To capitalize on Mulroney's unpopularity, Reform had run television ads dismissing the Charlottetown Accord as "Mulroney's deal."[66] The party, which claimed to represent the new Canada, kept speaking to the older Canada in the 1993 election, attacking bilingualism, multiculturalism, and immigration from non-traditional sources.[67] It captured the majority of seats in the West formerly held by Conservatives, and although it won just one seat east of Manitoba, the party ran second in fifty-six of Ontario's ninety-nine constituencies, establishing its bona fides as more than a party of regional protest.

Bloc Québécois: Nationalist Insurgency

Mulroney's coalition of western Conservatives and Québécois nationalists papered over the longstanding differences between them; the constitutional imbroglio demonstrated the challenge. Like Reform, the Bloc was engaged in a crusade with a subversive itinerary. If the Progressives and Social Credit were Reform forerunners, the short-lived federal Bloc Populaire of the 1940s served a similar role for the BQ. However, the BQ added a new dimension: a federal party championing Quebec's sovereignty. What united Bloc MPs, they said, was "national allegiance" to Quebec and a commitment to serve as an "instrument of Quebec in Ottawa."[68]

Six Quebec Conservative MPs, together with future Liberal cabinet minister and Quebec lieutenant Jean Lapierre, initially constituted the Bloc. Its leader Lucien Bouchard became Quebec's new nationalist exponent after resigning from the Conservative cabinet in protest against Mulroney's willingness to accommodate the objections of the provinces that had not signed on to the Meech Lake Accord. Quebecers' perception that they had been humiliated made the Bloc instantly popular; a month after its appearance in 1990, future party leader Gilles Duceppe won a by-election; two months after that, the Bloc was the front-running party in the province.[69]

As the federal avatar of the sovereigntist Parti Québécois, the Bloc drew on the same supporters: 88 per cent of PQ supporters planned to vote for it. Although Bouchard refused financial help from the PQ, he accepted the services of staff paid by the PQ. The PQ's strength – it had won 40 per cent of the vote in the 1989 provincial election – attested to the Bloc's potential. Both parties worked in concert to defeat the Charlottetown Accord. The Bloc had no specific legislative policies initially. Compelled to spell some out as the 1993 election loomed, it turned to PQists who offered policies with a social democratic bent.[70]

Bloc and Reform policies exposed the ideological differences of the parties: Reform touted the private sector, the Bloc wanted government to invest billions in job creation; Reform proposed user fees and the end of universality in social programs, the Bloc wanted no program cuts or means tests; Reform called for stricter parole conditions and deporting non-citizen criminals, the Bloc challenged "law and order" rhetoric.[71]

The animus between Reform and the Bloc was intense: Said Manning, "We want to take away from the promoters of separatism that soft, mushy ground of sovereignty-association which they offer to Quebeckers as intermediate ground between independence and Canada."[72] Manning reflected much of the attitude in English Canada. The Bloc's stunning performance in the 1993 election – wining half the vote in Quebec, capturing fifty-four of its seventy-five seats, and all but four seats in constituencies in which francophones made up 70 per cent or more of the population – led to charges of resentful Québécois tribalism in the anglophone media: "Its only agenda is racist."[73]

The 1993 election ended the historic balance between the two parties of Confederation. The Conservatives were as unceremoniously rejected, indeed even more so, as they had been enthusiastically embraced in 1984. In his failed pursuit of Quebec's constitutional accommodation and as a consequence of the West's alienation, Mulroney shrank his party; every Conservative candidate west of Quebec was rejected. The splintering and thrashing of the Conservatives produced two new parties composed of former Conservative voters. The dramatic rise of Reform and the Bloc Québécois represented transformational change in the party system.[74]

Conservative initiatives on free trade and the GST also represented transformational change. They set the stage for Canada's economic growth and a return to fiscal balance. More than two decades after his departure from politics, a poll of twelve prominent environmental activists led to a celebration of Mulroney as "Canada's greenest prime minister" for his government's Environmental Protection Act, an acid rain treaty with the United States, the creation of eight new national parks, and Canada's accession to the United Nations Framework Convention on Climate Change.[75] These Conservative achievements prepared the way for a Liberal government's ratification of the Kyoto Protocol in 1997, from which a future Conservative government led by former Reform MP Stephen Harper withdrew. Once again, the major parties traded places on policy.

Reform and the Bloc, beneficiaries of the Conservative party's implosion, brought one of Canada's three historical fault lines to the fore: regionalism. The Conservatives of the 1980s and early 1990s left enduring marks on the other two durable axes around which national politics have revolved: the French-English divide, and Canada's colonial cultural and economic relationships, first with Britain and then the United States. The triumphant Liberals of the 1990s became the major beneficiaries of the pratfalls of the Conservatives, Canada's regional divisions, and the reconfiguration of the party system.

Chapter Eight

Division and Reconfiguration

At a certain point in their historical lives, social groups become detached from their traditional parties.[1]

Antonio Gramsci

The multiparty parliament produced by the 1993 election indicated a new stage in party politics had arrived; regionalism and regional parties became the new motif characterizing party politics for the next decade.

Multiparty parliaments are common in the world and Canada has been no exception. Generally, majority governments emerge after some parties coalesce when no one party holds a majority of seats. However, coalition governments have not been part of the Canadian parliamentary tradition and one was not necessary in the 1990s, because the Liberal party benefitted from the regional character of each party's support. The Parliaments of the 1990s looked like a sliced pizza pie, each slice a different party. Different from earlier multiparty Parliaments, the Parliaments between 1993 and 2003 featured two large opposition parties, the Bloc Québécois and the Reform-cum-Canadian Alliance party, offering duelling visons of national identity.

Change in the party system, glacially slow after the election of Pierre Trudeau's Liberals in 1968, occurred suddenly in 1993. Since the 1920s third parties have occasionally held the balance of power in Parliament, but no party other than the Liberals or Conservatives had ever served as government or official opposition. In the 1990s third parties catapulted to becoming major parliamentary players while the principal party of Confederation, the Conservatives, were crushed, relegated to a peripheral role. The NDP, the traditional third party in what had become a de facto two-and-a-half party system in the 1970s and 1980s, also lost ground, losing its status as an officially recognized party in

Parliament in 1993. The Bloc Québécois and the Reform party took turns as the official opposition party in the 1990s, gaining the attention that the position warrants. No third party had been the second-largest in Parliament since the Progressives in the 1920s and they had refused to take the mantle of official opposition. Early in the twenty-first century, a reconfigured Reform party, the Canadian Alliance, which now included some former Conservatives and a new leader, Stockwell Day, became the major alternative to the dominant Liberals.

The Bloc and Reform had sharp differences but they also shared some characteristics and some interests. Breaking political habits, the Bloc detached francophone Quebecers from the Liberal and Conservative parties while Reform replaced the Conservatives as the voice of the West. Unlike Reform, however, the Bloc had no aspiration to govern the country or, for that matter, Quebec. It claimed only to represent Quebec's interests in Parliament until Quebec gained sovereignty. It renounced the federal system and sought to reconstruct Canada's relationship with Quebec. Reform wanted to transform some of the institutions that underpinned the political system. Both parties proposed a more decentralized state, reducing Ottawa's role in policymaking in areas of provincial jurisdiction such as culture and natural resources.

Both the Bloc and Reform rejected the discourse of diversity that the other parties, led by the NDP, had come to embrace by promoting de facto quotas for groups such as women and visible minorities in party affairs and public administration. Reform dropped its founding slogan "The West Wants In," but the sentiment that led to the catchphrase remained. Party leader Preston Manning and the party's brain trust resided in Alberta. Tactical considerations made cooperation between the Bloc and Reform/Canadian Alliance plausible; indeed, Day's Alliance refused to write off potential collaboration to dislodge the Liberals, and the Bloc did not categorically denounce the prospect of such an odd-couple arrangement.[2]

The pan-Canadian political appeals made by parties in earlier years gave way as the regionalization of the party system intensified: the Conservatives were competitive only in Atlantic Canada, the Bloc dominated Quebec, Reform/Alliance was supreme in the far west, and the NDP had small pockets of scattered strength. Only the Liberals had some strength everywhere, but they also took on some features of a regional party, bolstered by their remarkable stranglehold on Ontario, where they won 98 of the 99 seats in 1993, and 101 and 100 seats respectively of 103 seats in the 1997 and 2000 elections. They dominated the province, even though their popular vote in the province did not exceed 53 per cent in any of the elections.

C.B. Macpherson, studying the long-serving Social Credit regime in Alberta that followed a long-serving farmers' government, theorized that a "quasi-party system," where one party is overwhelmingly dominant, as in Alberta, was the product of quasi-colonial economic and political status. In Macpherson's view, regional subordination combined with relative class homogeneity leads voters to flock to a single party.[3] When he wrote in the early 1950s, he suggested that Canada might also have a quasi-party system because the federal Liberals had enjoyed many years of uninterrupted rule, as many as Social Credit in Alberta, and because of Canada's similar quasi-colonial relationship to the United States. The Liberals governed Canada in all but five of the years between 1935 and 1957. Applied to the Canada of the 1990s, Macpherson's thesis collapsed under its own weight; western Canada had no homogeneous class structure when it turned to Reform and the Alliance. Moreover, Saskatchewan and Manitoba were no less in the orbits of Ottawa and Bay Street than Alberta and British Columbia, yet the enthusiasm for Reform in Saskatchewan, and especially in Manitoba, was quite subdued initially; the Liberals won many more votes and seats than Reform in both provinces in 1993.

Maurice Pinard's explanation for a third party's sudden, stunning federal breakthrough focused on examining Social Credit's rise in Quebec in the 1960s. He pointed to grievances resulting from the divergence between people's expectations and their conditions. Pinard argued that third parties like Social Credit can break through when voters perceive that the traditional opposition party, the Conservatives in Quebec, is too weak electorally to unseat the government party.[4] However, while Quebecers were certainly dissatisfied with the resolution of Quebec's constitutional status in the 1990s, Pinard's condition – a traditional opposition party being dismissed as too weak to defeat a governing party – cannot explain the rise of the Bloc in 1993, since the Conservatives, the traditional opposition party, were the government.

Seymour Martin Lipset and Martin Robin downplayed the economic factors highlighted by Macpherson and Pinard in explaining the rise of third parties. They linked the parliamentary and electoral systems to the fragmentation of the party system.[5] Lipset contended that strong party discipline in Canada restrains dissension within a party, militating against alliances across party lines and impelling dissenters, like the MPs who formed the Bloc and the West's disaffected Conservatives, to create their own party. Canada's constituency-based electoral system permits parties with concentrated regionalized support, like the Bloc, Reform, and Social Credit and the Progressives before them, to emerge.[6]

No single cause can explain the unprecedented turbulence manifested in the 1993 election; there were many. They include the vagaries of the first-past-the-post electoral system, distinct regional political cultures, changing economic and fiscal conditions, and the incompetent campaign conducted by the governing Conservatives. Restive westerners in the early 1990s, always unsympathetic to Quebec's aspirations, resented the Conservatives for seeking to accommodate Quebec. Economically Canada was facing fiscal and economic crises: successive huge deficits, unprecedented levels of debt, program spending cuts, a barely growing economy, and stubbornly high unemployment.[7]

In the aftermath of the Conservatives' defeat in 1993, party leader Kim Campbell lamented the electoral system's lack of proportionality. She observed that the popular vote for her party was not very different from that of the Bloc and Reform, yet this "was not reflected in seats."[8] However, her government had created a Royal Commission on Electoral Reform and specifically prohibited it from considering alternatives to the first-past-the-post electoral system.[9] In this respect and others, the Conservatives contributed to their decisive humiliation, dropping from the 169 seats they won in 1988 to 2 seats in 1993.

Once the Bloc and Reform established themselves as major parliamentary players, the die was cast for the Conservative party; they would flail about ineffectually for the next decade. Partisanship took a new form for many right-wing voters in the West; Reform became their strategic voting option in 1993 and subsequently. For right-wing as well as left-wing Québécois nationalists, the Bloc became the vehicle. It gained a following sufficient to consolidate its position in Parliament, doggedly promoting Quebec's brief in Ottawa. With the Conservatives victims of regionally driven voting patterns, the Liberals faced scattered and divided opponents. Neither Reform nor certainly the Bloc, with their narrow regional appeals, could hope to overtake the Liberals. However, they could intensify regional tensions, which the Liberals, like the Conservatives before them, were challenged to alleviate. The latent danger to the Liberals in the context of their unrivalled dominance was the growing division over leadership within their ranks.

The Liberals: Divided Within

Recognizing that party leader Jean Chrétien was not particularly popular, the Liberal campaign in 1993 drew attention to his "team" of star candidates. He repeatedly insisted that his ministers would have great discretion in his government.[10] In office, however, Chrétien lorded over his cabinet, making decisions such as signing the Kyoto Protocol without consulting them. A senior Privy Council official described him as the "king," with Chrétien saying as much: "The Prime Minister is the

Prime Minister, and he has the cabinet to advise him. But at the end of the day, it is the Prime Minister who says 'Yes' or 'No.'"[11]

The Liberals had won power promising to lower unemployment and to eschew austerity. However, within two years spending cuts with a view to balancing the budget became their overriding priority. Urged on by Reform, in 1995 the Liberals addressed with dispatch the government's deficit and debt challenges in a draconian budget; they introduced the most sweeping structural change in Canadian finances in postwar history. Beyond that, Chrétien's Liberals appeared to have no agenda, a party "inspired less by the big vision model of Pierre Trudeau than the cautious formula practised ... by Mackenzie King," according to party historian Stephen Clarkson.[12] As in that earlier era, a contented and supportive corporate community led by the banks provided more than half the money raised by the party.[13]

With keen political instincts Chrétien, for no convincing reason, overrode his MPs' objections in calling for early elections in both 1997 and 2000. In 1997 his rationale lacked credibility: "We did not want an election that will last like Americans, six months."[14] In 2000, referring again to "American-style" elections, he charged that the Alliance party had begun campaigning as soon as Day became its leader.[15] In neither case could Chrétien state his real reason for it would have revealed blatant opportunism: the Liberals had solid leads in the polls, the conservative movement was divided, and Chrétien wanted to capitalize on the weakness of his rivals before a scandal or some embarrassing mistake could narrow his window of opportunity. Senior Liberals believed that the election call in 2000, which had been opposed by the party's election readiness committee, was intended to forestall a challenge to Chrétien's leadership and to quell mounting caucus discontent.[16]

Although the regionalized party system aided the Liberals, they too played to narrow regional sentiments while presenting themselves as the only truly pan-Canadian party. Regionally tailored Liberal television ads responded to salient issues raised by their primary opponents in each region.[17] Given the splintered party system, no party could present a substantial challenge to Liberal power. As one consequence, the Liberals became inward looking. Conflict within the party began to consume it, extending the cycle of conflict over leadership that had begun when Trudeau resigned. Just as an entourage around Chrétien had undermined John Turner's leadership, a Paul Martin entourage began to wrest control of the party's machinery, penetrating local party constituency associations and the ranks of the party's provincial boards of directors.

Chrétien's abrasiveness behind closed doors, and sometimes publicly – he once grabbed an intrusive protester by the throat with enough force to knock out the protester's dental bridges[18] – contributed to strengthening Martin's image within the caucus and among party activists. Many Liberals chafed at Chrétien's governing style and some of his policy decisions. As an example, he threatened his backbenchers with an immediate election call if they refused to defeat a Reform motion to compensate victims who had contracted hepatitis from tainted blood transfusions.[19]

Martin came to be lauded within and without the party as the finance minister who had turned around the government's sorry fiscal situation by delivering on his pledge to balance the budget, "come hell or high water."[20] A bitter falling out between Martin and Chrétien – it remains unclear whether Martin was fired, resigned, or left the cabinet by mutual consent – freed him from cabinet solidarity. He then devoted himself to full-time campaigning for the party's leadership. At one point in their rivalry after Martin left the government, Chrétien taunted Martin's caucus supporters, suggesting they could vote against his government and cause yet another early election.[21]

After Chrétien announced that he would resign and a leadership race began, Martin's control of the party was so overwhelming that substantial candidates including former cabinet minister and Newfoundland premier Brian Tobin, as well as senior ministers such as Allan Rock and John Manley, withdrew from the race. Martin amassed enough caucus followers, constituency delegates, and money to turn the leadership convention into an anticlimactic, predictable coronation. His organizers had mobilized significant blocs of supporters within some ethnic communities. In British Columbia, for example, Indo- and Chinese Canadians constituted two-thirds of the party's membership while Caucasians, who were three-quarters of the provincial population, accounted for less than 20 per cent of the membership.[22] Martin's leadership campaign raised so much money that he gave the party almost four million dollars, wiping out its debt.[23] Characterized by the media as a serious policy thinker and a man of action as finance minister, the same media depicted Martin as a ditherer after he became prime minister.[24]

What became known as the sponsorship scandal – the misuse and misdirection of federal government advertising funds in Quebec – threatened to undermine Liberal dominance even before a new consolidated Conservative party led by Stephen Harper appeared in 2003. Citing fictitious contracts and invoices, the auditor general caught the public's attention by using unusually expressive language to castigate the government: "Senior public servants broke about every rule in the book."[25] In the subsequent election, the Liberals were reduced to a minority government. Eager to demonstrate transparency, Martin, who had repeatedly talked of rectifying a "democratic deficit," established a public enquiry into the scandal. Since he had been finance minister and vice-chair of Treasury Board, which had authorized the budget of the sponsorship program, his attempt to distance himself from the scandal was suspect.[26] After a damning report by the enquiry commission described political involvement in the administration of the program,[27] Martin's minority government fell on a vote of confidence.

The sponsorship scandal became a popular coda for the Chrétien/ Martin years, but it was actually the RCMP's announcement during the election campaign of a criminal investigation into leaked information from the Department of Finance[28] that brought the Liberals down. They had led all fifty-eight polls published between the issuance of the election writ and the RCMP's announcement; three polls in the week preceding the announcement pointed to a Liberal majority government. In contrast, in all but one of the sixty-two polls after the RCMP's intervention, the Conservatives led.[29] The RCMP's announcement of a criminal investigation effectively corroborated Conservatives' accusations of Liberal corruption.

The RCMP's extraordinary intervention may have been motivated by their resentment of implicit criticism by Liberal MPs, including Martin, of an RCMP raid on the home of a journalist.[30] Police intervention tainted the Liberal government, although none of its members were ever identified as leakers. In a context of high public trust in police officers (73 per cent) and low trust in politicians (9 per cent),[31] public opinion turned against the Liberals. Most of the media also turned, from ally to nemesis.

Reform and the Canadian Alliance: Appropriating the Conservative Brand

A year before the party swept into Parliament with fifty-two seats in 1993, Reform's national assembly reflected the makeup and temperament of the party's membership. Over half the almost 900 delegates were from Alberta and British Columbia, more than 60 per cent were over fifty years of age, and only 3 had French as their mother tongue. The policy views of delegates were decidedly right of centre: 96 per cent thought "welfare makes people less likely to look after themselves" and 99 per cent wanted to "reduce deficits as much as possible." Reformers were also unhappy with a changing Canada: 98 per cent opposed a constitutional veto for Quebec and 97 per cent opposed government efforts to further multiculturalism.[32]

The party's 1993 platform, which repeatedly used the populist formulation "the common sense of the common people," promised a
Triple-E (elected, equal provincial representation, effective) Senate,
public ratification of constitutional changes by referendum, parliamentary approval of Supreme Court nominees, constitutional entrenchment
of property rights, parliamentary and electoral reform, and subjecting
the regional distribution of federal revenues and expenditures to "fairness tests." Echoing the Progressives of the 1920s, Reform proposed
free votes in Parliament, the right of voters to initiate a referendum and
to recall their MP, and eliminating the power of party leaders to veto
candidates nominated by their local party associations. Reform advocated dismantling the Department of Multiculturalism and, like John
Diefenbaker's Conservatives of an earlier era, it rejected the language
of "hyphenated" Canadians. It also dismissed "the conception of Canada as 'a meeting of two founding races, cultures, and languages.'"[33]

Despite the party's populist image, party documents and correspondence showed that party leader Manning was a strong discipli-
narian, sometimes acting autocratically.[34] To senior party insider Tom
Flanagan, Manning practised "ever-fluid populism," citing his attitude
to the Charlottetown Accord. Having fought for constitutional reform,
Manning argued within senior party circles after the accord was formulated that there ought to be a five-year moratorium on constitutional
negotiations. Before coming down firmly on the "No" side in the referendum on the accord, he told a private audience of Ontario Reformers to postpone deciding how to vote until they saw how opinion was
heading in other provinces.[35]

Some media reports conveyed the sense that Reform was tainted by
nativism and racism and driven by Christian evangelicals. The party
proposed to reduce the numbers of immigrants; one of its candidates,
subsequently disowned by the party, denounced immigrants as "taking
away jobs from the gentiles," saying that by "gentiles" he meant white
people.[36] A party insider was quoted referring to the "God Squad," the
nickname for almost a third of Reform MPs, including Manning, who
were evangelical Christians. Both he and Alliance leader Day proposed
referenda on moral issues such as abortion, with Manning advocating a
constitutional amendment to protect the unborn, and a referendum on
capital punishment. He also mused about removing maternity benefits
from the unemployment insurance system.[37] Deeply religious, Day did
not campaign on Sundays. Detractors pilloried him for his creationist
creed: "There is scientific support for both creationism and evolution,"
he opined, and if dinosaurs existed they did so at the same time as
Adam and Eve.[38]

In contrast to the other parties, neither Reform nor the Alliance gave specific societal groups special status in party organs – no women's, youth, or campus clubs. Hostile to "social engineering," organized feminism, and affirmative action programs favouring individuals belonging to groups known to have been discriminated against previously, Reform criticized the Liberals for appointing female candidates in selected ridings. The party opposed state-funded day care for children and public funding for women's organizations.[39] Unsympathetic to Quebec, Manning suggested during the 1997 election campaign that the country had had too many prime ministers from the province.[40]

Reformers focused their ire upon the Conservatives in 1993, the Liberals in 1997, and the Bloc Québécois throughout the Chrétien years. Their truculence, however, did not bring them any nearer to power. Their inability to win any seats in Ontario in 1997 led them to launch a United Alternative campaign, proposing joint nomination meetings and other forms of local cooperation with the Conservatives to end vote-splitting among right-wing voters. Conservative leader Joe Clark rejected the idea, but some Conservative notables such as Alberta premier Ralph Klein and some Ontario cabinet ministers signed on to the United Alternative. Reformers then voted overwhelmingly to fold themselves into the new Canadian Alliance party.

Under Day, who defeated Manning for the party's leadership, the Alliance made only modest gains in the 2000 election. Faced with a caucus revolt[41] – some MPs broke away to form a self-styled Democratic Representation Caucus – Day resigned and former Reform MP Stephen Harper became the Alliance leader. He pursued merger with the Conservatives after Peter MacKay became their new leader. MacKay's condition for a merger was that conventions of a new Conservative party provide for equal representation for constituencies. In contrast the Alliance, like Reform, provided for member equality and disregarded constituencies. MacKay's condition meant that the large number of Alliance members in the sixty constituencies the party held in Alberta and British Columbia would have less weight than the relatively few party members the Alliance and MacKay's Conservatives had in Quebec's seventy-five constituencies. Harper won the leadership of the new Conservative party in 2003, but it was runner-up Belinda Stronach, a unilingual anglophone, who won overwhelmingly in Quebec because her financial resources allowed her to hire more organizers to sign up members in the province's many "rotten boroughs," constituencies with few members.[42] Since each constituency was allotted 100 points in the leadership selection process, the voting weight of a Quebec constituency with a handful of members equalled that of an Alberta constituency with thousands of members.

The Bloc Québécois: Sovereigntists in Parliament

The simultaneous appearance of Reform and the Bloc Québécois in Parliament in 1993, with the Bloc serving as the official opposition, escalated the clash between Quebec and the rest of the country over Quebec's status in Canada. Born in the ashes of the Meech Lake Accord, the Bloc was the federal manifestation of the sovereigntist movement that had taken root a quarter century earlier in Quebec provincial politics. After Trudeau's Liberals had swept the province in 1980, many Québécois became disillusioned with his cosmopolitan image of Canada. Chrétien, who had been Trudeau's justice minister when the Constitution was patriated over Quebec's objection, became the first native son leading a major party to be rejected by the Québécois in a federal election. However, they did flock to another native son, Lucien Bouchard, venerated for his unconventional and apparently selfless behaviour in giving up a cabinet post in Brian Mulroney's Conservative government.[43] Without the trusted Bouchard, who combined passion with cool logic, the BQ would not have emerged as a significant force.

Bouchard cited the recently signed Maastricht Treaty that founded the European Union (and eventually led to the creation of the euro) as a model for Canada-Quebec relations.[44] He described the Bloc as a "doomed" party: if Quebecers voted for sovereignty in a referendum there would be no need for the party in Ottawa and the BQ would decamp. If Quebecers rejected sovereignty, the Bloc would abide by their wishes and disband. However, almost two-thirds of Quebecers wanted the Bloc to continue, whatever the result of a referendum, so even before it was held the BQ rationalized remaining in Parliament on the grounds that this was essential for the defence of Quebec's vital interests.[45] Support for sovereignty hovered around 40 per cent, but support for the Bloc receded. After winning half the vote in the province in 1993, it lost a quarter of that support in 1997. Some sovereigntists may have voted for other parties or abstained from voting because the Bloc had no prospect of governing, appearing more as a protest movement.

Bouchard's declaration that Canada was "not a real country"[46] outraged many English Canadians. Quebec's irrepressible nationalism, not English Canada's politics of left, right, and centre, was the stronger force driving Quebec's representation in Ottawa. The rural conservative base of Bloc support had supported Maurice Duplessis's Union Nationale and Réal Caouette's Créditistes in earlier decades. However, urban intellectuals led the party and styled it social democratic. A former Conservative MP-cum-Bloc MP who was expelled from the Bloc caucus observed that "in order to rid the party of everything that was not appropriately social democratic, it [engaged in] several purges."[47]

The BQ argued that sovereignty would permit the rest of Canada to pursue its own objectives without having to accommodate Quebec. Some media coverage of the Bloc reinforced an image of Canada as two solitudes at the heart of a federal state, a body with two languages, two cultures, two hearts, and two brains. The English-Canadian press did not devote much coverage to the BQ's activities, while Quebec's francophone media barely reported on developments west of Parliament Hill unless there was a perceived injury to francophones.

The Bloc's representation in Parliament sank from fifty-four to forty-four to thirty-eight seats between the 1993 and 2000 elections. Its official opposition status, a one-time fluke, was forfeited to Reform in 1997. Michel Gauthier, selected by a group of fewer than 160, became the second leader of the party after Bouchard left to become Quebec's premier.[48] Gauthier resigned the leadership soon after the 1997 election setback (and two decades later joined the Conservative party). The 480,000-member Quebec Federation of Labour contributed to the Bloc's decline by not endorsing it as it had in 1993. During the election campaign, the QFL leader questioned the Bloc's usefulness: "Does it help the cause? Does it harm the cause? Is it still pertinent?"[49]

Former Maoist Gilles Duceppe, a hospital orderly fired for his militant union activities, succeeded Gauthier but the BQ's position did not at first improve. The Liberals overtook it as the party holding most of Quebec's seats when BQ candidates were defeated in two 2003 by-elections in ridings that had voted "yes" in the sovereignty referendum and had elected Bloquistes since 1993. With the defeat of the Parti Québécois in 2003, the Bloc became the main protagonist of sovereignty. The PQ defeat underscored the Bloc's reasoning that its presence in Parliament was indispensable. With the Bloc in danger of withering, the scandal around the sponsorship program, which had been designed by the Liberals to dampen sovereigntist sympathies, ironically breathed new life into the BQ. It once again won fifty-four seats in the 2004 election. Duceppe conducted himself so ably that literary icon Margaret Atwood later declared that she would vote for the Bloc if she lived in Quebec.[50]

The 2004 election resulted in another pizza parliament: it produced a minority Liberal government while strengthening the Bloc's position as never before because it held the balance of power. However, the Bloc revealed how co-opted it had become in holding a joint press conference and signing a joint letter with Harper and NDP leader Jack Layton.

Addressed to the governor general, it asked her to consult with them should Martin request that Parliament be dissolved and an election called.[51] The Bloc changed the world of Canadian party politics while becoming fully incorporated into Canada's political culture.

The Progressive Conservatives: Failure and Collapse

The old Conservative party never recovered from what party historian Peter Woolstencroft termed the "electoral tsunami" that hit them in 1993.[52] Although over two million Canadians voted for the party, only two Conservative MPs were elected. In contrast, just over five-and-a-half million Liberal votes yielded 177 Liberal MPs. Thus the Liberals gained an MP for every 31,909 votes for their party while the Conservatives gained an MP for every 1,093,211 Conservative votes.

Similar if less dramatic distortions befell the Conservatives in the 1997 and 2000 elections. Three leaders – Kim Campbell, Jean Charest, and Joe Clark – led the party in the three campaigns. They offered common themes: tax and regulatory cuts, reduced benefits for MPs, and expanded free trade. Under Charest the Conservatives gained slightly in the popular vote and won twenty seats, but only two were west of Quebec. Under Clark the party lost seats. Nevertheless both Charest and Clark claimed that the Conservatives were the only national party alternative to the Liberals. There was some logic to this contention, given Reform/Alliance dominance in the West and absence east of Ontario, the Bloc's exclusive presence in Quebec, and the NDP's weakness almost everywhere. However, since the electoral system rewards parties with concentrated regional support and penalizes small parties with diffused national support, the assertion by the Conservatives of primacy among the opposition parties rang hollow.

Campbell left the leader's post in part because major party donors were reluctant to help pay down the party's debt if she stayed on.[53] Charest left to lead the Quebec Liberals, and Clark left after the disappointing 2000 election in which the Conservatives barely retained official party status, which required that a party have twelve MPs. Clark, like his successor Peter MacKay, had pledged not to merge the party with the Alliance. Indeed MacKay signed an agreement to that effect when he became party leader in 2003, but calculating that the Conservatives had no future he subordinated his reservations and soon agreed to negotiate his party's merger with the Alliance.

Conservative party veterans Clark and Flora MacDonald, a senior cabinet minister during the Mulroney era, attacked MacKay's decision.[54] Another former Mulroney minister, Senator Lowell Murray, who had worked for Diefenbaker's justice minister and had served as chief of staff to Robert Stanfield, aired his forceful opposition by contrasting the thinking of the older conservatism of the Progressive Conservatives and the new conservatism represented by the Reform/Alliance: "We believe that government's job is to provide stability and security against the excesses of the market. Democratic politics must define the public interest and ensure it always prevails over more private ambitions. To that extent the forces of technology and globalization need to be tamed.... Reform conservatism which is what the Alliance practises relies on people's fear of moral and economic decline.... It spoils all the good arguments for the market economy by making a religion of it, pretending there are market criteria and market solutions to all of our social and political problems."[55]

The protests proved ineffective: more than 90 per cent of the party membership voted in favour of merging with Harper's Alliance.[56] Soon after, Harper's rejection of a local party association's nomination of former Saskatchewan Conservative premier Grant Devine, a nominee MacKay endorsed, revealed the further waning influence of former Progressive Conservatives in the new Conservative party.[57]

The NDP: Not Going Away

The NDP's performance in the 1993 election – the lowest-ever vote (7 per cent) for the CCF-NDP and the loss of official party status in Parliament – led the party's founding partner, the Canadian Labour Congress, to reassess their relationship.[58] Hobbled, the party nevertheless persisted and kept the support of organized labour. Reflecting the continuing strength of social democracy at the provincial level, Ontario, British Columbia, Saskatchewan, Quebec, and Yukon, whose populations constituted over three-quarters of Canadians, had governments in 1995 that called themselves social democratic.

Deviating from the party's western roots and its urban Ontario support, NDP members selected Nova Scotia's Alexa McDonough as their new leader, after Audrey McLaughlin, who had replaced Ed Broadbent as party leader in 1989, departed. Much was made of the party's Atlantic breakthrough in the 1997 election because it had won eight seats in the region, as many as in British Columbia and Saskatchewan together.[59] However, the NDP's performance in Nova Scotia was the contingent product of the quirky electoral system; the Conservatives outpolled the NDP but won no seats in the province, while the NDP won six. Nationally, the party's gains were marginal and once again disappointing.

With the NDP vote rising between 2000 and 2004 from 9 to 16 per cent under new leader Jack Layton, the party exceeded the 15 per cent average it had won in the elections between its founding in 1961 and 2000. More significantly, it gained sufficient power in Parliament to extract concessions from Paul Martin's minority Liberal government, inducing the Liberals to add nearly five billion dollars in social program spending to their 2005 budget. However, after the enquiry into the sponsorship program exposed the extent of skulduggery, the NDP turned against the Liberal government and with Harper's new Conservative party and Duceppe's Bloc brought it down.

Reflecting strains between some elements of the labour movement and the NDP, the president of the autoworkers' union, Buzz Hargrove, the country's most prominent labour leader, endorsed the Liberals in the ensuing election.[60] At the same time, Manitoba's NDP government loosened labour-party relations by prohibiting financial contributions from unions.[61] Continuing on a path adopted in the 1980s, the federal party strengthened its identification with the "new social movements" of environmentalists, women, gays and lesbians, Indigenous peoples, and racialized groups. Under Layton's leadership, according to a leading NDPer, the party's economic policies evinced "ideological moderation," and party organization experienced increasing "professionalization."[62]

When Harper's newly united Conservative party defeated the Martin Liberals in the 2006 election, one pizza parliament with a minority government replaced another. Minority governments often result in a return to the polls in a short time; their average duration has been eighteen months. Harper's minority government proved an exception because it lasted longer than two years. Furthermore, when its end did come in 2008, it was Harper rather than the opposition parties who brought it down. Harper gambled that he could convert his minority government to a majority by winning more seats in Quebec; opinion polls indicated that support for the Bloc had receded. He lost the gamble but remained in power, continuing to put the stamp of the new conservatism on the public policy agenda.

Chapter Nine

Conservatism: Old and New

The rediscovery of the conservative agenda requires us to maintain the coalition of ideas that is the heritage of enlightenment liberalism and Burkean conservatism.[1]

Stephen Harper

The next distinctive era in party politics begins with the merger of the Progressive Conservative party and the Canadian Alliance in 2003. The motif for this period, running from 2003 to the 2015 election, is the appearance of an uncompromising new right-wing Conservative government led by Stephen Harper and opposed by a divided left that included an atypically strong federal NDP.

Quite different credos have informed older and newer conservative thought. English Canada's early conservatism or toryism may be traced to the retreating and expelled American Loyalists such as Virginian Christopher Robinson. Robinson had served in the Queen's Rangers during the American Revolution under the command of John Graves Simcoe, Upper Canada's first governor. Robinson's failed bill in Upper Canada's new legislature, "to enable persons migrating into this province to bring their negro slaves," echoed colonial Virginia's master-slave society.[2] Robinson's son, John Beverley Robinson, a War of 1812 veteran, became Upper Canada's attorney general. An "old [Family] Compact Tory," he opposed a wide electoral franchise, the separation of church and state as had occurred in the United States, and advocated a centrally controlled banking system and privileging the Church of England.[3]

By the late nineteenth century many politicians and political thinkers identifying themselves as conservatives still maintained a tory or classical conservative streak in their thinking. However, they accommodated themselves to the growing liberalism of Canada's market society. As classical conservatives, they thought stable, authoritative, respected, and established institutions best anchored a community, making for social order. Institutions rooted in the past had evolved organically and by nature were hierarchical, inegalitarian, and class-based. Rank and subordination among different groups exist in this conservative cosmology of community but class amity prevails; the higher classes, melding elitism with a sense of noblesse oblige, pursue the common good of the whole community. Moral and legal sanctions reinforce personal self-restraint.

As ideas of the individual as the owner of his own capacities grew stronger in English Canada's frontier society, the individual was decreasingly seen through the classical conservative lens of the larger social whole. In a New World not hidebound like the Old, notions of possessive individualism – the self-made man seeking to maximize his advantages – gained easy traction.[4] Establishing a class system as it operated in Britain proved challenging to Canada's early Tories. Nevertheless the toryism of Upper Canada's early elite lingered, buttressed by its philosophical connection to British toryism. Toryism in the political culture abated as Canada's ties to Britain diminished and Britain's class system weakened.

Currents of thought in the United States – the first new nation championing unalloyed liberalism as the model for social, political, and economic development – slowly gained influence in English Canada. William Lyon Mackenzie and his radical allies in the 1820s drew heavily on American examples on subjects such as education, the structure of government, and primogeniture, the right of the eldest son to inherit all the father's property. A century later, the Progressive party patterned itself on the populist Progressive party south of the border, formed in 1912 by Theodore Roosevelt, and North Dakota's Non-Partisan League, organized in 1915. Like the NPL, Canada's Progressives wanted to replace parties with direct democracy, undo cabinet domination of the legislature, and permit constituents to control their MPs.[5]

Quebec's philosophical counterparts to English-Canadian toryism, ultramontane Catholicism and a quasi-feudal seigneurial system, manifested earlier Gallic expressions of classical conservatism. Cut off from the liberalism of revolutionary France and hemmed in by anglophones, the Québécois sustained their corporatist pre-Enlightenment values after the British Conquest. Historian and priest Lionel Groulx approvingly cited the dicta of Maistre, the counter-Enlightenment proponent of aristocratic power and monarchy as stable, divinely sanctioned institutions.[6] Groulx's La naissance d'une race, describes the French-Canadian nation as possessing "through its faith and from its ancestors the sovereign law of hierarchic progress ... the dignity of morals, respect for the laws of life, the peace of families," and placing them "above all material grandeurs."[7] Thomas Chapais's *Cours d'histoire du Canada* lauded the British conquest of New France for "providentially" saving French Canada "from the horrors of the French revolution, the anti-clericalism, and materialism of modern France."[8]

Twentieth-century liberal principles increasingly clouded conservative thinking. Simultaneously collectivist social reform connotations muddied liberal thinking. Liberal thinkers and politicians modified older liberal thinking about primordial, competing, atomistic, free individuals. As an example, when the Liberals selected Mackenzie King as their party leader in 1919, they also outlined a social welfare agenda for government. King's pedantic and largely indigestible *Industry and Humanity* propounded the nebulous principle of "industrial democracy" in which equal numbers of delegates representing workers and managers would oversee their enterprise.[9] As classical liberal ideas infected and grew among Conservatives, some older tory notions of the state's social welfare obligations infected the Liberals, moving them in the direction of welfare liberalism, endorsing a regulated free market economy and accepting responsibility for citizens unable to avail themselves of the minimal provisions for a good life.

Prodded by a growing labour movement and the CCF-NDP, Liberal governments introduced major social reforms as twentieth-century affluence increased. Possessive individualist thinking became increasingly identified with the Conservative party. Declining labour movement activism after the 1960s and the NDP's inability to break out of its third-party status left more political space for Conservatives to preach free markets. Growing numbers of Conservatives and conservative thinkers favoured individual enterprise and consumption over collective goals. Taxes came to be considered economically burdensome and social programs overly generous, centralized, paternalistic, and bureaucratic.

The economic and political models of the United States attracted the re-normed Canadian conservatism of the late twentieth and early twenty-first centuries. Proximity to America's own evolving neoliberalism pollinates the new conservatism. It rejects the post–Second World War Keynesian economic paradigm that maintains government policy responses can mitigate economic recessions. As ardent laissez-faire and free-market supporters, these new conservatives, like neoliberals, seek to shrink the state, deregulate industries, privatize state enterprises, liberalize trade regimes, cut social entitlements, and outsource state functions to profit-motivated contractors.[10] The new fiscal conservativism, rejecting state management, believes private enterprise acting freely boosts the economy. "Social engineering" by government in the form of affirmative action and other programs for disadvantaged groups are ridiculed as inequitable for setting arbitrary quotas.

A modern variant of the old liberalism, the new conservatism, defines communities as associations of free-willed individuals. It prioritizes the individual over the community, viewing society as the sum of self-governing, equal, individuals. Margaret Thatcher's observation, "There is no such thing as society, only individuals and families," captures this contemporary conservative sentiment, depicting society as a one-class citizenry rather than as composed of social and economic classes.[11] Hesitant to wield the instrumentality of government for broad community interest at the expense of private freedoms, the new conservatism embraces the negative liberties – freedom from interference by others and external restraints – of autonomous individuals. Where the new conservatives have been keen to retain state power are in the realms of policing and war-making.

The new conservatism jettisons the tory conceptualization of state and society as ancient bonds linking past, present, and future generations. The new conservatism sees government as based on popular impulse, an ever-changeable compact among equal citizens. Contemporary Conservatives, most of whom subscribe to the new conservatism, consider the state a constantly renewed voluntary arrangement. New conservatives may criticize hierarchical institutions as archaic remnants of the past.

Contemporary conservatives divide on some ethical issues: abortion, suicide, homosexuality, pornography, drug use, prostitution, capital punishment. Social conservatives fear moral anarchy. They tend to the puritanical, believing government must not be neutral on such issues. They wish to preserve traditional values and institutions such as the patriarchal family: schools and the law ought to promote them. They consider teaching religious tenets in schools part of the bedrock function of education. Other contemporary conservatives, libertarians upholding liberty and autonomy as core principles, advocate the church of the self on moral issues such as abortion and prostitution. They would leave the teaching of religious doctrines to the educational marketplace.

Libertarians and social conservatives concur on shrinking state intrusion in economic matters. New conservatives would place much beyond the reach of government, reducing the capacity of the administrative state to act. Wedded to free-market solutions, the new conservatism would limit the pursuit of social justice by government but not by voluntary associations such as churches.

Conservative leader Robert Stanfield and other "red" tory communitarians, emphasizing the connection between the individual and the community, recognized the need to temper conflict among classes. Red tory George Grant, for whom Canadian values lay within the British conservative tradition of Edmund Burke and not the American liberal tradition of John Locke, lamented the end of the distinctive Canadian identity, which could counter American influence.[12] Grant and former Conservative party president Dalton Camp stood apart from the new conservatives who were business- and individual-oriented "blue" tories. They dominate the new Conservative party formed in 2004. Camp "regarded himself as a Red Tory" railing against the "Real Right," which he identified as the Reform and Canadian Alliance parties.[13]

Former Conservative cabinet ministers David MacDonald and Flora MacDonald expressed their tory tinge by preferring the NDP to the Liberals, the Reform party, and Stephen Harper's new Conservative party; David MacDonald ran as an NDP candidate, Flora MacDonald voted for the party at least once.[14] Like Joe Clark, they felt the Progressive Conservative party they had known had left them by merging with the Alliance party. A familial link between red toryism and socialism could be seen in the Laytons; father Robert had served as a Conservative cabinet minister, son Jack took the reins of the NDP.

Conservatives: Old and New

As Canada changed, the ideas of the old Conservative party changed. Reminiscent of the plutocratic posture of the high Tory right of Upper Canada's Family Compact and Lower Canada's Chateau Clique, John A. Macdonald's Conservatives at first opposed calls by labour leaders to extend the franchise. However, in 1872 Macdonald's Conservatives twinned the interests of labour and capital in their Trade Union Act.[15] Artfully designed to woo workers, it led to large labour rallies and workingmen's candidates running on behalf of the party for the first time. Articulating the conservatism of class cooperation, Henry Witton, endorsed by the *Ontario Workman* and elected as a Conservative Labour candidate, spoke of deferring to his "natural superiors."[16] Conservative popularity in labour circles subsequently declined as the party did little else for workers; they flocked to the Liberals after Ontario premier Oliver Mowat flexed provincial powers, introducing social and labour legislation in the late 1880s.[17]

Macdonald had brokered a coalition of Catholics and Protestant Orangemen, but the execution of Métis leader Louis Riel, the suppression of French-language schooling in New Brunswick, Ontario, and Manitoba, and the Conservatives' turn to conscription in the First World War distanced the party from the Québécois. The Conservatives failed to win more than four Quebec seats in any of the four elections between 1917 and 1926, winning none in 1921. Six decades later not much had changed; there were only two Quebec MPs in Joe Clark's governing caucus in 1979. No French Canadian led the party until the 1990s when, in its death spiral, Jean Charest took the helm.

The support base of the old Conservative party lay in the Maritimes and Loyalist Ontario. Long-established families and churches, a pervasive localism, dominance by self-perpetuating political elites, and other elements of a traditional conservative political culture such as low levels of urbanization and a decelerating economy characterized the Maritimes. Hyperbolically and disdainfully, Frank Underhill, the long-time dean of students of Canada's parties, dismissed the state of politics in the region: "Nothing, of course, ever happens down there."[18] Upper Canada's Loyalists furnished the ideological nucleus for the Conservatives, and Ontario came to yield a lopsided number of Conservative MPs; in every election between 1921 and 1958, the percentage of Conservative MPs from Ontario exceeded the percentage of Conservative voters in the province.

After the Second World War, Conservatives differentiated themselves from the Liberals by proposing a less muscular state; party leader George Drew promised to "lift the burden of taxation and arbitrary controls" by government.[19] As the immediate post-war years grew more distant, a loss of public memory set in about the former consensus and sense of collective solidarity behind the building of the welfare state. Surveys of party activists at Conservative, Liberal, and NDP conventions in the 1980s revealed that very few NDPers thought welfare programs were abused, while many more Conservatives thought so. The attitudes of Liberals fell in between.[20]

Studies by the Fraser Institute, a right-wing think tank advocating personal responsibility, greater individual choice, and unfettered competitive markets, reinforced Conservative party thinking. Brian Mulroney's Conservatives had privatized many Crown corporations, but after the party's devastating loss in the 1993 election, the Reform party became the primary standard-bearer for right-wing conservatism, proposing to scale back welfare programs, place many public services in the hands of the private sector, and deregulate the energy, transportation, and telecommunications sectors. As a senior Reform party policy adviser, Harper drew on a Fraser Institute study to contend that social justice groups were vested in exaggerating the prevalence of poverty: "There's absolutely no doubt that there's an agenda in some circles to maximize poverty as an issue."[21]

The success of Republicans in the United States inspired Reformers. Executive director of the Canadian Taxpayers Association Jason Kenney, a future Reform MP, Harper cabinet minister and Alberta premier, opined that Newt Gingrich, speaker of the United States House of Representatives, had "made real conservative ideas and policies more acceptable to talk about in Canada."[22] Gingrich and Reform leader Preston Manning praised each other on television as they compared notes on taxes and deficit cutting.[23]

The old Conservative party had come to look upon social issues such as abortion and gay rights more favourably than the Reform/Alliance party. Alliance leader Harper advocated a union of social and economic conservatives as a way to undercut Liberal support in ethnic and immigrant communities harbouring traditional views of the family. He thought the welfare state had damaged local communities and institutions such as the family. Criticizing the old Conservatives for the "continued progression of liberal pluralism in Canada ... by incrementally embracing it," he termed "group rights" a form of "tribalism." For Harper, "moral relativism, moral neutrality, and moral equivalency" lead to "moral nihilism." Prepared to "lose some old "Conservatives' like ... the Joe Clarks," in building a new conservative coalition, he nevertheless spoke of the "need to rediscover the virtues of Burkean conservatism." This meant articulating a social conservatism that appealed to different denominations, "even different faiths."[24]

Like Edmund Burke, Harper believed "real gains are inevitably incremental." Harper advocated building a "coalition of ideas that is the heritage of enlightenment liberalism and Burkean conservatism."[25] Tom Flanagan, his campaign director in the 2004 election, also cited Burke, urging Harper's Conservatives to pursue "moderation" and "incrementalism."[26] Imposing strict messaging on his party's candidates, Harper shrewdly insisted there be no abortion plank in the party's platform. He recognized, as studies showed, that the values of Canadians after the 1980s had moved on moral and family issues such as abortion, prostitution, and single-parent families; social conservative attitudes were not congruent with the libertarian attitudes of right-wing economic conservatives.[27]

A fixed election date law, one of the new Conservative government's achievements, was supported by all the parties. Harper had vowed it would "prevent governments from calling snap elections for short-term political advantage" and "stop leaders from trying to manipulate the [election] calendar," as Jean Chrétien had done.[28] However, Harper soon resorted to the tactic himself. After polls showed the Conservatives in a virtual tie with the Bloc Québécois in Quebec, and Liberal support collapsing among francophones,[29] he asked the governor

general to dissolve Parliament in 2008. To his chagrin, the election produced another Conservative minority government.

Some fiscal Conservatives felt betrayed by their government. After
having denounced the Liberals as spendthrifts, Harper's government
increased deficits and the national debt to unprecedented levels; their
first two budgets increased spending by more than 7 per cent annually
while inflation was running near 2 per cent. During the global financial crisis of 2008, his government intervened aggressively in the free
market with a multi-billion-dollar bail-out for the auto industry. The
Conservatives also expanded public sector employment at a higher
rate than the Liberals had.[30] "Who would have thought that Harper,
the former Reform MP, the noted fiscal hawk, the man who once led
the right-wing National Citizens Coalition, would ever be the one who
would recklessly plunge Canada into a sea of red ink?" moaned Gerry
Nicholls, who had been vice-president of the NCC when Harper had
been its president: "It's no wonder Canada's conservative community,
those Canadians who actually believe in things like minimal government and balanced budgets and fiscal prudence are currently in a state
of shock.... Stephen Harper was supposed to be their champion. He was
the guy who was going to roll back the state, make government smaller
and usher in a new conservative Canada. They expected Harper to be
Canada's Ronald Reagan. What they got instead was Bob Rae."[31]

Nevertheless the Conservatives came out of the 2011 election with a
majority government. Their 44 per cent of the vote in Ontario – where
the NDP and Liberals split the non-Conservative vote evenly, an unprecedented phenomenon – was higher than their 39 per cent of the
vote nationally. The Conservatives overtook the Liberals in many constituencies with large immigrant populations. As the new Conservative minister of multiculturalism, a portfolio Harper's Reform party
had promised to scrap, Jason Kenney boasted of record high levels of
immigration. He assiduously courted ethnic fraternal organizations
and their media. A video titled "Canada's Home-Grown 'Monarch,'"
produced at a Filipino-sponsored affair, showed Kenney cloaked in a
robe and crowned on a throne with a sash festooned across his chest
proclaiming him the "King of Multiculturalism."[32]

Liberals: Big and Little Red Machines

Paul Martin's resignation after the 2006 election put the Liberals on a fast
track to reconstruction. Contending to succeed him, Scott Brison, labelled
by the media a "Red Tory," had deserted the new Conservative party because he had "no interest in being part of a right-wing debating club where

we get together at conventions and debate how to privatize sidewalks."[33] Former cabinet minister Stéphane Dion, winning less than 18 per cent of the vote on the first ballot at the leadership convention, emerged the victor, despite having delivered a lengthy and uninspiring speech.

Not the choice of his caucus and unpopular in Quebec, Dion focused on environmental issues. Under his leadership the Liberals lost a by-election in Outremont, a seat they had held since 1993, and finished third and fourth in by-elections in two other Quebec constituencies, failing to win 10 per cent of the vote in either. Exhibiting weak political instincts, Dion ignored the warning of his party's pollster that his plan for a carbon tax was a "vote loser, not a vote winner."[34] Rebuffing local Liberals, Dion decided against fielding a Liberal candidate in a Nova Scotia riding being contested by Green party leader Elizabeth May. Dion then led the Liberals to their worst-ever popular vote result in 2008, 26 per cent.

Re-elected, the cash-rich Conservatives planned to starve the opposition parties by eliminating their public subsidies. This led the Bloc Québécois, the party most dependent on subsidies, to back a proposed Dion-led Liberal-NDP coalition government of eighteen Liberals and six NDPers. In a nationally televised address, Harper forcefully, if inaccurately, argued that the coalition would include Quebec "separatists" and undermine democracy by overturning the election results. Dion's televised rebuttal, compounded by technical malfunctions, looked as ineffective as his own leadership.[35] A forthcoming party convention was set to undo him if he did not resign.[36] Dion became the first Liberal leader since Edward Blake who failed to serve as prime minister.

The Liberals replaced Dion with Michael Ignatieff, the choice of the caucus and a sampling of constituency association presidents. A celebrity academic and journalist, Ignatieff had lived abroad since 1969 and was better known in Britain and the United States than in Canada before his return. He had described himself as "a Martian outsider" when delivering the Massey lectures, an annual series on a political, cultural, or philosophical topic given by a noted scholar, in 2000.[37] Billing him "Trudeauesque," leading Liberals lured him back to Canada, clearing his political path in 2005 by parachuting him into a riding with which he had no connection and despite objections by the local Liberal association.[38]

Ignatieff could have become the prime minister in 2009 but backed out of the coalition agreement he and the rest of the Liberal caucus had signed with the NDP. The Conservatives continued governing. Ignatieff's formal crowning as party leader came at a convention of about 1,500 delegates, a third of the 4,605 delegates who had attended the 2006 convention that had selected Dion. Urged on by former leadership candidate Bob Rae, who had served as Ontario's NDP premier in the 1990s, the convention decided to do away with delegated leadership conventions in the future in favour of a direct primary system, giving every party member a vote. "The Liberal party is not a private club," Rae intoned. "It's an organization that belongs to the people of Canada."[39]

The Conservatives depicted Ignatieff, of patrician air and demeanour, as a political tourist. The NDP attacked him for having supported the invasion of Iraq by the United States. According to a journalist who set out to write his biography, "He thought if he loved the country enough it would love him back, and it doesn't work that way."[40] When the 2011 election came, the Liberals lost more than 800,000 votes and were left with fewer than half the number of seats they had won under Dion. Ignatieff lost his seat, resigned as leader, and became the second Liberal leader since the 1870s to not serve as prime minister. He returned to the United States, confirming a Conservative advertisement that he had been "just visiting."[41]

Finishing third for the first time, financially strained, and with a sagging membership, the Liberals allowed anyone registering on their website as a "supporter" to be eligible to vote for their next leader. The objective was to harvest data to enable recruiting volunteers and soliciting funds for a future election. Nearly 300,000 signed on to the website but well fewer than half of them registered to vote, and well fewer than the 400,000 party members when Paul Martin became party leader in 2003.[42] Like the Conservatives, the Liberals allocated 100 points to each constituency, with points awarded to candidates proportionately based on the first preference votes they received on a preferential ballot. In total 104,552 votes were cast. With considerable help from his name recognition and his father's reputation, Justin Trudeau won in a landslide.

The Liberals entered the 2015 election campaign below 30 per cent in the polls. With 70 per cent of the electorate wanting a change in government,[43] the campaign revolved around which party, the NDP or the Liberals, was best positioned to defeat the Conservatives. Two months after the campaign began the Liberals were ushered into office. Some thought Trudeau had no program; "His program is that he's not Stephen Harper," said Mulroney.[44]

NDP: Expanding the Orange Tent

A new legal regime introduced in the aftermath of the Liberals' sponsorship scandal limited organized labour's ability to support the NDP financially. Another change was recasting union representation in the selection of the party leader; the party adopted a one-member, one-vote system. Affiliated unions lost their guaranteed representation at leadership conventions, eliminating the top-down model of union representation. This undid what had been established at the party's foundation in 1961 when the CCF partnered with the Canadian Labour Congress.[45] Nevertheless the intimate relationship between the union movement and the NDP continued; Elections Canada ordered the NDP to pay back money it had collected from unions sponsoring events at the party's 2011 convention.[46]

Minority parliaments have afforded the NDP potential leverage; the party shaped much of the 2005 Liberal budget, termed "an NDP budget" by Harper.[47] However, unlike Martin's Liberal minority government, Harper's two Conservative minority governments were not amenable to NDP pressure. The party also faced the continuing challenge of strategic voting, with many voters who would normally have voted NDP opting for the Liberals in an effort to block the Conservatives.

Recruited by party leader Jack Layton, former Liberal Quebec cabinet minister Tom Mulcair joined the NDP and successfully contested a 2007 by-election, giving the NDP a Quebec beachhead. Layton anointed Mulcair as the party's deputy leader but the party remained at the fringe of political consciousness in Quebec, mustering just 12 per cent of the vote in the 2008 election. The NDP had performed better in Quebec two decades earlier under Ed Broadbent.

When the 2011 election campaign began, the NDP in Quebec stood not much higher than it had in 2008 and faced, as many times before, the challenge of fielding a full slate of candidates. Layton's performances on *Tout le monde en parle*, a TV program with a mass audience, and on the French-language televised leaders' debate turned around a lacklustre campaign. He galvanized support for the NDP. To a Québécois ear, Layton's dialect and expressions were those of an anglophone who had grown up in Quebec. In contrast, the Liberal Ignatieff's French was European, and Harper's French sounded like he had taken a language-training program for civil servants. With his witty quips in the televised debates and his cane at rallies signalling his vulnerable physical condition as a cancer patient, Layton evoked sympathy. His talk of cooperating with other parties in Parliament also resonated with many listeners.

A widely publicized photograph of Layton at a Montreal bar in a Canadiens hockey jersey, beer mug in hand, cheering the team's victory in a playoff game, further boosted the NDP's image in Quebec. Support for the party surged, while Liberal and Conservative support faltered; according to two polling firms, the Liberals lost support in all fifteen Quebec constituencies surveyed, the Conservatives in fourteen.[48] With

Quebecers representing almost a quarter of the Canadian public, their shift to the NDP boosted the party's national poll numbers, leading some traditional Liberal voters in other regions to vote strategically, switching to the NDP. For the first time, the NDP's national vote exceeded that of the Liberals.

In forming the official opposition in 2011, the NDP moved from the periphery to the centre of the party system. In another first for the CCF-NDP, its share of seats exceeded its share of the vote. Much was made of an "orange wave"[49] across the country, but the gains rested almost wholly on Quebec; the party won only 8 additional seats of the 233 in the rest of Canada. The Conservatives won 28 additional seats, resulting in a Conservative majority government. The results reduced the NDP's ability to influence Parliament's policy direction but raised its profile as the second-largest party.

Many were struck by the party's politically inexperienced and youthful Quebec contingent of MPs: five were McGill university students, one of whom defeated the Conservative foreign affairs minister. A first-year student at l'Université de Sherbrooke, still a teenager, became the youngest-ever MP. Some of the successful candidates had not set foot in the constituencies that elected them, including an Ottawa bartender who vacationed in Las Vegas during the campaign. Yet another freshly minted party MP had once run as a Communist party candidate against Bloc Québécois leader Gilles Duceppe.[50]

An exit poll of over 39,000 voters revealed that the NDP had gained support among all demographic groups.[51] The party did better among voters who had been in the country less than ten years and among visible minorities than in the population at large. Where the NDP did not do as well, running well below their national average, was among immigrants who had been in the county longer than a decade.

In Parliament the NDP served more as a defender of past welfare achievements than as a proponent of major new economic reforms. Rising wages and an expanded social safety net sapped some urgency from the party's traditional demands for greater economic democracy. The party increasingly courted middle-class voters. After Layton's death, former Bloc Québécois member Nycole Turmel served as the party's interim leader before Mulcair was elected leader at a convention. He so impressed as leader of the opposition in Parliament that Brian Mulroney described him as "as the best opposition leader since John Diefenbaker and I've known them all and seen them all."[52]

As the 2015 election campaign began, the NDP was the front-runner conducting a front-runner's campaign; Mulcair refused to answer journalists' questions on the campaign's first day.[53] He declared he would not participate in a leaders' debate unless Harper also participated. In the French-language debate, after Mulcair offered a principled defence of a woman's right to wear a niqab at a citizenship ceremony, a deeply unpopular attitude in Quebec, support for the party collapsed in the province and the party finished a distant third in the federal election.[54]

Bloc Québécois: Staying or Going?

With the Liberals discredited by the sponsorship scandal and the Conservatives weak in Quebec, the Bloc hoped to win more than half the Quebec vote in the 2006 election and more than the fifty-four seats it had won two years earlier. The party's leaders believed this would set the stage for a successful referendum on Quebec's sovereignty. However, the Bloc's performance in the election – 42 per cent of the vote and fifty-one seats – was a "sour tasting victory."[55] In 2008 it appeared that the party would lose many seats to the Conservatives but, through no doing of their own, they recovered; a widely viewed and reported upon YouTube video by two popular Québécois comedians skewered the Harper government for having cut funding for the arts.[56] Conservative support fell and the Bloc held on to forty-nine seats.

Proposing that Quebec "opt out of Canadian multiculturalism," which "encourages various communities to live in isolation," the Bloc had made some specific appeals to immigrants and ethno-cultural communities in 2006.[57] Some academics discerned a "breakthrough among members of cultural communities in Montreal"[58] and, in 2008, the party fielded a higher percentage of racial minority candidates than either the Liberals or the Conservatives and as many as the NDP.[59] Nevertheless popular support for the BQ continued to decline, falling from 49 per cent in 2004, to 42 per cent in 2006, to 38 per cent in 2008.

On the eve of the 2011 campaign, the BQ enjoyed a commanding lead in Quebec; with 41 per cent support in an opinion poll, it was more than 20 percentage points ahead of all the other parties.[60] However, by the end of the campaign the party was at its lowest point ever, 23 per cent of the vote. Duceppe could not point to anything that had outraged Quebec's voters – no scandals, no federal cuts to culture programs as in 2008, and no "humiliation" of Quebec such as had occurred with the rejection of the Meech Lake Accord that led to the BQ's creation.

Formerly a beneficiary of the first-past-the-post electoral system, the Bloc became its victim. After having won an average of forty-eight seats in the six previous elections the decimated Bloc was reduced to four seats, losing its status as a recognized party in Parliament. Duceppe lost his own seat and resigned after fourteen years as party leader.

Quebecers demonstrated once again that they could switch partisan allegiance en masse. Some argued that many Bloquiste voters remained in tune with the party's underlying social democratic message but, unhappy with the BQ downplaying sovereignty, decided to vote for a "real" social democratic party, the NDP.[61] However, since 1921, the Liberals, as in the 2015 election, have been the major beneficiary of block voting in Quebec, resulting in many national elections not being very competitive.

Support for the Bloc declined further in 2015, to less than one in five voters. However, as the result of the vagaries of the electoral system the party won ten seats compared to four in 2011 and was still denied official standing as a party in Parliament. The drive for sovereignty, though not at a dead end, appeared to be in remission. For the first time in a generation, the issue of sovereignty was not at the centre of political life in Quebec. Originally intended by its founding leader Lucien Bouchard to be a temporary party, the Bloc seemed to have reached its expiry date. The assumption that as older federalist Quebecers died, a young sovereigntist cohort would prevail in a future referendum was undone.

Greens: A Party of One

Founded in 1983, the Green Party was inspired by the success of West Germany's Greens, who had won parliamentary representation that same year. The Canadian party proved unable to gain more than 1 per cent of the vote until 2004 when former Progressive Conservative Jim Harris was its leader.[62] A 2005 survey of party members revealed that they were younger and more educated than members of the other parties. However, unlike Green parties elsewhere, whose position was "on the left of the left-to-right ideological" spectrum, the Canadian party was "located at the centre of the political spectrum."[63]

Stepping down as executive director of the Sierra Club, Elizabeth May became the party's leader in 2006. The only foreign-born (United States) leader, May had served as an environmental policy adviser in Mulroney's Conservative government. She had been an NDP and, briefly, a Liberal party member.[64] After running for Parliament and losing – the first time in 1980 under the unofficial banner of the Small Party,[65] the second in 2008 – May finally succeeded in 2011, defeating a Conservative cabinet minister in a British Columbia constituency that included the Gulf Islands, a counterculture bastion where environmental consciousness is highest in Canada. Nevertheless the federal vote for the Greens fell from almost 7 per cent to less than 4 per cent. As a party of one, May, like the Bloc's MPs, was denied membership on parliamentary committees and not assured a regular turn in Question Period. Like the NDP but unlike the other parties, the Greens advocated proportional representation.

Peter Newman's requiem, *When the Gods Changed: The Death of Liberal Canada*, concluded that the dismal showing of the Liberals in 2011 marked "the end of the Liberal Party.... I'm sorry to say it. But it's not hard to document that this is the end of it."[66] Three consecutive Conservative governments led a leading pollster, Darrell Bricker, and a well-known journalist, John Ibbitson, to discern a seismic change with power shifting irreversibly to the West and to new immigrants holding conservative social values. They argued that the "Laurentian consensus" of metropolitan Ontario and Quebec, the base of Liberal dominance, was now outmoded.[67]

Two years later, in 2015, the Laurentian consensus was back: Montreal provided a Liberal prime minister and his foreign minister; Bay Street contributed the finance minister. In a governing caucus of 184, only 29 Liberal MPs were from the West, just 12 from the prairies. Constituencies with large numbers of immigrants returned to voting for the Liberals who won thirty-five of the forty-one constituencies in which visible minorities were the majority.[68] Inclusion and diversity issues changed the behaviour of parties; the Liberals proved the most successful in presenting a range of candidates coming from various identity communities. Of the forty-seven visible minority MPs elected, thirty-nine were Liberals. Only six were Conservatives. Mulcair had said he would "wipe the floor" with Justin Trudeau in the election, and Harper's spokesperson said that if Trudeau "comes on stage with his pants on, he will probably exceed expectations" in the leaders' televised debate.[69] Hubris led to the undoing of both their parties.

Party politics had reverted to their historical norm: a Liberal majority government, a competitive Conservative opposition, and the NDP as the distant third party. It appeared that the more things changed, the more they remained the same. What changed was how the parties operated.

Conclusion: The Ever-Changing Party

Party is the madness of many for the gain of a few.[1]

Jonathan Swift

This book began with an observation that today's political parties would be unrecognizable to the party leaders, activists, and voters of nineteenth-century Canada. It then chronicled many of the ideas and policies motivating the parties as different motifs characterized party politics in different eras in Canada's history. They required the parties to reinvent themselves.

It has become axiomatic that a hallmark of a democratic political system is competing political parties. Canadian democracy is no exception. Nevertheless the internal operations of the parties themselves may not be democratic. Notions of democracy have grown and changed over time, making party democracy a contentious issue. Parties in the nineteenth century were little more than small cadres of MPs; "Extra-parliamentary organization (beyond constituency associations) did not exist; the party was the caucus."[2] Local party associations were once isolated entities, but technological developments, from air travel to the internet, led to the emergence of national networks of partisans. Techniques of mobilizing support have also been modernized. What has not changed is that parties continue to be ineffective vehicles for citizen participation.[3]

Canada's parties began as clique-driven cadre parties, dominated by small elite groups of activists. Cadre parties like the Conservatives and Liberals in the nineteenth century relied on a small number of large financial contributors. The party's leaders determined party policy. As the democratic impulse grew in the twentieth century, with demands for more participatory democracy and transparency, mass parties like

the Progressives, the CCF, the Communists, Reform, and the Parti
Québécois appeared. Mass parties rely on a large number of small
contributors. Their essential constituents are the party's members; in
theory, they determine and drive their party's policies. The older and
established Conservative and Liberal parties transformed themselves –
at least nominally – into mass parties over time. Conversely, self-styled
mass parties have always had some features associated with cadre
parties.

Parties have changed their modes of competition and self-presentation.
Party discipline in Parliament, once weak, has steadily become sturdier.
In the early years of party politics, power flowed from leaders of the
governing party to local activists rewarded for their fealty. Today party
members, many of whom are transients, determine who rises to the
top, sometimes including the prime ministership. The number of MPs
has nearly doubled since Confederation, but they wield less influence
collectively and individually.

Unelected entourages surrounding party leaders now overshadow
MPs, including most cabinet ministers. As an example, former Liberal
leader Stéphane Dion had only one meeting with prime minster Justin
Trudeau in his fourteen months as foreign minister.[4] Ministers once appointed their staffers, the team of people surrounding them; the prime
minister's office now generally appoints them, their major tasks being
to implement directives of the office and deal with criticisms by government MPs.[5]

Parties once had no constitutions and no legal status. Their operations
were no business of the state. The government now registers parties –
in 2019 there were sixteen, including inconsequential players like the
Marijuana Party, the Marxist-Leninist Party, and the Rhinoceros Party –
and party finances are regulated by law.[6] The courts, which once played
no role in party affairs, have been called upon to adjudicate intra-party
disputes, deal with violations of election finance laws, and decide how
many candidates for parliamentary office constitute a party.[7]

Links between federal and provincial parties of the same name have
become more tenuous. Party finance legislation at both levels of government makes the integration of fund-raising efforts of federal and provincial parties that go by the same name challenging; a contribution must
be designated as going to the federal or provincial party rather than, as
once was possible, to the party as such.[8] Despite laws pushing them in
the direction of independence, provincial and federal parties sporting
the same colours nevertheless maintain strong informal ties, especially
during election campaigns.[9] Many politicians move easily from federal
to provincial and provincial to federal levels while representing the

same party brand. However, former provincial premiers are much less likely to serve in federal cabinets than in the past, and provincial party leaders are less likely to think of their parties as inferior to their federal counterparts or to consider their interests identical. In the second half of the twentieth century, conflicts between provincial parties and their federal counterparts became more common. Policy fields such as energy, the environment, free trade, equalization payments, and constitutional issues have evoked substantial divisions between federal and provincial Liberals, Conservatives, and NDPers.

The demands of governing have also changed how parties operate. To be sure, some corrupt practices and patronage, the lifeblood of parties in the nineteenth century, have continued, but the form and focus of patronage have changed.[10] Direct personal face-to-face contacts between MPs and the individual beneficiaries of their patronage were once local and cellular. This elementary form of "clientelism," to use the vocabulary of social anthropology, gave way in the first half of the twentieth century. Regional chieftains or supra-local notables in the federal cabinet such as Saskatchewan's Jimmy Gardiner and Quebec's Ernest Lapointe directed party machines and were pivotal in selecting party candidates in their regions and overseeing the disbursement of patronage to their regions. A more sanitized and expanded form of distributing benefits now prevails: impersonally and bureaucratically dispensed, benefits are directed by governing parties to select groups scattered across the country such as students and families. This evolution in how people and causes are supported meshes with Canada's transformation from a rural to an advanced urban society.[11]

Ever-changing too have been the mechanics of leadership selection, the role of party members, and the financing of parties. New media platforms have reconfigured how parties communicate and operate. Voter fidelity, continuing loyalty and support for one party, has given way to more fluid and volatile patterns of partisan support. What has not changed is the pride Conservatives and Liberals take in their early leaders, John A. Macdonald and Wilfrid Laurier. Party leaders once took the pulse of the nation by consulting their MPs, who reported on what their constituents were saying at local community functions. Party leaders relied on their MPs as their political eyes, ears, and nose. The professionalization of political life has changed that. Survey research conducted by the national parties under the direction of the party leader and his entourage now offers a more accurate gauge of public opinion in a community than an MP can glean from her constituents.

Several developments have greatly weakened the independence of MPs. Leaders now pull MPs along in their slipstream, legally able to deny them and other prospective candidates the right to run for office under their party's banner. They can guarantee their MPs and other prospective candidates that they need not face nomination contests in their constituency. Manitoba statute law limits the independence of MLAs by prohibiting them from switching their party affiliation by crossing the floor to sit with another party, and the federal NDP has proposed legislation to the same effect.[12]

Party Leadership

The ways parties select their leaders reflect the times and the messages parties seek to communicate. Parliamentary caucuses, the MPs sitting together as a party, initially selected their party's leader, but they have become less important. Indeed they are often marginalized in leadership selection. Much has changed since the nineteenth century when the governor general played a part in determining Macdonald's successors as prime minister, and therefore as leader of the Conservative party.[13] One successor, John Abbott, led the party and the government from the Senate, a highly unlikely though not inconceivable scenario today. Many politicians have become party leaders without being members of Parliament, among them John Bracken, George Drew, Tommy Douglas, Brian Mulroney, Jean Chrétien, Jack Layton, Elizabeth May, and Jagmeet Singh. Pierre Trudeau, John Turner, Kim Campbell, and Paul Martin became prime ministers by virtue of their selection as party leaders, not by virtue of a general election.

Canada became the first country governed by a British parliamentary system in which a delegate convention chose a party leader, Liberal Mackenzie King, in 1919.[14] Constituency association representatives participated, but ex-officio delegates – MPs, senators, MLAs, and defeated party candidates – dominated. The federal Conservatives opted for a leadership convention in 1927 after Ontario's Conservatives held a convention in 1920 and after noticing that election victories followed the 1919 and 1920 conventions.[15] Provincial Liberal and Conservative parties began adopting the leadership convention model, the last being New Brunswick's Conservatives, whose caucus continued to select the party leader in the 1960s, reflective perhaps of the more traditional political culture of the Maritimes.[16]

The Progressive party after the First World War looked to an established parliamentarian, T.A. Crerar, to lead them. Crerar was a Liberal who had served in Robert Borden's Union government. In 1922 the United Farmers of Manitoba recruited John Bracken, the president of the Manitoba Agricultural College, as their leader and premier, although he had neither run nor voted in the election that brought him to power.[17] The NDP has continued the CCF's practice of voting on the party's leadership at biennial conventions. Social Credit's first parliamentary leader, John Blackmore, emerged from his party's federal caucus, but the party's de facto leader was Alberta premier William Aberhart. H.H. Stevens of the Reconstruction party in the 1930s and Lucien Bouchard of the Bloc Québécois in the 1990s were leaders of fragment parties, defined as parliamentary parties breaking off from an established parliamentary party.[18]

A corollary of election by convention is dismissal by convention. A Conservative convention in 1966 initiated this process by voting to hold a special leadership convention, despite the objection of leader John Diefenbaker, who believed the position was his until he voluntarily stepped down. The convention's decision prevailed and Robert Stanfield bested Diefenbaker and nine others the following year in the contest. At that convention and at the 1968 Liberal leadership convention that elected Pierre Trudeau, constituency delegates exceeded the number of ex-officio delegates for the first time.

After Nova Scotia's Liberals changed their constitution in 1993 to allow their annual meeting to vote on whether to hold a leadership convention, public servants, trade unionists, and others opposed to Liberal premier John Savage's labour legislation joined the party with the express purpose of defeating him as party leader. In panic, the party's executive postponed its annual meeting and changed the party's constitution so that a leadership review would happen only after an election loss.[19]

Conventions force leaders to be acutely sensitive to their extra-parliamentary party, the party's members who are not MPs, and make them less dependent on their caucus. In 2016 a majority of convention delegates rejected NDP leader Tom Mulcair, despite the support of his caucus. Conventions ease the way for a takeover of a party by a single-issue or crossover partisan candidate, someone who has been a member of another party. Pearson-era cabinet minister Paul Hellyer sought the Liberal leadership in 1968 and the Conservative leadership in 1976, and then led the miniscule Canadian Action Party in 1997. Anti–free trade crusader David Orchard pursued the Conservative leadership twice. Rebuffed, he considered bidding for the Liberal leadership, as did Belinda Stronach, who had failed in an earlier bid to lead the Conservatives.[20] Organizers for leadership aspirants have manipulated the selection of delegates by buying party memberships for many individuals in a brief period. This led the Liberals and Conservatives to adopt new rules that instituted greater central party control.

The leadership selection process continues to evolve. In 1985 the Parti Québécois became the first party to adopt a closed primary: direct election by party members.[21] In 1990 Conservative parties in Ontario and Prince Edward Island followed suit. Oddly the number of party members participating in PEI was smaller than that of party delegates at the previous convention.[22] Primaries permit parties to present themselves as being open, welcoming, and more transparent. Discounting maturity and past association with their party, the Liberals, Conservatives, and the NDP permit members as young as fourteen to vote in leadership races.

New techniques have been used that do not require members or delegates to meet to select leaders. Nova Scotia's Liberals pioneered televoting in 1992 and the Bloc Québécois used mail-in ballots in 1997. Ontario's Liberals adopted a hybrid system in which party members vote for both a leadership candidate and a slate of constituency delegates fielded by each of the leadership contenders. The federal NDP used a primary for its labour affiliates and five regional primaries before electing their leader at a delegate convention in 1996. The winner, Alexa McDonough, received only 18 per cent of the votes in the primaries and less than a third of the delegates' votes at the convention. Nevertheless she became leader by acclamation when the front-runner, Svend Robinson, withdrew after the first ballot.[23] The federal Progressive Conservatives, Alberta's Conservatives, and the Canadian Alliance have used run-off votes in which the two or three leading candidates compete a week or more after an initial vote in which no one has secured majority support.[24] Alberta's Ralph Klein became party leader and premier after his entourage signed up more members between the first and second round of voting. With 77,000 voting, new members swamped the party's 11,400 long-serving members.[25] In 2013 the federal Liberals adopted an open primary, making it possible for non-members to register on the party's website and cast their vote for leader.

Party Membership

There have always been party activists, but card-carrying party membership was instituted only against the backdrop of the intensifying democratic impulse in the twentieth century. However, as party membership grows, the role of party activists may shrink. Developments such as the rise of survey research, the proliferation of communications platforms, the fragmentation of messages, and the micro-targeting of discrete demographic and psychographic groups enhance and entrench the role of political professionals in party organizations.[26]

A list of mass-movement parties would include the Progressives (a loose coalition of provincial farmers' groups), the CCF (patterned on the British Labour model), Social Credit (which began as a movement of study groups), and the Parti Québécois. All four took on the form of party-movements in which party principles suffered in the drive for power.[27] The provincial CCF parties had dues-paying members, but the federal party had no provision for direct membership, as it was composed of affiliated provincial sections that issued memberships and provided for affiliated farm and labour organizations. Alberta's Social Credit had local constituency associations that proposed election candidates, but a small committee dominated by party leader William Aberhart selected them.[28] Like the CCF, the Liberal Party was a federation of provincial parties with no distinct federal membership until recently.

Membership in Canada's political parties appears to have increased while there has been a substantial decline in party membership in virtually all the European democracies.[29] However, membership numbers in Canada's parties have oscillated wildly; many people joining, attracted by a nomination or leadership contest may soon drift away; for example, almost 90 per cent of Conservatives in Quebec did so between the 1984 federal election and the following year.[30] Another example of extreme membership fluctuation is Ontario's Conservative party; it had 100,000 members in 2002 when it was choosing a party leader. Membership then plummeted to 3,000 in 2003 and ballooned again to 66,000 during another leadership contest in 2004.[31] In 2018 the party claimed over 200,000 members, but only 64,000 voted in the contest to choose the leader. In the Brampton East constituency, where the federal Conservatives won 10,600 votes in the 2015 election, the provincial party claimed an astounding 18,700 members. Yet only 811 of them registered to vote in the provincial party's leadership race and the party attracted only 12,600 votes in the 2018 election.[32] Clearly membership numbers are an unreliable indicator of attachment to a party. In federal leadership races in all three major parties, turnout rates by members have been below the turnout rates of the public in general elections.

The link between membership numbers and electoral performance is questionable. Deeming provincial Liberal party members to be members of their federal party, the Liberals boasted they had 531,536 members eligible to vote in their 2003 leadership contest. The New Brunswick Liberal party, granting lifetime memberships to anyone with any past or familial association with the party, claimed to have 148,000 members. This represented more than a fifth (including children) of the provincial population and made the membership of the New Brunswick Liberal party larger than the memberships of the federal Progressive Conservative, NDP, Canadian Alliance, or Bloc Québécois parties at the time. In British Columbia, Liberal campus clubs were entitled to four convention delegates each, but eleven clubs did not report that any of their members voted, and in other cases the number of votes cast was fewer than the number of delegates entitled to go to the convention. One constituency's single party member was theoretically able to elect twelve delegates.[33] Despite their large number of members in 2003, the federal Liberals were reduced to a minority government the following year after having won three consecutive majority governments with fewer members.

In recent years Indo-Canadians, especially Sikhs, have been a particularly active group in all the major parties. Ujjal Dosanjh has served as an NDP premier in British Columbia and as a federal Liberal cabinet minister. All three contestants for the provincial Conservative nomination in the Brampton East constituency referred to above (with its 18,700 Conservative members) were Sikhs, but another Sikh, Gurratan Singh, won the seat for the NDP in the 2018 election. At the largest rally for any party in the 2015 federal election, the Liberals attracted over 5,000 people in Brampton, where over two thirds of the population are visible minorities.[34] Brampton is also the city that federal NDP leader Jagmeet Singh represented as an MPP. In the party's leadership race in 2017, nearly 30 per cent of his national fundraising came from the city, and 1,200 of his 5,500 contributors were named Singh or Kaur.[35]

Sikhs are also politically active in Britain, but none was elected in that country's 2015 election, while seventeen (sixteen of whom were Liberals) were elected in Canada's 2015 election.[36] "Canada Now Has the World's Most Sikh Cabinet," headlined the *Washington Post*, noting it had four Sikh ministers. Playfully Justin Trudeau told a Washington audience, "I have more Sikhs in my Cabinet than [Indian prime minister Narendra Modi] does."[37]

Party Finance

Without funds, parties cannot mount election campaigns and communicate their message, although in the age of social media some costs may be minimized. Much has been written about party finance since it became more strictly regulated in the 1970s.[38] Finances are, of course, quantifiable and the mesmerizing precision of money totals perennially appeals to journalists and academics.

In the first major post-Confederation political scandal, John A. Macdonald solicited election funds in exchange for the Canadian Pacific Railway contract, resulting in the resignation of his government. Money followed the leaders of both parties. After the former leaders of the Ontario, New Brunswick, Manitoba, Saskatchewan, and Alberta Liberal parties joined Robert Borden's Union cabinet, their "party war chests had gone with them."[39] In the early 1930s the federal Liberals received a huge sum of money to speed approval of a hydroelectric project.[40] The "Beauharnois" scandal led to the creation of the National Liberal Federation with the aim of distancing fundraising from the party's parliamentary leadership,[41] offering it plausible deniability, denying knowledge of or responsibility for any damnable actions committed by others. The era of non-elected party fundraisers, colloquially known as bagmen, arose. However, there was a dearth of information about party finance, because it went largely unregulated.

Small donations from party members and supporters proved inadequate to finance election campaigns. The Liberals and Conservatives therefore decided to solicit large contributions from a relatively small number of large corporations and wealthy individuals, with the Liberals proving to be more successful. Dependent on the contributions of party supporters, the CCF struggled, especially during the Cold War, when its membership declined. As the NDP, the party depended heavily on trade union contributions. Social Credit relied almost wholly on funds raised in Alberta and British Columbia; the party's Quebec offshoot, the Créditistes, enjoyed initial but not sustained success at fundraising by using paid television programming featuring their fiery leader, Réal Caouette.

Research findings in a 1966 report by a parliamentary Committee on Election Expenses led to the recommendation to limit the dependence of parties on a few big donors.[42] The assumption that campaign spending influences voting behaviour led in 1974 to legislation imposing a ceiling on the amount of spending permitted during election campaigns, requiring disclosure of expenses, providing partial public financing of the expenses of parties and candidates, and a tax write-off for individuals contributing to parties.[43] The prevailing attitude was that although limiting expenditures intruded on abstract liberty, unlimited spending undermined the equal treatment of parties. In the 1970s the Conservatives began a productive direct mail fundraising program, reducing their reliance on corporations and surpassing the efforts of the other parties. Some donors, not realizing that their donation did not include party membership, were turned away at nomination meetings.

In 2003, in the aftermath of the sponsorship scandal in which Liberal-linked Quebec advertising firms received money in return for little or no work, the governing Liberals hurt themselves by legislating limits on corporate and union contributions to parties. Corporations accounted for almost half of the Liberals' income that year, while the Conservatives, the BQ, and the NDP respectively received 20 per cent, 7 per cent, and virtually none of their funds from corporations. Unions contributed over half of the NDP's income. Liberal party president Stephen LeDrew called his party's reform, which party leader Jean Chrétien insisted upon, "dumb as a bag of hammers."[44] The public annual allowances to parties achieving a prescribed vote threshold came to account for between half and three-quarters of the income for all the parties.

Like that of membership numbers, various election results point to the questionable power of money in determining election outcomes. In 1993, for example, the Conservatives spent almost $25 million and elected two MPs, while the Reform Party spent just over $6 million and elected fifty-two MPs. In the third quarter of 2015, on the eve of the election campaign, the NDP had raised more money from more donors, 64,000, than the previous quarterly record for any political party, while the Liberals raised less than half that amount from half as many donors.[45] Nevertheless the Liberals won the election easily and the NDP was humbled.

Governing parties generally change finance regimes to improve their re-election prospects. In 2015, to capitalize on having more money than the other parties combined had, the governing Conservatives changed the law to permit a pro-rated increase to election campaign spending limits for each day beyond the required minimum writ period of thirty-seven days. By having the governor general issue the writ, which orders the holding of an election, seventy-seven days before election day, they became entitled to spend the $54 million in their bank account, far in excess of the other parties' available funds. However, this additional spending was to little avail; they lost the election.

Regulatory changes have contributed to the centralization of power in the national offices of parties at the expense of their local party associations. The national party organizations also have easier access to the technologies, techniques, professionals, and funds required to fashion personalized appeals to specific groups of voters. Solicitation of support and more funds comes by way of the internet, telephone, and direct mail. In contrast, legal spending limits on local party associations, run by volunteers, effectively limit the use of such techniques and the professionals required to deploy them.[46]

Media

Nineteenth-century party newspapers served as vehicles for publicity, attacking partisan foes, contributing to party discipline, and boosting morale. There was often a cosy relationship between parties and newspaper editors; the Toronto *Globe*'s George Brown, for example, was the power behind the federal Liberal government of 1873–8, and Macdonald launched Toronto's *Empire* in the 1880s after the Conservative *Mail* declared its editorial independence.[47] Lavish government printing contracts rewarded faithful papers, which in turn generously praised the governing party. Conservative papers presented the Conservatives as the party of tradition and patriotism while characterizing the Liberals as dangerous, pro-American, and radical. Liberal papers depicted the Conservatives as reactionary elitists, presenting their own party as reforming progressives.

Party papers did not attack partyism, as independent papers often did, but the independent papers could offer no practical alternative to party politics. By the first decade of the twentieth century, the circulation of independent newspapers eclipsed that of party papers. Newspaper owners who had unabashedly championed one party as a way of building a stable, loyal readership succumbed to the economic need for larger audiences. With increased literacy, the paid circulation of newspapers grew from 17 per cent of households in 1867 to nearly 110 per cent in 1915 as some households subscribed to more than one paper.[48] Close links between owners, editors, and parties persisted. For example, Liberal cabinet minister Clifford Sifton owned the influential *Manitoba Free Press*, which was edited by John Dafoe, Laurier's biographer and a confidant of Mackenzie King.[49] Nevertheless the marriage of party and media became increasingly stormy as politicians and journalists came to see politics differently. For the parties, politics was a contest among rivals; for journalists, politics became increasingly a war of ideas in which right ought to triumph.

The appearance of radio and its spread to most households in the 1930s offered parties an unmediated link to voters. Social Credit would not have swept to power in Alberta without Aberhart's weekly *Back to the Bible Hour* broadcasts.[50] Radio also benefitted the Saskatchewan CCF in the 1940s as the charismatic Tommy Douglas spoke directly to the public. Of course radio was no guaranteed remedy for difficulties, as Conservative leader R.B. Bennett learned in 1935 when he used it to try to forestall the defeat of his government. In order to achieve some equity in broadcasting opportunities, in the late 1930s a government White Paper, presenting potential policies and inviting opinions, recommended free broadcast time for all parties. The CBC soon made this a permanent feature.[51]

The arrival of television in the 1950s further transformed campaigning. The introduction of television to the House of Commons in 1977 converted Question Period into a theatrical performance. Parties began to frame their positions in sound bites with a view to having newscasts use pithy clips of their message. Staged events by the parties during election campaigns generally occur in the early morning so that television newscasts will play them the rest of the day.

The cheap, efficient, digital technologies of recent decades have neither improved the quality of political communication by parties nor made the parties more open and participatory.[52] Parties have used digital technologies to draw even greater attention to party leaders, facilitate negative messaging, and engage in permanent campaigning.[53] Technology has also been used nefariously: during the 2011 federal election, misleading automated calls to 6,700 phone lines in Guelph were "a deliberate and considered course of criminal conduct specifically designed to subvert the inherent fairness of the electoral process," according to a judge.[54] New communications technologies and the premium placed on the management and manipulation of large data sets has led to the triggering of subconscious urges in specific sets of voters and, some contend, distracted parties from engaging in national political discussions.[55]

The rise of think tanks and "spin doctors" – spokespersons employed to give favourable interpretations of events on behalf of their party – have also contributed to changing the relationship between parties and media. Left- and right-leaning think tanks such as the Canadian Centre for Policy Alternatives and the Fraser Institute produce studies that the media report. The think tanks aid parties in policy research and help to shape party policies.

A love-hate relationship often develops between party leaders and the media. In 1993, for example, after casting a positive light on Kim Campbell's spontaneity and freshness, most media turned to presenting her as hopelessly impolitic for saying that an election campaign was too short a time to engage in a debate over serious matters. "She was captured and used, and she ended up discarded on the shelf."[56] Similarly, most media at first lauded Paul Martin for his determination to tackle budget deficits but later dismissed him as a "ditherer."[57] Because the media generally prefer to emphasize negatives and to embarrass party leaders after they have held office for a few years, John Diefenbaker, Lester Pearson, Pierre Trudeau, and Brian Mulroney all complained of unfair treatment. Stephen Harper tried to tame the media by limiting their access, and in the 2015 election he exerted some control of coverage by dictating in which televised debates and on which subjects he would participate. Justin Trudeau initially basked in the media spotlight, but after a while the domestic media turned dim.[58] In contrast, the international media continued to fawn over him and the unique character of the Canadian political system; as a major scandal broke in

2019 regarding a possible obstruction of justice by Trudeau's office, a *New York Times* headline declared, "Thank God for Canada! Our Boring Neighbor is a Moral Leader of the Free World."[59]

Party Fidelity and Voter Volatility

In recent decades Canadian voters have become volatile, more volatile than American voters. Although there is no generally accepted measure of party identification, Canadians are less likely than Americans to have party affiliations ingrained into their personal identities.[60] One reason is that Americans on average have many more opportunities to vote each year, and since many of their ballots are pages long, many voters just vote the party ticket, which voting machines allow. There are fewer "durable" and more "flexible" partisans in Canada,[61] and flexibility has grown over time. Perhaps Canadians are less faithful to a party than Americans because they are not offered the option, as are Americans in most states, of registering to vote as partisans. Canadians have also been more supportive than Americans of upstart third parties. The parliamentary system is more conducive to their rise than the American congressional system.[62]

Exemplifying the low volatility of the past, the provincial Conservatives were the undisputed party of Ontario's eastern counties, and the Liberals of its western counties through most of the nineteenth and twentieth centuries: "If the rule were reduced to a township-to-township basis it becomes clearer and truer: some towns and townships never voted anything but Grit, and some never anything but Tory."[63] Stability once characterized Ontario's political system; between the 1940s and 1980s the Conservative party governed for forty-two years, the longest uninterrupted reign by a Canadian party in the century. Abruptly, stability gave way to volatility: the three elections between 1987 and 1995 produced three successive majority governments led by three different parties.

Incumbency and constituency service are less vital to the fortunes of party candidates in Canada than in the United States, where 97 per cent of incumbents contesting the 2016 election to the House of Representatives were re-elected. In contrast the turnover of MPs in Canada has averaged more than 40 per cent in the twentieth century. An astounding 69 per cent turnover occurred in 1993.[64] Party brand and party leaders in Canada drive voting behaviour more than do local candidates, making Canada's parties very much personal parties.[65]

Social determinants of voting such as religion, education, language, region, and economic class have weakened. Familial cross-generational partisanship has waned, although not completely; when asked when he had joined his party, one delegate at a leadership convention in the 1970s responded, "At conception."[66] Religion was once by far the strongest influence on party preference, dwarfing the impact of other social variables; Catholics preferred the Liberals and Protestants the Conservatives. The Catholic-Protestant divide began to decline noticeably in the 1960s. Of course the religious effect did not disappear altogether; in the 1972 election, it was as strong as it had been in the watershed election of 1917 when Quebec's French Catholics overwhelmingly rejected the conscription stance of the Conservatives.[67] Although the Catholic-Protestant divide is less significant than in the past, the level of religiosity has gained in importance; in the 2011 election, religious citizens were more likely to vote Conservative while the NDP was more heavily dependent on the votes of secular citizens.[68]

It may be that voters, increasingly accustomed to behaving as consumers, opt for choosing the policy positions of parties rather than signing up to their comprehensive world views. However, with the exception of elections such as those that revolved around freer trade with the United States in 1891, 1911, and 1988, it is difficult to tie party choice to specific issues. In every election, some will vote for a party whose position on a particular issue, like free trade, does not correspond with theirs.

Frank Underhill suggested that federalism influences the choices of voters. As the federal Liberal dynasty continued into the 1950s, he proffered a balance theory of party choice: "By some instinctive subconscious mental process the Canadian people have apparently decided that, since freedom depends upon a balance of power, they will balance the monopolistic power of the Liberal government, not in Ottawa but in the provincial capitals."[69] There is scant empirical evidence to buttress this creative suggestion and some evidence to the contrary; Prince Edward Island's voters installed provincial administrations of the same party banner as the federal governing party in fifteen consecutive elections between the late 1920s and late 1970s. The chance of that occurring in a perfectly competitive two-party system is roughly one in 33,000![70]

Declining party loyalty has gone hand-in-hand with the rise of a more educated, more secular, and more urban electorate. The adage delivered at nineteenth-century pulpits that "Heaven is blue and hell is red" had purchase in Quebec, where scientific education, secularism, and the rise of the urban family lagged other regions. Residents of the province generally voted for the winning party; it was overrepresented much more frequently than any other region in the federal caucus of the governing party in the twenty-four Parliaments between 1879 and 1980.[71] Since then, with a dramatic rise in educational levels and a no less dramatic decline in religiosity and the rural family, federal as well as provincial party politics in Quebec have exhibited significant volatility. The way Quebecers identify politically may contribute to explaining their exceptional electoral volatility in recent decades; in a survey of young adults in the five Anglo-American democracies, only among Canada's young Québécois did ethnicity overshadow the self-identification of respondents as a leftist or rightist in predicting the direction of their responses to questions about equality, women, minorities, and the role of government.[72]

In recent decades the waning significance and effectiveness of Canada's parties has been alleged. This has been attributed to a host of factors, including the rise of think tanks, social movements, post-materialist values, and the bureaucratic state. The "decline of party" school also points to a growing number of large interest groups, lower voter turnout, technological changes, ideological convergence, demands for direct democracy, and more private behaviour or "cocooning."[73] Political parties are thought to be in decline because they appear increasingly unwilling or unable to fulfil functions traditionally associated with them such as organizing public opinion, integrating citizens, and aggregating interests. Such critiques imply that there was once a golden age of party politics.

To be sure, there is more disillusionment with Canada's parties today than in the past but they continue to dominate the political landscape. Without parties political life could degenerate to squabbles among small factions, each promoting their narrow self-interest. Political parties continue to hold sway over nominations for public office. They continue to recruit and train the country's leaders and to operate the levers of government. They are vital instruments in the operation of parliamentary democracy in Canada.

In focusing on federal political parties, this book has dealt only tangentially with provincial parties. Federalism, the existence of two orders of government, and the presence of parties at both the federal and provincial levels add complexity to fathoming Canada's parties. Passing references in earlier chapters cited theorists including Seymour Lipset, C.B. Macpherson, and Maurice Pinard who accounted for third parties such as the CCF and Social Credit becoming prominent. Their studies began by examining the politics of individual provinces: Saskatchewan, Alberta, and Quebec. Their findings spoke to Canada's diverse political cultures, demonstrating that party politics in each province is a big world unto itself.[74]

Political parties offer to lead but they must also reflect. New federal and provincial parties emerged to challenge the parties of

Confederation as Canada grew, as society became more diverse, the economy became more complex, and new technologies appeared. The values of Canadians evolved and new identities emerged. Political parties have contributed to these changes. More than a century and a half after Confederation the two original parties, the Liberals and Conservatives, remain as the major parties. A third party, the CCF, created almost a century ago as a labour-socialist party, persists as the NDP. Other parties have come and gone. New ones may yet appear, as have the Greens. What is striking about Canada's established parties is the continuity of their representation in Parliament. What is no less striking beyond Parliament Hill since the nineteenth century is the discontinuity in how party leaders are selected, how parties are financed, how they and the media relate to each other, and how they go about courting a more fickle electorate.

This study presented themes that distinguish different eras in the history of Canada's political parties. The themes range from the late nineteenth-century debates regarding Canada's relationship to Britain and the United States to the rise of a Conservative government offering a new brand of conservatism early in the twenty-first century until its defeat in 2015 by the Liberal party. The re-election of the Liberals in 2019 spoke to their weakness, not their strength; they retained power with the lowest-ever vote share by a winning party; fewer votes were cast for them than for the Conservatives.

Recast and different motifs will inevitably drive party politics in the unpredictable future. History tells us nothing about the future of Canada's political parties except that they will continue to surprise.

Notes

Introduction

1 Donald Creighton, *John A. Macdonald: The Young Politician* (Toronto: Macmillan, 1952); Creighton, *John A. Macdonald: The Old Chieftain* (Toronto: Macmillan, 1955); John English, *Citizen of the World: The Life of Pierre Elliot Trudeau, 1919–1968* (Toronto: Alfred A. Knopf, 2006); and English, *Just Watch Me: The Life of Pierre Elliot Trudeau, 1968–2000* (Toronto: Alfred A. Knopf, 2009).

2 Richard Johnston, *The Canadian Party System: An Analytical History* (Vancouver: UBC Press, 2017); William Cross, *Political Parties* (Vancouver: UBC Press, 2004); and R.K. Carty, "Three Canadian Party Systems: An Interpretation of the Development of National Parties," in *Party Democracy in Canada*, ed. George Perlin, 15–30 (Scarborough, ON: Prentice-Hall, 1988).

3 Canada Elections Act (SC 2000, c 9).

4 Charles Taylor, "Can Canada Survive the Charter?," *Alberta Law Review* 30, no. 2 (1992): 427–47; and Alan C. Cairns, *Charter versus Federalism: The Dilemmas of Constitutional Reform* (Montreal: McGill-Queen's University Press, 1992).

5 R. Kenneth Carty, *Big Tent Politics: The Liberal Party's Long Mastery of Canada's Public Life* (Vancouver: UBC Press, 2015), 23, fig. 2.4.

6 Peter Woolstencroft, "The Conservatives: Rebuilding and Rebranding, Yet Again," in *Canadian Parties in Transition*, ed. Alain-G. Gagnon and A. Brian Tanguay, 4th ed. (Toronto: University of Toronto Press, 2017), 151.

1. Four Party Types: Nineteenth-Century Party Politics

1 Quoted in E.B. Biggar, *Anecdotal Life of Sir John Macdonald* (Montreal: John Lovell, 1891), 252.

2 Preston Manning and André Turcotte, "Whither Our Political Parties?," *Globe and Mail*, 10 February 2014, A11.

3 Carol Wilton, *Popular Politics and Political Culture in Upper Canada, 1800–1850* (Montreal and Kingston: McGill-Queen's University Press, 2000), 36, 245.

4 Gordon T. Stewart, *The Origins of Canadian Politics: A Comparative Approach* (Vancouver: UBC Press, 1986), 29.

5 William Menzies Whitelaw, *The Maritimes and Canada before Confederation* (Toronto: Oxford University Press, 1934), 46–56.

6 Alexander H. McLintock, *The Establishment of Constitutional Government in Newfoundland, 1783–1832* (London: Longmans, Green, 1941).

7 43 Geo. III, cap. 138.

8 In collaboration, "Hunter, Peter," in *Dictionary of Canadian Biography (DCB)*, vol. 5, http://www.biographi.ca/en/bio/hunter_peter_5E.html; and Frederic F. Thompson, "Pickmore, Francis," in *DCB*, vol. 5, http://www.biographi.ca/en/bio/pickmore_francis_5E.html.

9 W.S. McNutt, *The Atlantic Provinces: The Emergence of Colonial Society, 1712–1857* (Toronto: McClelland and Stewart, 1965), chap. 6.

10 Robert Thorpe, quoted in W. Stewart Wallace, *The Family Compact* (Toronto: Glasgow Brook, 1915), 4–5.

11 Elwood H. Jones, "Willcocks (Wilcox), Joseph," *DCB*, vol. 5, http://www.biographi.ca/en/bio/willcocks_joseph_5E.html.

12 Frank MacKinnon, *The Government of Prince Edward Island* (Toronto: University of Toronto Press, 1951), 54.

13 William L. Mackenzie, *Sketches of Canada and the United States* (London: E. Wilson, 1833), 409.

14 James Hannay, *History of New Brunswick* (St. John, NB: J.A. Bowes, 1909), 161.

15 J. Murray Beck, *The Government of Nova Scotia* (Toronto: University of Toronto Press, 1957), 20–2 and appendix C, 349; and Norah Story, "The Church and State 'Party' in Nova Scotia, 1749–1851," in *Collections of the Nova Scotia Historical Society* (Halifax), 27: 33–57.

16 James H. Lambert, "Ryland, Herman Witsius," in *DCB*, vol. 7, http://www.biographi.ca/en/bio/ryland_herman_witsius_7E.html.

17 Fernand Ouellet, *Lower Canada 1791–1840* (Toronto: McClelland and Stewart, 1980), 61, 69.

18 William E. Lass, "The Northern Boundary of the Louisiana Purchase," *Great Plains Quarterly* 35, no. 1 (2015): 28.

19 W.L. Morton, *The Kingdom of Canada* (Toronto: McClelland and Stewart, 1969), 210.

20 Frederick H. Armstrong, *Handbook of Upper Canadian Chronology* (Toronto: Dundurn, 1985), 272.

21 Michael S. Cross, "The Shiners' War: Social Violence in the Ottawa Valley in the 1830s," *Canadian Historical Review* 54, no. 1 (1973): 1–26.

22 John M. Murrin, "The Great Inversion, or Court versus Country: A Comparison of the Revolutionary Settlements in England (1688–1721) and

America (1776–1816)," in *Three British Revolutions, 1641, 1688, 1776*, ed.
J.G.A. Pocock, 368–453 (Princeton: Princeton University Press, 1980).

23 Peter Baskerville, "MacNab, Sir Allan Napier," in *DCB*, vol. 9, http://
www.biographi.ca/en/bio/macnab_allan_napier_9E.html.

24 Gertrude E. Gunn, *The Political History of Newfoundland, 1832–1864* (Toronto:
University of Toronto Press, 1966), 11.

25 S.J.R. Noel, *Politics in Newfoundland* (Toronto: University of Toronto Press,
1971), 7–8.

26 Louis Massicotte, "Quebec: The Successful Combination of French Culture and
British Institutions," in *Provincial and Territorial Legislatures in Canada*, ed. Gary
Levy and Graham White (Toronto: University of Toronto Press, 1989), 71–2.

27 Fernand Ouellet, "Papineau, Louis-Joseph," in *DCB*, vol. 10, http://www
.biographi.ca/en/bio/papineau_louis_joseph_10E.html.

28 Marcel Rioux, *Quebec in Question*, trans. James Boake (1969; Toronto: James
Lorimer, 1978), 48–9.

29 Ouellet, *Lower Canada 1791–1840*, 232.

30 Hartwell Bowsfield, "Maitland, Sir Peregrine," in *DCB*, vol. 8, http://
www.biographi.ca/en/bio/maitland_peregrine_8E.html.

31 Beck, *Government of Nova Scotia*, 49.

32 J. Murray Beck, *Joseph Howe: Voice of Nova Scotia* (Toronto: McClelland and
Stewart, 1964), part 1; and J. Murray Beck, "Joseph Howe: Opportunist
or Empire-Builder?," in *Historical Essays on the Atlantic Provinces*, ed. G.A.
Rawlyk (Toronto: McClelland and Stewart, 1967), 146.

33 Hugh G. Thorburn, *Politics in New Brunswick* (Toronto: University of Toronto
Press, 1961), 7–9.

34 Upper Canada House of Assembly, *The Seventh Report from the Select
Committee of the House of Assembly of Upper Canada on Grievances* (Toronto:
M. Reynolds, 1835).

35 Leonard Cooper, *Radical Jack: The Life of John George Lambton, First Earl of
Durham, Viscount Lambton, and Baron Durham* (London: Cresset, 1959); and
Arthur Berriedale Keith, *Responsible Government in the Dominions* (Oxford:
Clarendon, 1912), 15.

36 *Lord Durham's Report: An Abridgement of Report on the Affairs of British North
America by Lord Durham*, ed. G.M. Craig (Montreal and Kingston: McGill-
Queen's University Press, 2007).

37 Jacques Monet, "La Fontaine, Sir Louis-Hippolyte," in *DCB*, vol. 9, http://
www.biographi.ca/en/bio/la_fontaine_louis_hippolyte_9E.html.

38 Quoted in Donald Creighton, *John A. Macdonald: The Young Politician* (Toronto:
Macmillan, 1952), 199.

39 Paul Craven and Tom Traves, "Canadian Railways as Manufacturers,
1850–1880," *Historical Papers*, Canadian Historical Association (1983),
254–81.

40 Ron Baker and Morina Rennie, "Net Debt in the Canadian Public Accounts: Its Emergence, Evolution and Entrenchment," *Canadian Public Administration* 54, no. 3 (2011): 359–75.

41 Beck, *Government of Nova Scotia*, 78–85, 143.

42 Quoted in C.M. Wallace, "Fisher, Charles," in *DCB*, vol. 10, http://www.biographi.ca/en/bio/fisher_charles_10E.html.

43 Thorburn, *Politics in New Brunswick*, 11.

44 Noel, *Politics in Newfoundland*, 25.

45 J.M. Bumsted, "Davies, Sir Louis Henry," in *DCB*, vol. 15, http://www.biographi.ca/en/bio/davies_louis_henry_15E.html; and MacKinnon, *Government of Prince Edward Island*, 187.

46 T.W. Acheson, "The Maritimes and 'Empire Canada,'" in *Canada and the Burden of Unity*, ed. David Jay Bercuson, 87–114 (Toronto: Macmillan, 1977).

47 *The Citizens Insurance Company of Canada and the Queen Insurance Company v Parsons (Canada)* [1881] UKPC 49; and *Liquidators of the Maritime Bank of Canada v Receiver-General of New Brunswick* [1892] AC 437.

48 Beck, *Government of Nova Scotia*, 147, 155–6.

49 MacKinnon, *Government of Prince Edward Island*, 187–8.

50 Frank MacKinnon, "David Laird of Prince Edward Island," *Dalhousie Review* 27 (January 1947): 412–13.

51 Noel, *Politics in Newfoundland*, 30.

52 Escott M. Reid, "The Rise of National Parties in Canada," in *Party Politics in Canada*, ed. Hugh G. Thorburn and Alan Whitehorn, 8th ed. (Toronto: Prentice-Hall, 2001), 10.

53 Paul Rutherford, *A Victorian Authority: The Daily Press in Late Nineteenth-Century Canada* (Toronto: University of Toronto Press, 1982), 213, and table 30, 218–19.

54 Quoted in S.J.R. Noel, *Patrons, Clients, Brokers: Ontario Society and Politics, 1791–1896* (Toronto: University of Toronto Press, 1990), 306.

2. Imperialism, Continentalism, Nationalism

1 "Our History," Imperial Order Daughters of the Empire, http://www.iode.ca/our-history.html.

2 Margaret Morton Fahrni and W.L. Morton, *Third Crossing: A History of the First Quarter Century of the Town and District of Gladstone in the Province of Manitoba* (Winnipeg: Advocate Printers, 1946).

3 W.D. Lighthall, *Canada: A Modern Nation* (Montreal: Witness Printing, 1904), 78.

4 Carl Berger, *The Sense of Power: Studies in the Ideas of Canadian Imperialism, 1867–1914* (Toronto: University of Toronto Press, 1970), 259.

5 D.P. Gagan, "The Relevance of 'Canada First,'" *Journal of Canadian Studies* 5, no. 4 (1970): 40; and Donald Creighton, *John A. Macdonald: The Old Chieftain* (Toronto: Macmillan, 1955), 84–5.

6 Goldwin Smith, *Essays on Questions of the Day: Political and Social* (Boston: Macmillan, 1893), v.

7 Quoted in Edgar McInnis, *The Commonwealth Today* (Sackville, NB: Mount Allison University Publications, 1959), 7.

8 Frank Underhill, *In Search of Canadian Liberalism* (Toronto: Macmillan, 1960), 220.

9 Ben Forster and Jonathan Swainger, "Blake, Edward," in *DCB*, vol. 14, http://www.biographi.ca/en/bio/blake_edward_14E.html.

10 Raymond Tatalovich, "Revisiting Post-Confederation Fiscal Policy: Liberal Dissent from Conservative Deficits," *Journal of Canadian Studies* 47, no. 2 (2013): 180–214.

11 Christopher Pennington, *The Destiny of Canada: Macdonald, Laurier, and the Election of 1891* (Toronto: Penguin Group, 2011), 75.

12 Jeffrey A. Keshen, "Hopkins, John Castell," in *DCB*, vol. 15, http://www .biographi.ca/en/bio/hopkins_john_castell_15E.html.

13 André Siegfried, *The Race Question in Canada* (New York: Appleton, 1907).

14 J. Castell Hopkins, *Life and Work of the Rt. Hon. Sir John Thompson, P.C., K.C.M.G., Q.C., Prime Minister of Canada* (Toronto: United, 1895), 165.

15 Donald Creighton, *John A. Macdonald: The Old Chieftain* (Toronto: Macmillan, 1955), 553.

16 Quoted in J.S. Willison, *Sir Wilfrid Laurier and the Liberal Party: A Political History* (Toronto: George N. Morang, 1908), 170.

17 Quoted in D. Owen Carrigan, *Canadian Party Platforms: 1867–1968* (Urbana: University of Illinois Press, 1968), 28.

18 Patricia K. Wood, "Defining 'Canadian': Anti-Americanism and Identity in Sir John A. Macdonald's Nationalism," *Journal of Canadian Studies* 36, no. 2 (Summer 2001): 64.

19 Richard Cartwright, *Reminiscences* (Toronto: William Briggs, 1912), 283.

20 Pennington, *Destiny of Canada*, 171.

21 "Mr. Blake's Views," *Globe* (Toronto), 6 March 1891, 6.

22 Charles Tupper, "How I Would Federate the Empire," *Review of Reviews* 4, no. 22 (October 1891): 386; and Carrigan, *Canadian Party Platforms: 1867–1968*, 39.

23 *Official Report of the Liberal Convention, Held in Response to the Call of Hon. Wilfrid Laurier, Leader of the Liberal Party of the Dominion of Canada: Ottawa, Tuesday, June 20th and Wednesday, June 21st, 1893*, 7, https://archive.org/details/cihm_09048.

24 J.S. Willison, *Sir Wilfrid Laurier and the Liberal Party: A Political History* (Toronto: George N. Morang, 1903), 321.

25 Berger, *Sense of Power*, 3.

26 Joseph Schull, *Laurier: The First Canadian* (Toronto: Macmillan of Canada, 1965), 387.

27 Norman Penlington, *The Alaska Boundary Dispute: A Critical Reappraisal* (Toronto: McGraw-Hill Ryerson, 1972), 43.

28 M.E. Nicholls, "A Forecast of the General Elections," *Canadian Magazine* 15 (October 1900), 547.

29 Michèle Brassard and Jean Hamelin, "Tarte, Joseph-Israël," in *DCB*, vol. 13, http://www.biographi.ca/en/bio/tarte_joseph_israel_13E.html.

30 H. Blair Neatby, *Laurier and a Liberal Quebec: A Study in Political Management* (Toronto: McClelland and Stewart, 1973), 107–8.

31 Donald Avery and Peter Neary, "Laurier, Borden and a White British Columbia," *Journal of Canadian Studies* 12, no. 4 (1977): 27.

32 Quoted in Penlington, *Alaska Boundary Dispute*, 105.

33 Quoted in Andrew Macphail, *Essays in Politics* (London: Longmans Green, 1909), 251–2.

34 Quoted in J. Holland Rose, A.P. Newton, and E.A. Benians, eds., *The Cambridge History of the British Empire* (Cambridge: Cambridge University Press, 1930), 518.

35 Quoted in *The Annual Register: A Review of Public Events at Home and Abroad for the Year 1904*, ed. Edmund Burke (London: Longmans, Green, 1905), 451.

36 Gerald Lynch, "Stephen Leacock," *The Canadian Encyclopedia*, http://www.thecanadianencyclopedia.ca/en/article/stephen-leacock/.

37 Stephen Leacock, *The Social Criticism of Stephen Leacock*, intro. Alan Bowker (Toronto: University of Toronto Press, 1973), xxxix.

38 Quoted in Robert C. Sibley, *Northern Spirits: John Watson, George Grant, and Charles Taylor: Appropriations of Hegelian Political Thought* (Montreal and Kingston: McGill-Queen's University Press, 2008), 44.

39 James S. Olson and Robert Shadle, eds., *Historical Dictionary of the British Empire* (Westport, CT: Greenwood, 1996), 1: 548.

40 *The Liberal-Conservative Platform as Laid Down by R.L. Borden, M.P., Opposition Leader, at Halifax, August 20th, 1907* (Halifax?: 1907), 5.

41 J. Castell Hopkins, *Canadian Annual Review of Public Affairs 1904* (Toronto: Canadian Review Co., 1905), 175.

42 W.L. Morton, "Direct Legislation and the Origins of the Progressive Movement," *Canadian Historical Review* 25, no. 3 (1944): 281.

43 "The Great Victory in Canada," *National Review* 58 (November 1911): 381–92.

44 "Mr. Johnson's Address," in G.F. Chipman, *The Siege of Ottawa* (Winnipeg: Grain Growers' Guide, 1910?), 56, http://peel.library.ualberta.ca/bibliography/3397.html.

45 Quoted in Robert Bothwell, Ian Drummond, and John English, *Canada, 1900–1945* (Toronto: University of Toronto Press, 1987), 47.

46 Carrigan, *Canadian Party Platforms: 1867–1968*, 65.

47 Quoted in David Kimmel, "Walker, Sir Byron Edmund," in *DCB*, vol. 15, http://www.biographi.ca/en/bio/walker_byron_edmund_15E.html; and

Barbara Ruth Marshall, "Sir Edmund Walker, Servant of Canada" (MA thesis, York University, 1969), 55.

48 *Le Devoir*, "The Reciprocity Agreement and Its Consequences as Viewed from the Nationalist Standpoint," 12 February 1911.

49 Robert L. Borden, *The Naval Aid Bill: Speech Delivered by R.L. Borden, 5th December, 1912*. (n.p.: 1912), 6; and *Vancouver Daily World*, "Premier Borden," 17 September 1913.

50 Robert L. Borden, *Canada in the Commonwealth: From Conflict to Co-operation* (Oxford: Clarendon, 1929), 88.

51 J.L. Granatstein, and J.M. Hitsman, *Broken Promises: A History of Conscription in Canada* (Toronto: Oxford University Press, 1977), 14.

52 *Manitoba Free Press*, "An Explanation," 22 August 1917, 9.

53 Martin F. Auger, "On the Brink of Civil War: The Canadian Government and the Suppression of the 1918 Quebec Easter Riots," *Canadian Historical Review* 89, no. 4 (2008): 503–40.

54 J.A. Stevenson, "Canadian Foreign Policy," *Pacific Affairs* 7, no. 2 (June 1934): 153; and D.C. Watt, "Imperial Defence Policy and Imperial Foreign Policy, 1911–1939: A Neglected Paradox?," *Journal of Commonwealth Political Studies* 1, no. 4 (May 1963): 269.

55 *Initiative and Referendum*, pamphlet, 27 January 1913, R.A.C. Manning Papers, Provincial Archives of Manitoba.

56 Bothwell, Drummond, and English, *Canada, 1900–1945*, 232.

57 A.E. Safarian, *Foreign Ownership of Canadian Industry* (Toronto: University of Toronto Press, 1973), 7, and table 1, 10.

58 Neatby, "King, William Lyon Mackenzie," in *DCB*, vol. 17, http://www .biographi.ca/en/bio/king_william_lyon_mackenzie_17E.html; and W.L.M. King, *Industry and Humanity: A Study in the Principles Underlying Industrial Reconstruction* (Toronto: Houghton Mifflin, 1918).

59 Liberal and Conservative Party, Publicity Committee, *The National Liberal and Conservative Handbook* (Ottawa: Ottawa Printing, 1921), 17; and Liberal Party of Canada, *The National Liberal Convention, Ottawa, August 5, 6, 7, 1919* (n.p.: 1919), 203.

60 Lorna Lloyd, "Loosening the Apron Strings," *Round Table* 92, no. 369 (2003): 292–3; *Daily Mail and Empire* (Toronto), "Canada's Aid Vital to Empire Declares Hon. Mr. Meighen," 23 September 1922, 1, 5.

61 Quoted in Joseph T. Jockel and Joel J. Sokolsy, "Dandurand Revisited: Rethinking Canada's Defence Policy in an Unstable World," *International Journal* 48, no. 2 (Spring 1993): 380.

62 Robert Bothwell, "Canada's Isolationist Tradition," *International Journal* 54, no. 1 (Winter 1999): 77.

63 Neatby, "King, William Lyon Mackenzie."

64 W.L. Mackenzie King, *The Message of the Carillon, and Other Addresses* (Toronto: Macmillan, 1927), 106, 164, 183.

65 Larry A. Glassford, *Reaction and Reform: The Politics of the Conservative Party under R.B. Bennett, 1927–1938* (Toronto: University of Toronto Press, 1992), 79.

66 Anthony Patrick O'Brien and Judith A. McDonald, "Retreat from Protectionism: R.B. Bennett and the Movement to Freer Trade in Canada, 1930–1935," *Journal of Policy History* 21, no. 4 (October 2009): 331–65.

67 Harold A. Innis, "Great Britain, the United States and Canada," in *Essays in Canadian History* (Toronto: University of Toronto Press, 1956), 404–5.

68 Quoted in "Federal-Provincial Conference of First Ministers on the Constitution," verbatim transcript, Ottawa, 8–13 September 1980 (Ottawa: Canadian Intergovernmental Conference Secretariat, n.d.).

69 Frédéric Bastien, *The Battle of London: Trudeau, Thatcher, and the Fight for Canada's Constitution*, trans. Jacob Homel (Toronto: Dundurn, 2014), 186.

70 Quoted in Nelson Michaud and Kim Richard Nossal, "Out of the Blue: The Mulroney Legacy in Foreign Policy," in *Transforming the Nation: Canada and Brian Mulroney*, ed. Raymond B. Blake (Montreal and Kingston: McGill-Queen's University Press, 2007), 115.

71 Jane Taber, "Liberals Vote to Keep Monarchy, Legalize Pot at Convention," *Globe and Mail*, 15 January 2012, http://www.theglobeandmail.com /news/politics/ottawa-notebook/liberals-vote-to-keep-monarchy-legalize -pot-at-convention/article620760/#dashboard/follows/.

3. Industrialization, Urbanization, and Depression: The Rise of Third Parties

1 Quoted in Seymour Martin Lipset, *Agrarian Socialism: The Cooperative Commonwealth Federation in Saskatchewan; A Study in Political Sociology* (Garden City, NY: Doubleday Anchor, 1968), 169.

2 Richard Pomfret, *The Economic Development of Canada* (Toronto: Methuen, 1981), 148, 184.

3 Pedro S. Amaral, "The Great Depression in Canada and the United States: A Neoclassical Perspective," *Review of Economic Dynamics* 5, no. 1 (2002), table 7, 57.

4 University of Minnesota Department of Applied Economics, "The World Wheat Situation, 1931–32: A Review of the Crop Year," 86n2, ageconsearch .umn.edu/bitstream/139600/2/wheat-1932-12-09-03.pdf.

5 Victor Howard, *"We Were the Salt of the Earth!" A Narrative of the on-to-Ottawa Trek and the Regina Riot* (Regina: University of Regina Press, 1985).

6 Doug Owram, "Economic Thought in the 1930s: The Prelude to Keynesianism," *Canadian Historical Review* 66, no. 3 (1985): 344–77.

7 Martin Robin, *Shades of Right: Nativist and Fascist Politics in Canada, 1920–1940* (Toronto: University of Toronto Press, 1992), 266.

8 John Meisel, "The Stalled Omnibus: Canadian Parties in the 1960s," *Social Research* 30, no. 3 (1963): 367–90.

9 J.R. Mallory, *Social Credit and the Federal Power in Canada* (Toronto: University of Toronto Press, 1954), 189.

10 Governor General's Speech, *House of Commons Debates,* 17th Parliament, 6th Session, 17 January 1935, 3; 17th Parliament, 4th Session, 27 Feb. 1933, 2509.

11 Escott Reid, "The Canadian Election of 1935 – and After," *American Political Science Review* 30, no. 1 (1935): 117.

12 "The Farmers' Platform, 1921," in W.L. Morton, *The Progressive Party in Canada* (Toronto: University of Toronto Press, 1950), 302.

13 Quoted in Ramsay Cook, ed., *The Dafoe-Sifton Correspondence, 1919–1927* (Winnipeg: Manitoba Record Society, 1966), 196.

14 George Hoffman, "The 1934 Saskatchewan Provincial Election Campaign," *Saskatchewan History* 36, no. 2 (1983): 5n49; William Calderwood, "Pulpit, Press and Political Reactions to the Ku Klux Klan in Saskatchewan," in *The Twenties in Western Canada: Papers of the Western Canadian Studies Conference, March 1972,* ed. Susan Mann Trofimenkoff, 191–229 (Ottawa: History Division, National Museum of Man, 1972).

15 Quoted in Thomas Peterson, "Manitoba: Ethnic and Class Politics," in *Canadian Provincial Politics: The Party Systems of the Ten Provinces,* ed. Martin Robin (Scarborough, ON: Prentice-Hall, 1978), 84.

16 Rose T. Harasym, "Ukrainians in Canadian Political Life, 1923–45," in *A Heritage in Transition: Essays in the History of Ukrainians in Canada,* ed. Manoly R. Lupul (Toronto: McClelland and Stewart, 1982), 119.

17 Theodore Saloutos, "The Rise of the Non-Partisan League in North Dakota," *Agricultural History* 20, no. 1 (1946): 43–61.

18 *Re The Initiative and Referendum Act* (1919) AC p. 935.

19 W.L. Morton, *The Progressive Party in Canada* (Toronto: University of Toronto Press, 1950), 95.

20 Foster J. K. Griezic, "The Honourable Thomas Alexander Crerar: The Political Career of a Western Liberal Progressive in the 1920s," in *The Twenties in Western Canada,* ed. S.M. Trofimenkoff (Ottawa: History Division, National Museum of Man, 1972), 118.

21 F.F. Schindeler, *Responsible Government in Ontario* (Toronto: University of Toronto Press, 1969), 179.

22 Quoted in Augustus Bridle, *The Masques of Ottawa* (Toronto: Macmillan, 1921), 19.

23 J. Castell Hopkins, *Canadian Annual Review of Public Affairs 1922* (Toronto: Annual Review Pub. Co., 1923), 216.

24 Statistics Canada, *Canada Year Book, 1929*, 466–635, https://www66.statcan
    .gc.ca/eng/1929-eng.htm.
25 J. Blanchard, *A History of the Canadian Grain Commission 1912–1987* (Ottawa:
    Canadian Grain Commission, 1987), 28; Paul F. Sharp, *The Agrarian Revolt
    in Western Canada: A Survey Showing American Parallels* (Minneapolis:
    University of Minnesota Press, 1948), 81.
26 Walter D. Young, *The Anatomy of a Party: The National CCF, 1932–61* (Toronto:
    University of Toronto Press, 1969).
27 Grace MacInnis, *J.S. Woodsworth: A Man to Remember* (Toronto: Macmillan,
    1953), 188.
28 Quoted in Seymour Martin Lipset, *Agrarian Socialism: The Cooperative
    Commonwealth Federation in Saskatchewan; A Study in Political Sociology*
    (Garden City, NY: Doubleday Anchor, 1968), 135–6.
29 Peter R. Sinclair, "The Saskatchewan CCF: Ascent to Power and the Decline
    of Socialism," *Canadian Historical Review* 59, no. 4 (1973): 423; and Lipset,
    Agrarian Socialism, 220, table 32, 228, and table 16, 202.
30 J.S. Woodsworth, *Strangers within Our Gates* (Toronto: Stephenson, 1909);
    Woodsworth, *My Neighbour* (Toronto: Missionary Society of the Methodist
    Church, 1911).
31 Michael Shevell, "A Canadian Paradox: Tommy Douglas and Eugenics,"
    Canadian Journal of Neurological Sciences 39, no. 1 (2012): 35–9.
32 Quoted in David Lewis, "Socialism across the Border: Canada's C.C.F.,"
    Antioch Review 3, no. 1 (1943): 475.
33 League for Social Reconstruction, *Social Planning for Canada* (Toronto: Nelson,
    1935); and quoted in Michiel Horn, *The League for Social Reconstruction: Intel-
    lectual Origins of the Democratic Left in Canada, 1930–1942* (Toronto: University
    of Toronto Press, 1980), 93.
34 Martin Robin, *Radical Politics and Canadian Labour, 1880–1930* (Kingston:
    Industrial Relations Centre, Queen's University, 1968), 276.
35 J.E. Rea, "The Politics of Class: Winnipeg City Council 1919–1945," in *The
    West and the Nation*, ed. Carl Berger and Ramsay Cook (Toronto: McClelland
    and Stewart, 1976), 235.
36 Ian MacPherson, *Each for All: A History of the Co-operative Movement in English
    Canada, 1900–1945* (Toronto: Macmillan, 1979).
37 James Naylor, *The Fate of Labour Socialism: The Co-operative Commonwealth
    Federation and the Dream of a Working-Class Future* (Toronto: University of
    Toronto Press, 2016), 112.
38 Kenneth McNaught, *A Prophet in Politics: A Biography of J.S. Woodsworth*
    (Toronto: University of Toronto Press, 1959), 286–8.
39 Quoted in Nelson Wiseman, *Social Democracy in Manitoba: A History of the
    CCF-NDP* (Winnipeg: University of Manitoba Press, 1985), 22.
40 C.H. Douglas, *Social Credit* (London: Palmer, 1924).

41 Quoted in Janine Stingel, *Social Discredit: Ant-Semitism, Social Credit, and the Jewish Question* (Montreal and Kingston: McGill-Queen's University Press, 2000), 13.

42 McMillan v Brownlee, [1937] SCR 318, 1937 CanLII 28 (SCC), http://www.canlii.org/en/ca/scc/doc/1937/1937canlii28/1937canlii28.html.

43 W.E. Mann, *Sect, Cult, and Church in Alberta* (Toronto: University of Toronto Press, 1955), 4.

44 Josiah Austin Hammer, "Mormon Trek to Canada," *Alberta Historical Review* 7, no. 2 (1959): 7–16; and L.A. Rosenvall, "The Transfer of Mormon Culture to Alberta," *American Review of Canadian Studies* 12, no. 2 (1982): 51.

45 *Globe and Mail*, "Social Credit Moves East," 30 April 1938, 3.

46 Austin Albert Mardon and Ernest G. Mardon, *Alberta's Political Pioneers: A Biographical Account of the United Farmers of Alberta, 1921–1935* (Edmonton: Golden Meteorite, 2010), 52.

47 John Finlay, *Social Credit: The English Origins* (Montreal and Kingston: McGill-Queen's University Press, 1972).

48 Bob Hesketh, *Major Douglas and Alberta Social Credit* (Toronto: University of Toronto Press, 1997), chap. 5.

49 *Globe and Mail*, "Social Crediter Hints at Plot over Canada," 15 May 1936, 2.

50 *Globe and Mail*, "Dunning Calls Aberhart's Hand," 1 April 1938, 6.

51 James Powell, *A History of the Canadian Dollar* (Ottawa: Bank of Canada, 2005), 47.

52 Edward Bell, *Social Classes and Social Credit in Alberta* (Montreal and Kingston: McGill-Queen's University Press, 1994), 158, 128.

53 Anthony Mardiros, *William Irvine: The Life of a Prairie Radical* (Toronto: J. Lorimer, 1979), 146–7.

54 James Naylor, "Socialism for a New Generation: CCF Youth in the Popular Front Era," *Canadian Historical Review* 94, no. 1 (2013): 234–8.

55 Ian McLeod and Thomas H. McLeod, *Tommy Douglas: The Road to Jerusalem* (Calgary: Fifth House, 2004), 58–67.

56 Government of Alberta, *The Case of Alberta: Addressed to the Sovereign People of Canada and Their Governments* (Edmonton: 1938).

57 Arja Pilli, *The Finnish-Language Press in Canada, 1901–1939: A Study in the History of Ethnic Journalism* (Helsinki: Suomalainen Tiedeakatemia, 1982), 142.

58 Harasym, "Ukrainians in Canadian Political Life, 1923–45."

59 Quoted in D. Owen Carrigan, *Canadian Party Platforms: 1867–1968* (Urbana: University of Illinois Press, 1968), 118.

60 Jean-François Nadeau, *The Canadian Fuhrer: The Life of Adrien Arcand*, trans. Bob Chodos, Eric Hamovitch, and Susan Joanis (Toronto: James Lorimer, 2010), 222.

61 *Globe and Mail*, "Once Talked of March on Ottawa," 2 August 1967, 36.

62 John Manley, "'Communists Love Canada!': The Communist Party of Canada, the 'People' and the Popular Front, 1933–1939," *Journal of Canadian Studies* 36, no. 4 (2001–2): 74, 79.

63 A.E. Smith, *All My Life* (Toronto: Progress Books, 1949).

64 Harold Dingman, "Corporate State Aim of Quebec Fascists," *Globe and Mail*, 5 January 1938, 1.

65 Dingman, "Corporate State Aim of Quebec Fascists."

66 Quoted in J.R.H. Wilbur, "H.H. Stevens and the Reconstruction Party," *Canadian Historical Review* 45, no. 1 (1964): 1–2.

67 Mary Hallett, "The Social Credit Party and the New Democracy Movement," *Canadian Historical Review* 47, no. 4 (1966): 301–25.

68 Seymour Martin Lipset, *Continental Divide: The Values and Institutions of the United States and Canada* (New York: Routledge, 1991), 201.

69 Nelson Wiseman, "Provincial Political Cultures," in *Provinces: Canadian Provincial Politics*, ed. Christopher Dunn, 21–56 (Peterborough, ON: Broadview, 2006).

70 Richard Hofstadter, *The Age of Reform: From Bryan to F.D.R.* (New York: Vintage Books, 1955), 97.

71 John Maynard Keynes, *The General Theory of Employment, Interest and Money* (London: Macmillan, 1936).

4. Parties of Warfare and Welfare

1 Liberal Party election platform, 1945.

2 Gad Horowitz, "Conservatism, Liberalism, and Socialism in Canada: An Interpretation," *Canadian Journal of Economics and Political Science* 32, no. 2 (1966): 162.

3 *Globe and Mail*, "Cannot Be Neutral, Declares Dr. Manion; Against Conscription," 28 March 1939, 1.

4 Stephen Brooks, *Canadian Democracy* (Toronto: Oxford University Press, 2015), table 11.1, 341.

5 William D. Coleman and Kim Richard Nossal, "The State and War Production in Canada, 1939–1945," in *Organizing Business for War: Corporatist Economic Organization during the Second World War*, ed. Wyn Grant, Jan Nekkers, and Frans van Waarden, 47–74 (New York: Berg, 1991).

6 W.T. Easterbrook and Hugh G.J. Aitken, *Canadian Economic History* (Toronto: University of Toronto Press, 1988), 558; and Statistics Canada, "Union Membership in Canada, in Total and as a Percentage of Non-Agricultural Paid Workers and Union Members with International Affiliation, 1911 to 1975," table E175–177, http://www.statcan.gc.ca/pub/11-516-x/sectione/4147438-eng.htm#6.

7   Peter S. McInnis, *Harnessing Labour Confrontation: Shaping the Postwar Settlement in Canada, 1943–1950* (Toronto: University of Toronto Press, 2002), 113–14.

8   W.L. Mackenzie King, *Industry and Humanity: A Study in the Principles Underlying Industrial Reconstruction* (Boston: Houghton Mifflin, 1918).

9   A.J. Miller, "The Functional Principle in Canada's External Relations," *International Journal* 35, no. 2 (Spring 1980): 309–28.

10   House of Commons, *Debates*, 6 December 1945.

11   P.J. Philip, "Canada Expresses Doubt on Charter," *New York Times*, 21 October 1945, 17; and *Globe and Mail*, "'Finger in the Pie Again': Nations League Figures Block Success of UN, Socred Leader Charges," 1 February 1949, 3; Warren Baldwin, "He Knows His Dollars: Complex Monetary Pact Simple Under Rasminsky," *Globe and Mail*, 7 September 1949, 7; Baldwin, "Gold Production Gain Unlikely with Subsidy, Abbott Tells Commons," *Globe and Mail*, 7 April 1948, 3; and Baldwin, "Dependence of Canada on States Not Increased by Pact: Rasminsky," *Globe and Mail*, 13 December 1945, 3.

12   P.J. Philip, "Canada Expresses Doubt on Charter," *New York Times*, 21 October 1945, 17.

13   House of Commons, *Debates*, 1 April 1938, 2092.

14   Quoted in C.P. Stacey, *Canada and the Age of Conflict: A History of Canadian External Policies, vol. 2, 1921–1948: The Mackenzie King Era* (Toronto: University of Toronto Press, 1981), 213.

15   Escott Reid, "The Saskatchewan Liberal Machine before 1929," *Canadian Journal of Economics and Political Science* 2, no. 1 (1936): 27–40.

16   J.L. Granatstein, *Canada's War: The Politics of the Mackenzie King Government* (Toronto: Oxford University Press, 1975), 85.

17   Solon Low, "Socred Doctrine Will Avoid War," *Globe and Mail*, 13 May 1949, 14.

18   House of Commons, *Debates*, 10 June 1942.

19   F.R. Scott, "W.L.M.K.," in *The Blasted Pine: An Anthology of Satire Invective and Disrespectful Verse Chiefly by Canadian Writers*, ed. F.R. Scott and A.J.M. Smith (Toronto: Macmillan, 1957), 28.

20   Quoted in H. Blair Neatby, "Mackenzie King and French Canada," *Journal of Canadian Studies* 11, no. 1 (1976): 6.

21   Michael Bliss, introduction to *Report on Social Security for Canada* by Leonard Marsh (Toronto: University of Toronto Press, 1975), ix.

22   J.W. Pickersgill and D.F. Forster, *The Mackenzie King Record, vol. 3, 1945/1946* (Toronto: University of Toronto Press, 1970), 386–7.

23   Bruce Hutchison, *The Incredible Canadian: Mackenzie King: His Works, His Times, and His Nation* (Toronto: Longmans Green, 1952).

24   Reginald Whitaker, *The Government Party: Organizing and Financing the Liberal Party of Canada, 1930–58* (Toronto: University of Toronto Press, 1977), 420.

25   Quoted in *Globe and Mail*, "Now Push War, Says Manion," 26 October 1939, 1.
26   Quoted in J. Castell Hopkins, *Canadian Annual Review 1937–38* (Toronto: Annual Review Pub. Co., 1940), 57.
27   J.L. Granatstein, *The Politics of Survival: The Conservative Party of Canada, 1939–1945* (Toronto: University of Toronto Press, 1967), 112.
28   *Globe and Mail*, "Say Meighen Seeks Bracken as Successor," 28 November 1942, 10; and *Globe and Mail*, "Meighen Will Resign Leadership of Party, Developments Indicate," 9 December 1942, 1.
29   Thomas Peterson, "Manitoba: Ethnic and Class Politics," in *Canadian Provincial Politics: The Party Systems in the Ten Provinces*, ed. Martin Robin (Scarborough, ON: Prentice-Hall, 1972), 88.
30   Kenneth Cragg, "Conservative Party Policies Weighed at Port Hope: Conservative Laymen Ponder Party's Future," *Globe and Mail*, 5 September 1942, 7.
31   Quoted in W.H. McConnell, "The Genesis of the Canadian 'New Deal,'" *Journal of Canadian Studies* 4, no. 2 (1969): 33.
32   *Globe and Mail*, "Port Hope Plan Declared Basis of Convention," 27 November 1942, 4.
33   Charlotte Whitton, *The Dawn of Ampler Life* (Toronto: Macmillan, 1943).
34   *Globe and Mail*, 9 and 17 July 1943; and "The Constructive Platform of the Progressive Conservative Party in the Province of Ontario, July 3, 1943," quoted in Rand Dyck, *Provincial Politics in Canada: Towards the Turn of the Century* (Scarborough, ON: Prentice-Hall), 338.
35   Lawrence LeDuc, Jon H. Pammett, Judith I. McKenzie, and André Turcotte, *Dynasties and Interludes: Past and Present in Canadian Electoral Politics* (Toronto: Dundurn, 2010), 143–4.
36   P.J. Philips, "Meighen Will Quit Party Leadership," *New York Times*, 10 December 1942, 15.
37   *Toronto Daily Star*, 25 June 1949, 1.
38   James Naylor, "Pacifism or Anti-Imperialism? The CCF Response to the Outbreak of World War II," *Journal of the Canadian Historical Association* 6 (1997): 213–37.
39   Frank Underhill, "To Protect Our Neutrality," *Canadian Forum* 17 (February 1938): 375–7.
40   Walter D. Young, *Anatomy of a Party: The National CCF 1932–61* (Toronto: University of Toronto Press, 1969), 106–7.
41   Victor Huard, "Canadian Ideological Responses to the Second World War," *Peace Research* 25, no. 2 (1993): 67–81.
42   David Lewis and Frank Scott, *Make This Your Canada: A Review of CCF History and Policy* (Toronto: Central Canada Publishing, 1943); M.J. Coldwell, *Left Turn, Canada* (London: Victor Gollancz, 1945).

43 Canadian Institute of Public Opinion, "Find C.C.F. Leads Old Groups in Popular Favor," *Toronto Daily Star*, 29 September 1943, 3.

44 M.A. Sanderson, "Sugar-Coating the Arsenic," *Globe and Mail*, 29 July 1943, 2.

45 John Boyko, *Into the Hurricane: Attacking Socialism and the CCF* (Winnipeg: J. Gordon Shillingford, 2006), 112.

46 B.A. Trestrail, *Social Suicide* (Toronto: Public Informational Association, 1945).

47 Seymour Martin Lipset, *Agrarian Socialism: The Cooperative Commonwealth Federation in Saskatchewan: A Study in Political Sociology* (Berkeley: University of California Press, 1950).

48 Census of Canada, 1951, vol. 1, tables 9 and 13.

49 Fred Tipping, quoted in Nelson Wiseman, *Social Democracy in Manitoba: A History of the CCF-NDP* (Winnipeg: University of Manitoba Press, 1983), 75.

50 Gad Horowitz, *Canadian Labour in Politics* (Toronto: University of Toronto Press, 1968), 202.

51 Quoted in C.B. Macpherson, *Democracy in Alberta: Social Credit and the Party System* (Toronto: University of Toronto Press, 2013), 204.

52 Quoted in *Globe and Mail*, "Social Credit Caucus Held: Members Fear Trend toward Socialism," 2 November 1942, 10.

53 E.G. Smith, "Back Conscription Bill, 158 to 54: Single Men, Childless Widowers from 20 to 40 Called Up," *Globe and Mail*, 8 July 1942, 1; and Peter Melnycky, "Tears in the Garden: Alberta's Ukrainians during the Second World War," in *For King and Country: Alberta in the Second World War*, ed. K.W. Tingley (Edmonton: Provincial Museum of Alberta), 331.

54 Alvin Finkel, *The Social Credit Phenomenon in Alberta* (Toronto: University of Toronto Press, 1989), 75.

55 Tom Langford, "Why Alberta Vacillated over Wartime Day Nurseries," *Prairie Forum* 20, no. 2 (2003): 173–94.

56 Finkel, *Social Credit Phenomenon in Alberta*, 88.

57 *Globe and Mail*, "Social Credit Plans Future: Western Group to Issue Reconstruction Book," 21 December 1942, 8; and *Globe and Mail*, "Alberta Suggests Federal Scheme of Social Credit," 1 December 1945, 3.

58 Quoted in Finkel, *Social Credit Phenomenon in Alberta*, 138.

59 *Globe and Mail*, "Jeers, Catcalls Greet Solon Low at U of T Talk," 22 January 1948, 1.

60 *Toronto Daily Star*, "M.P. says CBC, Film Board Used to Spread Communism," 18 July 1946, 39.

61 *Globe and Mail*, "Social Credit Foe of All Ideologies," 5 April 1946, 13.

62 *New York Times*, "Aid to Social Credit Banned by Cardinal: Canadian Clergy Forbidden to Support," 8 February 1940, 9.

63 *Globe and Mail*, "Solon Low: Biblical Joseph Type Needed as Canadian Finance Minister," 6 June 1949, 3.

64 Michel Beaulieu, *Labour at the Lakehead: Ethnicity, Socialism, and Politics, 1900–35* (Vancouver: UBC Press, 2011), 206.

65 *Edmonton Journal*, "Ukrainians Here Declare Loyalty," 5 September 1939, 11.

66 Royal Canadian Mounted Police Headquarters, "Intelligence Bulletin, War Series No. 45" 19 July 1942 (Ottawa), 374.

67 *Globe and Mail*, "Maxime Raymond: Nationalist Led Splinter Group, Bloc Populaire," 17 July 1961, 9; and *Globe and Mail*, "Bloc Populaire Opposes Economic Dictatorship," 29 December 1943, 3.

68 Michael Behiels, "The Bloc Populaire Canadien: Anatomy of a Failure, 1942–1947," *Journal of Canadian Studies* 18, no. 2 (1983–4): 1–30.

69 Livio Di Matteo, *A Federal Fiscal History: Canada, 1867–2017* (Vancouver: Fraser Institute, 2017), 82, https://www.fraserinstitute.org/sites/default/files/federal-fiscal-history-canada-1867-2017.pdf.

70 J. Murray Beck, *Pendulum of Power: Canada's Federal Elections* (Scarborough, ON: Prentice-Hall, 1968), 227.

71 *Toronto Daily Star*, "Conservatives' Motion Means Margarine Sale but Doesn't Say So," 2 October 1948, 2; and George Perlin, *The Tory Syndrome: Leadership Politics in the Progressive Conservative Party* (Montreal and Kingston: McGill-Queen's University Press, 1980), 53.

72 Warren Baldwin, "George Drew: Vote for Liberals Is Vote for Coalition with CCF; PC's Pledge Tax Cuts," *Globe and Mail*, 23 May 1949, 3.

73 *Globe and Mail*, "Some Changes Have Been Made," 19 September 1959, 6.

74 Quoted in Dale C. Thomson, *Louis St. Laurent: Canadian* (Toronto: Macmillan, 1967), 266.

5. Minority Governments: The Diefenbaker-Pearson Years

1 Quoted in Sean O'Sullivan and Rod McQueen, *Both My Houses: From Politics to Priesthood* (Toronto: Key Porter, 1986), 49.

2 Alan Cairns, "The Electoral System and the Party System in Canada, 1921–1965," *Canadian Journal of Political Science* 1, no. 1 (March 1968): 55.

3 Clark Davey, "At Winnipeg Today: Confident PM Scorns Liberal Tax Cut Aim," *Globe and Mail*, 12 February 1958, 1; Liberal Party of Canada, "Speakers' Notes," in D. Owen Carrigan, *Canadian Party Platforms 1867–1968* (Toronto: Copp Clark, 1968), 319.

4 Quoted in Carrigan, *Canadian Party Platforms*, 208, 210, and 204; Frank Flaherty, "House Rejects Motion to Outlaw Communism but Drew Commended," *Globe and Mail*, 10 May 1950, 3.

5 Peter Newman, *Renegade in Power: The Diefenbaker Years* (Toronto: McClelland and Stewart, 1963); Newman, *The Distemper of Our Times* (Toronto: McClelland and Stewart, 1968).

6 Donn Downey, "Charles Lynch: Political Columnist Had Large Following," *Globe and Mail*, 22 July 1994, A12; Ralph Hyman, "Attack Press Record in House Coverage," *Globe and Mail*, 29 July 1964, 5.

7 Dalton Camp, *An Eclectic Eel* (Ottawa: Deneau, 1981), 49.

8 W.C. Soderlund, W.I. Romano, E.D. Briggs, and Ronald H. Wagenberg, "From a Single Medium to a Multimedia Society," in *Canadian Political Party Systems: A Reader*, ed. R.K. Carty (Peterborough, ON: Broadview, 1992), 275.

9 *The Confederation of Tomorrow Conference: Proceedings* (Toronto: s.n., 1968).

10 Harvey Hickey, "Fleming Bids St. Laurent Repent Stand," *Globe and Mail*, 28 November 1956, 1; and Eugene Griffin, "Canadian MPs Back Cabinet on Suez Policy: US Meekly Followed, Conservatives," *Chicago Daily Tribune*, 30 November 1956, 5.

11 Peter Woolstencroft, "The Conservatives: Rebuilding and Rebranding, Yet Again," in *Canadian Parties in Transition*, ed. Alain-G. Gagnon and A. Brian Tanguay, 4th ed. (Toronto: University of Toronto Press, 2017), 155.

12 *Toronto Daily Star*, "Tories Decline Shorter Name Frost Against," 14 December 1956, 1; and *Toronto Daily Star*, "Victory for Diefenbaker Seen Foreshadowing Pact," 15 December 1956, 3.

13 J.E. Beliveau, "Diefenbaker Win Seen Ending Tory Chances in Quebec," *Toronto Daily Star*, 15 December 1956, 3.

14 Bruce MacDonald, "St. Laurent, Frost Clash," *Toronto Daily Star*, 25 May 1957, 7; T.M. Eberlee, "Frost Sends Kelly to Woo Bennett, Manning for Diefenbaker Win," *Toronto Daily Star*, 4 October 1956, 1.

15 John Meisel, "Analysing the Vote," *Queen's Quarterly* 64, no. 4 (1958): 487.

16 *Washington Post*, "New Ballot Test Due in Canada," 12 June 1957, A5; and *Globe and Mail*, "A Crushing, Defeat," 11 June 1957, 6.

17 "Canada: Mr. Diefenbaker's Triumph," *Round Table* 48, no. 191 (June 1958): 290.

18 Elizabeth Wangenheim, "The Ukrainians: A Case Study of the 'Third Force,'" in *Nationalism in Canada*, ed. Peter Russell, 72–91 (Toronto: McGraw-Hill, 1965).

19 John G. Diefenbaker, *One Canada: Memoirs of the Right Honourable John G. Diefenbaker* (Toronto: Macmillan, 1975), 1.

20 Hugh Segal, *No Surrender: Reflections of a Happy Warrior in the Tory Crusade* (Toronto: HarperCollins, 1996), 1.

21 Eugene Griffin, "New Type Found among Canada's Office Holders: Claims Unhyphenated Ancestry," *Chicago Daily Tribune*, 13 September 1948, A3.

22 *Globe and Mail*, "Lauds Ukrainians for Contribution; Music Is Praised," 1 April 1957, 5.

23 Asa McKercher, "Sound and Fury: Diefenbaker, Human Rights, and Canadian Foreign Policy," *Canadian Historical Review* 97, no. 2 (June 2006): 165–94.

24 Marco Adria, "Arms to Communications: Idealist and Pragmatist Strains of Canadian Thought on Technology and Nationalism," *Canadian Journal of Communication* 27, no. 2 (2003): 167.

25 Newman, *Renegade in Power*, v.

26 *Newsday*, "Diefenbaker Is Out: Nuclear Rift Topples Canada Regime," 6 February 1963, 1.

27 George Grant, *Lament for a Nation: The Defeat of Canadian Nationalism* (Toronto: McClelland and Stewart, 1965), 63.

28 George Grant, *Technology and Empire: Perspectives on North America* (Toronto: House of Anansi, 1969).

29 Carl Berger, *The Writing of Canadian History: Aspects of English-Canadian Historical Writing, 1900–1970* (Toronto: Oxford University Press, 1976).

30 W.L. Morton, "Canadian Conservatism Now," *Conservative Concepts* 1 (Spring 1959): 7–8.

31 W.L. Morton, *The Canadian Identity* (Madison: University of Wisconsin Press, 1961).

32 Gerald Waring, "Convention Repudiates Diefenbaker," *Washington Post*, 16 November 1966, A16.

33 Gordon Donaldson, *The Prime Ministers of Canada* (Toronto: Doubleday Canada, 1997), 310.

34 Quoted in Peter Shawn Taylor, "Son of the Chief?: What Harper Shares with Diefenbaker, and the Lessons He Must Learn," *National Post*, 6 March 2007, A23.

35 Harvey Hickey, "MPs Blast US Envoy for Speech," *Globe and Mail*, 18 April 1956, 1.

36 R. Kenneth Carty, *Big Tent Politics: The Liberal Party's Long Mastery of Canada's Public Life* (Vancouver: UBC Press, 2015), 106.

37 Clark Davey, "Howe Warning Kept Secret: PM Blasts Timid Liberal Move, Seeking Office without Vote: New Leader under Fire First Day," *Globe and Mail*, 20 January 1958, 1.

38 Clark Davey, "Pearson Cracks Whip: Liberals Frank, Free and Tough in Party Discussions," *Globe and Mail*, 19 November 1958, 8.

39 L.B. Pearson, "Introduction," in *The Liberal Party*, by J.W. Pickersgill, vii–ix (Toronto: McClelland and Stewart, 1962).

40 Christina McCall-Newman, *Grits: An Intimate Portrait of the Liberal Party* (Toronto: Macmillan, 1982), 90–1.

41 Joseph Wearing, *The L-Shaped Party: The Liberal Party of Canada, 1958–1980* (Toronto: McGraw-Hill Ryerson, 1981), 72.

42 Barry Wilson, *Politics of Defeat: The Decline of the Liberal Party in Saskatchewan* (Saskatoon: Western Producer Books, 1980); and David E. Smith, *The Regional Decline of a National Party: Liberals on the Prairies* (Toronto: University of Toronto Press, 1981).

43 *Globe and Mail*, "A Polish Newspaper's Interview with Mr. Lester Pearson," 27 February 1958, 6.

44 Stephen Clarkson, *The Big Red Machine: How the Liberal Party Dominates Canadian Politics* (Vancouver: UBC Press, 2005), 11.

45 Canada, Report of the Task Force on the Structure of Canadian Industry, *Foreign Ownership and the Structure of Canadian Industry* (Ottawa: Queen's Printer, 1968).

46 Harold Greer, "Endorsation of a Political Disaster: The Conference at Kingston ..." *Globe and Mail*, 14 September 1960, 7.

47 Harold Greer, "St. Laurent–Howe Tradition Bypassed: Pearson Invites a Liberal New Look," *Globe and Mail*, 7 September 1960, 1; *Globe and Mail*, "Looking for New Ideas," 8 September 1960, 6; Greer, "Endorsation of a Political Disaster," 14 September 1960, 7; and Sandra Martin, "Political Thinker Had a Passion for Canada: Tom Kent Wasn't a Diehard Partisan – He was an Exemplar of the Intellectually Engaged Citizen," *Globe and Mail*, 10 December 2011, S11.

48 Robert Bothwell, Ian Drummond, and John English, *Canada since 1945: Power, Politics, and Provincialism* (Toronto: University of Toronto Press, 1989), 213.

49 Diefenbuck image: https://www.google.com/search?q=diefenbuck +image&tbm=isch&imgil=6Bdr66Ld1sL24M%253A%253BmTRr _hsOqh9C2M%253Bhttp%25253A%25252F%25252Fwww.coincommunity .com%25252Fforum%25252Ftopic.asp%25253FTOPIC_ID%2525253D151030 &source=iu&pf=m&fir=6Bdr66Ld1sL24M%253A%252CmTRr_hsOqh9C2M %252C_&usg=__OtufpqrsEihKiGqcf7jsp3LUQXU%3D&biw=1252& bih=559&ved=0ahUKEwjav6_G_eXRAhUJSyYKHbp9DIwQyjcINQ&ei =jSeNWJrFMomWmQG6-7HgCA#imgrc=6Bdr66Ld1sL24M%3A.

50 Ryan Edwardson, "'Kicking Uncle Sam Out of the Peaceable Kingdom': English-Canadian 'New Nationalism' and Americanization," *Journal of Canadian Studies* 37, no. 4 (Winter 2003): 131–50; and Michael Hart, "Twenty Years of Canadian Tradecraft: Canada at GATT, 1947–1967," *International Journal* 52, no. 4 (1997): 604.

51 Bruce MacDonald, "PM Leaves in Doubt Fate of $700,000,000 A-Weapons, Stresses Basic Arms," *Globe and Mail*, 26 January 1963, 3.

52 Quoted in Greg Donaghy, *Tolerant Allies: Canada and the United States, 1963–1968* (Montreal and Kingston: McGill-Queen's University Press, 2002), 130.

53 Anthony Westell, "Pearson Has Sarcastic Words for Authors," *Globe and Mail*, 8 November 1968, 10.

54 L. Ian MacDonald, "The Best Prime Minister of the Last 50 Years: Pearson, by a Landslide," *Policy Options*, June–July 2003, https://policyoptions.irpp .org/magazines/the-best-pms-in-the-past-50-years/the-best-prime -minister-of-the-last-50-years-pearson-by-a-landslide/.

55   Val Scott, "NDP Men in Negotiation Talk with Liberals 'Rank High in Party,'" *Toronto Daily Star*, 2 January 1964 6; and Vernon Singer, "Should the NDP Join: A Liberal Member of the Provincial Legislature ...," *Globe and Mail*, 23 May 1964, A6.

56   Bryan D. Palmer, *Canada's 1960s: The Ironies of Identity in a Rebellious Era* (Toronto: University of Toronto Press, 2009), 206.

57   Gad Horowitz, "The Future of the NDP," *Canadian Dimension* no. 3 (July–August 1966): 23.

58   Lorne Ingle to Don Swailes, 19 June 1950, CCF Records – Public Archives of Canada.

59   David Lewis, "A Socialist Takes Stock," [1956], quoted in Paul W. Fox, ed., *Politics: Canada*, 4th ed. (Toronto: McGraw-Hill Ryerson, 1997), 241.

60   Socialist History Project, "The Winnipeg Declaration of Principles (1956)," http://www.socialisthistory.ca/Docs/CCF/Winnipeg.htm.

61   Keith Archer, *Political Choices and Electoral Consequences: A Study of Organized Labour and the New Democratic Party* (Montreal and Kingston: McGill-Queen's University Press, 1990).

62   Stanley Knowles, *The New Party* (Toronto: McClelland and Stewart, 1961), 127.

63   Nelson Wiseman, *Social Democracy in Manitoba: A History of the CCF-NDP* (Winnipeg: University of Manitoba Press, 1983), 109.

64   Interview with author, February 1972.

65   Gerassimos Moschonas, *In the Name of Social Democracy: The Great Transformation, 1945 to the Present*, trans. Gregory Elliot (London: Verso, 2002).

66   Lynn MacDonald, *The Party That Changed Canada: The New Democratic Party, Then and Now* (Toronto: Macmillan, 1987); David Lewis, *The Good Fight* (Toronto: Macmillan. 1981), 293–4, 504; and Edward Broadbent, "Social Democracy or Liberalism in the New Millennium?," in *The Future of Social Democracy*, ed. Peter Russell, 73–93 (Toronto: University of Toronto Press, 1999).

67   Social Credit Association of Canada, *These Are Facts You Should Know* (Edmonton: SCAC, 1953).

68   *Globe and Mail*, "Quebec Party Liberal Alliance Perfidious: Low," 15 May 1956, 9; and George Bain, "Ottawa Letter," *Globe and Mail*, 16 May 1956, 6.

69   *Globe and Mail*, "Reform Plan: Socreds Offer 10 Points," 22 February 1958, 1.

70   Walter Gray, "A Reporter Looks Back: Social Credit as It Was 25 Years Ago," *Globe and Mail*, 25 April 1961, 7.

71   E.C. Manning, *Political Realignment* (Toronto: McClelland and Stewart, 1967).

72   Quoted in Malcolm G. Taylor, *Health Insurance and Canadian Public Policy: The Seven Decisions That Created the Canadian Health Insurance System* (Montreal and Kingston: McGill-Queen's University Press, 1978), chap. 4, and 338–40.

73   *Globe and Mail*, "Alberta Reports Record Budget over $116,000,000," 8 March 1952, 3.

74 *Globe and Mail*, "B.C. Social Crediters End 15-Year Joke Role," 15 March 1952, 10.

75 Ivers Kelly, "Three Fill the Bill: Teetotaler Seen Next B.C. Premier," *Globe and Mail*, 11 July 1952, 8.

76 Geoff Meggs and Rod Mickleburgh, *The Art of the Impossible: Dave Barrett and the NDP in Power, 1972–1975* (Madeira Park, BC: Harbour Publishing, 2012), 36.

77 Hugh MacLennan, *Two Solitudes* (Toronto: Collins, 1945).

78 Chaim I. Waxman, ed., *The End of Ideology Debate* (New York: Funk and Wagnalls, 1968).

6. Economy, Language, Unity

1 Quoted in *Toronto Daily Star*, "PM: 'Only Bleeding Hearts' Object to Army Guns," 14 October 1970, 9.

2 ICPSR, "The 1974–1979–1980 Canadian National Elections and Quebec Referendum Panel Study, 16 February 1992, https://www.icpsr.umich.edu /icpsrweb/ICPSR/studies/08079; ICPSR, "Most Important Issue," 16 February 1992, https://www.icpsr.umich.edu/icpsrweb/ICPSR/ssvd /studies/08079/datasets/0001/variables/V92?q=%22most+important +issue%22+canada.

3 Statistics Canada, *Canada Year Book, 1973* (Ottawa: Minister of Industry, Trade, and Commerce, 1973), 346–7, 458, 515.

4 Fred Lazar, "The National Economy," in *Canadian Annual Review of Politics and Public Affairs 1977*, ed. John Saywell, 309–10 (Toronto: University of Toronto Press, 1979); and Lazar, "The National Economy," in *Canadian Annual Review of Politics and Public Affairs 1979*, ed. R.B. Byers, 127–34 (Toronto: University of Toronto Press, 1981).

5 Michael Hawes, "The National Economy," in *Canadian Annual Review of Politics and Public Affairs 1984*, ed. R.B. Byers, 100–2 (Toronto: University of Toronto Press, 1987).

6 Robert J. Drummond, "Parliament and Politics," in Byers, *Canadian Annual Review of Politics and Public Affairs 1984*, 6–7.

7 Jeff Sallot, "Turner Apologizes for Patting Rears of Liberal Women," *Globe and Mail*, 14 August 1984, 1.

8 Statistics Canada, *Canada Year Book, 1973* (Ottawa: Information Canada, 1973), 344.

9 Parliament of Canada, "Women Candidates in General Elections: 1921 to Date," https://web.archive.org/web/20060305140947/ http://www.parl .gc.ca/information/about/process/house/asp/WomenElect.asp?lang= E&source=hoc.

10 Richard Cleroux, "'It's Not Wage, It's Income, Controls': Words Twisted on Freeze Issue, Stanfield Says," *Globe and Mail*, 31 May 1974, 8.

11 Donald S. Macdonald with Rod McQueen, *Thumper: The Memoirs of the Honourable Donald S. Macdonald* (Montreal and Kingston: McGill-Queen's University Press, 2014), 154.

12 Donald Newman, "Four Quebec Tories to Split with Party in Support of War Measures Imposition," *Globe and Mail*, 19 October 1970, 1.

13 D. Owen Carrigan, *Canadian Party Platforms 1867–1968* (Toronto: Copp Clark, 1968), 343.

14 Eugene Griffin, "270 in Quebec Seized under War Powers," *Chicago Tribune*, 17 October 1970, 1.

15 Donald Murray, "The Ralliement des creditistes in Parliament, 1970–71," *Journal of Canadian Studies* 8, no. 2 (1973): 24; and House of Commons, *Debates*, 3rd Session, 28th Parliament, vol. 1, 332.

16 Donald Newman, "NDP Adamant as House Backs Ottawa on War Measures Act by 190–16," *Globe and Mail*, 20 October 1970, 9.

17 Robert Sheppard, "Vote of 246–24 Sends Package to Senate: O Canada Hails Constitution Victory," *Globe and Mail*, 3 December 1981, 1.

18 Hugh Segal, "The Struggle to Save Canada: A Federalist Perspective," *Orbis* 41, no. 3 (1997): 464.

19 Michael Gillan, "Old Men Serve as Young Men Stand in Line," *Globe and Mail*, 7 January 1967, 5.

20 Robert McKenzie and Lotta Dempsey, "Pierre Trudeau: 'I Became Accustomed,'" *Toronto Star*, 8 April 1968, 8.

21 Hugh Winsor, "Grand Greeting for Trudeau as He Starts East African Tour," *Globe and Mail*, 8 August 1981, 4.

22 *Globe and Mail*, "Our Man in Ottawa," 6 April 1975, 6; and Edward Cowan, "Canadian Movement Seeking Home Rule for West," *New York Times*, 10 April 1970, 20.

23 Pierre Elliott Trudeau, *Federalism and the French Canadians* (Toronto: Macmillan, 1968), xix.

24 Max and Nemni Monique Nemni, *Young Trudeau: Son of Quebec, Father of Canada, 1919–1944*, trans. William Johnson (Toronto: McClelland & Stewart, 2006).

25 Trudeau, *Federalism and the French Canadians*, 151–81.

26 Michel Brunet to Gad Horowitz, 7 July 1968, personal papers of Gad Horowitz.

27 Peter H. Russell, "Aboriginal Nationalism and Quebec Nationalism: Reconciliation through Fourth World Decolonization," *Constitutional Forum* 8., no. 4 (1997): 117, and Indigenous and Northern Affairs Canada, "Statement of the Government of Canada on Indian Policy" (The White Paper, 1969), https://www.aadnc-aandc.gc.ca/eng/1100100010189/1100100010191.

28 Pierre Elliott Trudeau, "New Treason of the Intellectuals," and "Separatist Counter-Revolutionaries," in *Federalism and the French Canadians* (Toronto:

Macmillan, 1968). Originally published in *Cité Libre*, April 1962 and May 1964.

29 Ron Graham, *The Last Act: Pierre Trudeau, the Gang of Eight and the Fight for Canada* (Toronto: Allen Lane, 2011), 86.

30 Pierre Elliott Trudeau, "The Practice and Theory of Federalism," in *Social Purpose for Canada*, ed. Michael Oliver (Toronto: University of Toronto Press, 1961), 378.

31 Henry Giniger, "8 Premiers Planning a Parley," *New York Times*, 4 April 1981; and Jeffrey Simpson, "Clark 'Head Waiter' to Greedy Premiers, Trudeau Charges," *Globe and Mail*, 20 April 1979, 9.

32 Tom Traves and John Saywell, "Parliament and Politics," in Saywell, *Canadian Annual Review of Politics and Public Affairs 1977*; *Globe and Mail*, "Not on Program, Turner Still Big Draw," 28 March 1977, 25.

33 William Johnson, "Ottawa Awaiting Position of Premiers: Resignation of Richardson over Constitution Premature, Trudeau Says," *Globe and Mail*, 14 October 1976, 5.

34 Walter Stewart, "Like a Stone through a Stained Glass Window," *Globe and Mail*, 18 September 1971, 7.

35 Edwin R. Black, "Trudeau's Constitutional Coup d'Etat," *Queen's Quarterly* 84, no. 4 (Winter 1980): 577, and Peter Russell, *Constitutional Odyssey: Can Canadians Become a Sovereign People?* 3rd ed. (Toronto: University of Toronto Press, 2004), 118.

36 Jean Chrétien, *Straight from the Heart* (Toronto: Key Porter, 1985), 117.

37 Herman Bakvis, *Regional Ministers: Power and Influence in the Canadian Cabinet* (Toronto: University of Toronto Press, 1991).

38 Donald Savoie, "Power at the Apex: Executive Dominance," in *Canadian Politics*, ed. James Bickerton and Alain-G. Gagnon, 4th ed. (Peterborough, ON: Broadview, 2004), 146.

39 Stephen Clarkson, "The Defeat of the Government, the Decline of the Liberal Party, and the (Temporary) Fall of Pierre Trudeau," in *Canada at the Polls, 1979 and 1980: A Study of the General Elections*, ed. Howard R. Penniman (Washington: American Enterprise Institute for Public Policy Research, 1981), 152.

40 George C. Perlin, *The Tory Syndrome: Leadership Politics in the Progressive Conservative Party* (Montreal and Kingston: McGill-Queen's University Press, 1980).

41 Martin O'Malley, "The Stanfield Lunge," *Globe and Mail*, 8 July 1974, S5.

42 Geoffrey Stevens, *Stanfield* (Toronto: McClelland & Stewart, 1973), 184.

43 Geoffrey Stevens, "Pratfalls in Perspective," *Globe and Mail*, 16 January 1979, 6; and David L. Humphreys, *Joe Clark: A Portrait* (Ottawa: Deneau & Greenberg, 1978), 119.

44 Robert L. Stanfield, "Conservative Principles and Philosophy," in *Politics: Canada*, ed. Paul W. Fox and Graham White, 7th ed. (Toronto: McGraw-Hill Ryerson, 1991), 297–301.

45 Robert Krause and Lawrence LeDuc, "Voting Behaviour and Electoral Strategies in the Progressive Conservative Leadership Convention of 1976," *Canadian Journal of Political Science* 12, no. 1 (March 1979): fig. 2, 122.

46 Colin Campbell and William Christian, *Parties, Leaders, and Ideologies in Canada* (Toronto: McGraw-Hill Ryerson, 1996), 45.

47 Paul Gesell, "Visions of Canada: Joe Clark's Community of Communities; Mulroney Has Already Embraced His Old Rival's Recipe for National Unity and Expected to Appoint Him Federal-Provincial Relations Minister," *Ottawa Citizen*, 20 April 1991, B1.

48 Tom Hawthorne, "Jack Horner, Rancher and Politician: 1927–2004; 'Cactus Jack' Arrived in Ottawa as a Tory Cowpuncher Prepared to Duke It Out with His Opponents. In the End, He Shot Down His Own Career by Going Over to His Arch-Enemies, the Liberals," *Globe and Mail*, 22 November 2004, S1.

49 Traves and Saywell, "Parliament and Politics," in Saywell, *Canadian Annual Review of Politics and Public Affairs 1977*.

50 John Sawatsky, *Mulroney: The Politics of Ambition* (Toronto: McClelland & Stewart, 1991), 356.

51 John C. Courtney, *Do Conventions Matter? Choosing National Party Leaders in Canada* (Montreal and Kingston: McGill-Queen's University Press, 1995), 433n17.

52 John C. Crosbie with Geoffrey Stevens, *No Holds Barred: My Life in Politics* (Toronto: McClelland & Stewart, 1998), 226.

53 Stephen Brooks, *Canadian Democracy: An Introduction*, 8th ed. (Toronto: Oxford University Press, 2015), 99.

54 Canada, Report of the Task Force on the Structure of Canadian Industry, *Foreign Ownership and the Structure of the Canadian Industry* (Ottawa: Queen's Printer, 1968).

55 Resolution No. 133, Fifth Federal Convention of the New Democratic Party, Winnipeg, 28–31 October 1969.

56 Anthony Westell, "NDP Radicals Face Drubbing," *Winnipeg Free Press*, 28 October 1969, 1.

57 Alan Whitehorn, *Canadian Socialism: Essays on the CCF-NDP* (Toronto: Oxford University Press, 1992), 92.

58 Quoted in Jeffrey Simpson, "Convention Is Lacking in Fire, Rhetoric as NDP Opts for Moderation in Aims," *Globe and Mail*, 4 July 1977, 9.

59 *Toronto Star*, "The Best Choice for Canada," 21 May 1979, A8.

60 Traves and Saywell, "Parliament and Politics," in Saywell, *Canadian Annual Review of Politics and Public Affairs 1977*, 36; Judy Steed, *Ed Broadbent: The Pursuit of Power* (Markham, ON: Viking, 1988), 239–41; and Whitehorn, *Canadian Socialism*, 193.

61 Donald V. Smiley, *Canada in Question: Federalism in the Eighties*, 3rd ed. (Toronto: McGraw-Hill Ryerson, 1980), chap. 5; and Rand Dyck, "Links between Federal and Provincial Parties," in *Representation, Integration and Political Parties in Canada*, ed. Herman Bakvis, 129–77 (Toronto: Dundurn, 1991).

62 Whitehorn, *Canadian Socialism*, table 5.6, 109.

63 *Canada Year Book, 1973*, 353.

64 Maurice Pinard, *The Rise of a Third Party* (Englewood Cliffs, NJ: Prentice-Hall, 1971), 12.

65 Donald Murray, "The Ralliement des creditistes in Parliament, 1970–71," *Journal of Canadian Studies* 8, no. 2 (May 1973): 17; Claire Balfour, "Caouette Retains Leadership with Ease on First Ballot at Socred National Rally," *Globe and Mail*, 11 October 1971, 1; and "Platform of the Social Credit Party of Canada (1972)," 4, 10. (The text used comes from the collection of political texts made available at www.poltext.org by the Center for Public Policy Analysis [CAPP] from Laval University, with the financial support of the Fonds de recherche du Québec – Société et culture [FRQSC]).

66 John J. Barr, *The Dynasty: The Rise and Fall of Social Credit in Alberta* (Toronto: McClelland and Stewart, 1974), 172.

67 Denis Pilon, "Right-Wing Coalition Politics and Neoliberalism," in *Transforming Provincial Politics: The Political Economy of Canada's Provinces and Territories in the Neoliberal Era*, ed. Bryan M. Evans and Charles W. Smith (Toronto: University of Toronto Press, 2015), 286.

68 Claude Morin, *Quebec versus Ottawa: The Struggle for Self-Government* (Toronto: University of Toronto Press, 1976), 81.

69 John Saywell, *The Rise of the Parti Québécois, 1967–1976* (Toronto: University of Toronto Press, 1977), 140.

70 René Lévesque, *La Passion du Québec* (Montreal: Editions Québec/Amérique, 1979), 48; and Victor Malarek, "Leftists from around World Attend," *Globe and Mail*, 7 December 1981, 12.

71 Clinton Archibald, "Corporatist Tendencies in Quebec," in *Quebec: State and Society*, ed. Alain-G. Gagnon, 353–64 (Toronto: Methuen, 1984).

72 Kenneth McRoberts, *Quebec: Social Change and Political Crisis*, 3rd ed. (Toronto: McClelland & Stewart, 1988), 256.

73 Quoted in William Johnson, "Voting System Cries Out for PQ Reform," *Globe and Mail*, 11 December 1979, 8.

74 William Johnson, "First PQ Program Foreshadows Broad Control over Quebec Life," *Globe and Mail*, 9 March 1977, 1.

75 Edward McWhinney, *Quebec and the Constitution 1960–1978* (Toronto: University of Toronto Press, 1979), 118.

76 Graham Fraser, *René Lévesque and the Parti Québécois in Power* (Montreal and Kingston: McGill-Queen's University Press, 2001), 375.

77 *Globe and Mail*, "Hellyer Stars at Socred Meeting as Right-Wing Flirtation Continues," 11 October 1971, 9.

78 SC 1973–74, c 51.

79 *Globe and Mail*, "Bigotry Met Head-on," 30 May 1974, 6.

7. Trading Places

1   S.M. Crean, *Who's Afraid of Canadian Culture?* (Toronto: General Publishing, 1976), 275.

2   For example, in a 5 May 1984 speech in Toronto, Mulroney said, "Government at all levels, not just the political, must cooperate with the business community and organized labour." Four days later in his Toronto speech Turner said, "No economy can work where government does not reach out to its partners in the economy: business and labour." See "Managing Economic Change," 2, in "On the Issues: Brian Mulroney and the Progressive Conservative Agenda," July 1984, and "The Issues: John Turner Speaks Out," 10. (The texts used come from the collection of political texts made available at www.poltext.org by the Center for Public Policy Analysis [CAPP] from Laval University, with the financial support of the Fonds de recherche du Québec – Société et culture [FRQSC]).

3   Nicholas Mansergh, *The Commonwealth Experience, vol. 2, From British to Multiracial Commonwealth* (London: Macmillan, 1982), 11.

4   Michael Crawford Urban, "A Fearful Asymmetry: Diefenbaker, the Canadian Military and Trust during the Cuban Missile Crisis," *Canadian Foreign Policy Journal* 21, no. 3 (2015): 257–71; and Asa McKercher, "Principles and Partnership: Merchant, Heeney, and the Craft of Canada-US Relations," *American Review of Canadian Studies* 42, no. 1 (March 2012): 68.

5   Robert Bothwell, "Canada's Isolationist Tradition." *International Journal* 51, no. 1 (Winter 1999): 80.

6   Robert L. Stanfield, "Conservative Principles and Philosophy," in *Politics: Canada*, ed. Paul W. Fox and Graham White, 7th ed., 297–301 (Toronto: McGraw-Hill Ryerson, 1991).

7   *Royal Commission on Dominion-Provincial Relations* (Rowell-Sirois] Report, Book I (1940), 36.

8   Grace MacInnis, *J.S. Woodsworth: A Man to Remember* (Toronto: Macmillan, 1953), 188.

9   Kenneth Bryden, *Old Age Pensions and Policy-Making in Canada* (Montreal and Kingston: McGill-Queen's University Press, 1974), 88.

10   House of Commons, *Debates*, 12 July 1966.

11   Quoted in Patrice Dutil, *The Guardian: Perspectives on the Ministry of Finance of Ontario* (Toronto: University of Toronto Press, 2011), 326–7.

12   Quoted in Malcolm G. Taylor, *Health Insurance and Canadian Public Policy: The Seven Decisions That Created the Canadian Health Insurance System* (Montreal and Kingston: McGill-Queen's University Press, 1978), chap. 4, 338–40.

13   Quoted in Brenda Crossman and Judy Fudge, eds., *Privatization, Law, and the Challenge to Feminism* (Toronto: University of Toronto Press, 2002), 3.

14   Quoted in Colin Campbell and William Christian, *Parties, Leaders, and Ideologies in Canada* (Toronto: McGraw-Hill Ryerson, 1996), 52.

15 Herschel Hardin, *A Nation Unaware: The Canadian Economic Culture* (Vancouver: J.J. Douglas, 1974), 54.

16 Reg Whitaker, *A Sovereign Idea: Essays on Canada as a Democratic Community* (Montreal and Kingston: McGill-Queen's University Press, 1992), 20.

17 Brian Mulroney, *Where I Stand* (Toronto: McClelland and Stewart, 1983).

18 W.T. Stanbury, "Privatization and the Mulroney Government, 1984–1988," in *Canada under Mulroney: An End-of-Term Report*, ed. Andrew B. Gollner and Daniel Salée (Montreal: Véhicule, 1988), 119.

19 Joseph Brean, "Diplomatic One-Liners," *National Post*, 17 November 2014, A6; and Douglas Martin, "Ottawa Playing Down Trudeau's Differences with Reagan," *New York Times*, 12 June 1984, A9.

20 "Mulroney and Reagan Sing 'When Irish Eyes Are Smiling,'" https://www.youtube.com/watch?v=vJqehECa2VY; and quoted in David Shribman, "Canada Day and July 4th: A Tale of Two National Holidays," *Globe and Mail*, 4 July 2017, A3.

21 Donald J. Savoie, *Thatcher, Reagan, Mulroney: In Search of a New Bureaucracy* (Toronto: University of Toronto Press, 1994).

22 L. Ian Macdonald, *Mulroney: The Making of a Prime Minister* (Toronto: McClelland and Stewart, 1985), 295.

23 Sylvia Bashevkin, "Confronting Neo-Conservatism: Anglo-American Women's Movements under Thatcher, Reagan and Mulroney," *International Political Science Review* 15, no. 3 (1994): 279.

24 Quoted in Tasha Kheiriddin and Adam Daifallah, *Rescuing Canada's Right: Blueprint for a Conservative Revolution* (Mississauga, ON: J. Wiley, 2005), 15.

25 David Jay Bercuson, J. L. Granatstein, and William Robert Young, *Sacred Trust?: Brian Mulroney and the Conservative Party in Power* (Toronto: Doubleday, 1986), 5–6.

26 Quoted in Jeff Sallot, "Mulroney Trips over 'Jokes' on Patronage," *Globe and Mail*, 17 July 1984, 1.

27 Guy Gendron, *Brian Mulroney: L'homme des beaux risques* (Montreal: Québec Amerique, 2014), 147.

28 Eric Mintz, "The Canadian General Election of 1984," *Electoral Studies* 4, no. 1 (1985): 73.

29 Quoted in *Montreal Gazette*, "Quebec Completes Constitutional Plans," 15 May 1985, A4.

30 Quoted in Lawrence Martin, "US President Man of Guts, Crosbie Says," *Globe and Mail*, 1 June 1983, 9.

31 James Farney, "The Personal Is Not Political: The Progressive Conservative Response to Social Issues," *American Review of Canadian Studies* 39, no. 3 (2009): 242, 247; and Michael Lusztig and J. Matthew Wilson, "A New Right? Moral Issues and Partisan Change in Canada," *Social Science Quarterly* 86, no. 1 (2005): 117.

32 Stanley Tromp, "How Mulroney Buried the Move to Reinstate Capital Punishment," *Globe and Mail*, 13 October 2007, A12.

33 Michael I. Krauss, "Mulroney's Save," *Policy Review* 48 (1989): 48.

34 Mollie Dunsmuir, "The Senate: Appointments under Section 26 of the Constitution Act, 1867," August 1990, http://publications.gc.ca/Collection-R/LoPBdP/BP/bp244-e.htm#LEGISLATIVE.

35 Gallup Canada, "Campbell Would Best Liberals, Poll Says," *Toronto Star*, 12 April 1993, A15.

36 L. Ian MacDonald, "The Best Prime Minister of the Last 50 Years: Pearson, by a Landslide," *Policy Options*, June–July 2003, https://policyoptions.irpp.org/magazines/the-best-pms-in-the-past-50-years/the-best-prime-minister-of-the-last-50-years-pearson-by-a-landslide/.

37 Stephen Clarkson, *The Big Red Machine: How the Liberal Party Dominates Canadian Politics* (Vancouver: UBC Press, 2014), 111.

38 Lawrence Martin, "Turner Backs Quebec Law on Language," *Globe and Mail*, 12 April 1984, 1.

39 Robert J. Drummond, "Parliament and Politics," in *Canadian Annual Review of Politics and Public Affairs 1984*, ed. R.B. Byers (Toronto: University of Toronto Press, 1987), 12–13.

40 "The Issues: John Turner Speaks Out," 9 May 1984, 3. (The text used comes from the collection of political texts made available at www.poltext.org by the Center for Public Policy Analysis [CAPP] from Laval University, with the financial support of the Fonds de recherche du Québec – Société et culture [FRQSC]).

41 Quoted in Raymond M. Hébert, *Manitoba's French-Language Crisis: A Cautionary Tale* (Montreal and Kingston: McGill-Queen's University Press, 2004), 176.

42 Richard Cleroux, "Manitoba PC Chief Assails Mulroney," *Globe and Mail*, 15 March 1984, 1–2.

43 Quoted in Christina McCall Newman, *Grits: An Intimate Portrait of the Liberal Party* (Toronto: Macmillan, 1983), 356.

44 *On the Issues: Brian Mulroney and the Progressive Conservative Agenda* (Ottawa: July 1984).

45 Richard Johnston, André Blais, Henry E. Brady, and Jean Crête, *Letting the People Decide: Dynamics of a Canadian Election* (Montreal and Kingston: McGill-Queen's University Press), 133.

46 Graham Fraser, *Playing for Keeps; The Making of the Prime Minister, 1988* (Toronto: McClelland & Stewart, 1989), 308–27.

47 Brooke Jeffrey, *Divided Loyalties: The Liberal Party of Canada, 1984–2008* (Toronto: University of Toronto Press, 2010), 168.

48 Terry Mercer, quoted in Jeffrey, *Divided Loyalties*, 176.

49 Harold D. Clarke and Allan Kornberg, "Partisan Dealignment, Electoral Choice and Party-System Change in Canada, *Party Politics* 2, no. 4 (1996): 464.

50 Stephen Clarkson, "Yesterday's Man and His Blue Grits: Backward into the Future," in *The Canadian General Election of 1993*, ed. Alan Frizzell, John H. Pammett, and Anthony Westell (Ottawa: Carleton University Press, 1994), 32–3.

51 Quoted in James Travers, "Don't Trust Campaign of Secrecy," *Ottawa Citizen*, 25 September 1993, A10.

52 Rosemary Speirs, "Tory TV Ad Hits 'a New Low in Politics,' Chrétien Says," *Toronto Star*, 15 October 1993, A1; and Peter Woolstencroft, "'Doing Politics Differently': The Conservative Party and the Campaign of 1993," in Frizzell, Pammett, and Westell, *Canadian General Election of 1993*, 21, n16.

53 Kenneth Whyte, "The Face That Sank a Thousand Tories," *Saturday Night* 109, February 1994, 14.

54 John Geddes, "The Campaign: Jobs, Jobs, Jobs; Economic Leadership the Ley Issue," *Financial Post*, 8 September 1993, 9.

55 Ian Brown, "The Awful State of, umm ... ORATORY," *Globe and Mail*, 1 September 1984, 10.

56 *Toronto Star*, "NDP Could Win Next Election Based on Poll Analyst Says," 26 June 1987, A1; and *Globe and Mail*, "New Poll Puts NDP 6 Points Up," 17 July 1987, A4.

57 Harold D. Clarke, Jane Jenson, Lawrence LeDuc, and Jon H. Pammett, *Absent Mandate: Interpreting Change in Canadian Politics*, 2nd ed. (Toronto: Gage, 1991), tables 5.3–5.5, 97–100.

58 Tom Langford, "Politics of the Canadian New Middle Class: Public/Private Sector Cleavage in the 1980s," *Canadian Journal of Sociology* 21, no. 2 (1996): 153–83.

59 Lawrence LeDuc, "The Leaders' Debates: Critical Event or Non-Event?," in Frizzell, Pammett, and Westell, *Canadian General Election of 1993*, 135–6.

60 Quoted in Hugh Winsor, "Election 93: Attacks Will Backfire, Manning Says Ignore 'Politics-of-Fear' Campaign Waged by Other Parties, Backers Urged," *Globe and Mail*, 13 October 1993, A4.

61 Alan Whitehorn, "The NDP's Quest for Survival," in Frizzell, Pammett, and Westell, *Canadian General Election of 1993*, 55.

62 Keith Archer and Faron Ellis, "Opinion Structure of Party Activists: The Reform Party of Canada," *Canadian Journal of Political Science* 27, no. 2 (1994): 304.

63 Peter McCormick, "The Reform Party of Canada: New Beginning or Dead End?," in *Party Politics in Canada*, ed. Hugh G. Thorburn and Alan Whitehorn, 7th ed. (Scarborough, ON: Prentice-Hall, 1996), 343.

64 Reform Party of Canada, *Platform and Statement of Principles* (n.p.: 1988).

65 David Laycock, "Reforming Canadian Democracy? Institutions and Ideology in the Reform Party Project," *Canadian Journal of Political Science* 27, no. 2 (1994): 213–47.

66 Miro Cernetig, "Referendum 1992: Reform Party's TV Ads Slam 'Mulroney's Deal,' Strategists Bank on PM's Low Popularity," *Globe and Mail*, 13 October 1992, A6.

67 Haroon Siddiqui, "Don't Blame Multiculturalism," in Janice Stein, David Robertson Cameron, John Ibbitson, Will Kymlicka, John Meisel, Haroon Siddiqui, and Michael Valpy, *Uneasy Partners: Multiculturalism and Rights in Canada* (Waterloo, ON: Wilfrid Laurier University Press, 2007), 24.

68 Patricia Poirier, "Sovereigntist MPs to Form Quebec Bloc in Commons: Will Not Become Party or Vote the Same Way," Globe *and Mail*, 26 July 1990, A1.

69 Robert McKenzie, "Tories Hit PM with Quebec Headache: Mulroney Faces Push from Ridings for Radical Plans to Change Canada," *Toronto Star*, 27 October 1990, A9.

70 Manon Cornellier, *The Bloc* (Toronto: James Lorimer, 1995), chap. 5.

71 *Globe and Mail*, "Election '93: A Voters' Guide to the Issues," 2 October 1993, A7.

72 Richard Mackie, "Reform Chief Takes Aim at Bouchard," *Globe and Mail*, 2 October 1993, A6.

73 Diane Francis, "Canada's 'Fringe' Parties Reflect Global Trends," *Financial Post*, 28 September 1993, 19.

74 R. Kenneth Carty, William Cross, and Lisa Young, *Rebuilding Canadian Party Politics* (Vancouver: UBC Press, 2000).

75 Jane Taber, "Mulroney: Blue Tory, Green Leader," *Globe and Mail*, 18 April 2006, A1; and CBC, "Mulroney Honoured for Environmental Record," 20 April 2006, http://www.cbc.ca/news/canada/mulroney-honoured-for-environmental-record-1.616580.

8. Division and Reconfiguration

1 Quoted in David Forgacs, ed., *The Gramsci Reader: Selected Writings, 1916–1935* (New York: New York University Press, 2000), 217–18.

2 Alexander Panetta, "BQ Offers Friendly Reception to Day's Partnership Idea," *Winnipeg Free Press*, 30 July 2000, A4.

3 C.B. Macpherson, *Democracy in Alberta: The Theory and Practice of a Quasi-Party System* (Toronto: University of Toronto Press, 1953).

4 Maurice Pinard, *The Rise of a Third Party: A Study in Crisis Politics* (Englewood Cliffs, NJ: Prentice-Hall, 1971).

5 Seymour Martin Lipset, *Continental Divide: The Values and Institutions of the United States and Canada* (London: Routledge, 1990), 203; and Martin Robin, *Radical Politics and Canadian Labour, 1880–1930* (Kingston: Queen's University Press, 1968), 273.

6 Alan C. Cairns, "The Electoral System and the Party System in Canada, 1921–1965," *Canadian Journal of Political Science* 1, no. 1 (1968): 55–80.

7 Robert Everett, "Parliament and Politics," in *Canadian Annual Review of Politics and Public Affairs, 1992*, ed. David Leyton Brown (Toronto: University of Toronto Press, 1998), 29.

8 Quoted in Murray Campbell, "Middle Kingdom: How Rep by Pop Wins Converts," *Globe and Mail*, 27 October 1993, A19.

9 Law Commission of Canada, *Voting Counts: Electoral Reform for Canada* (Ottawa: Law Commission, 2004), 30.

10 *Vancouver Sun*, "Vote Not Just for Me but for My Team, Leader Says," 16 January 1993, A8; and Jane Taber, "Liberal Strategy Will Emphasize Team Spirit, Keep Chretien under Wraps," *Ottawa Citizen*, 26 August 1993, A2.

11 Donald J. Savoie, *Governing from the Centre: The Concentration of Power in Canadian Politics* (Toronto: University of Toronto Press, 1999), 283; Savoie, "Power at the Apex: Executive Dominance," in *Canadian Politics*, ed. James Bickerton and Alain-G. Gagnon, 4th ed. (Peterborough, ON: Broadview, 2004), 153; and Hugh Winsor, "'Penalty Killer' PM Plays Rough," *Globe and Mail*, 1 December 2000, A4.

12 Stephen Clarkson, *The Big Red Machine: How the Liberal Party Dominates Canadian Politics* (Vancouver: UBC Press, 2005), 208.

13 Robert Everett, "Parliament and Politics," in *Canadian Annual Review of Politics and Public Affairs, 1995*, ed. David Leyton-Brown (Toronto: University of Toronto Press, 2002), 31.

14 Quoted in Edward Greenspon, "Following the Trail of Campaign '97," in *The Canadian General Election of 1997*, ed. Alan Frizzell and Jon H. Pammett (Toronto: Dundurn, 1997), 23.

15 Shawn McCarthy and Paul Adams, "Chrétien Defends Early Vote," *Globe and Mail*, 23 October 2000, A1.

16 Brooke Jeffrey, *Divided Loyalties: The Liberal Party of Canada, 1984–2008* (Toronto: University of Toronto Press, 2010), 341.

17 R. Kenneth Carty, William Cross, and Lisa Young, *Rebuilding Canadian Party Politics* (Vancouver: UBC Press, 2000), 198.

18 Colin Nickerson, "Civility Cracking in Canada Prime Minister's Tussle with Protester Stirs Furor," *Boston Globe*, 17 February 1996, 2.

19 Jim Brown, "PM Draws Line in Sand on Hepatitis C," *Winnipeg Free Press*, 23 April 1998, 6.

20 *Hamilton Spectator*, "Quotables," 2 January 1995, A8.

21 Paul Samyn, "Come Get Me, PM Tells Critics Chretien Dares Martin Allies to Force an Early Election," *Winnipeg Free Press*, 5 June 2002, A1.

22 Peter O'Neil, "Ethnic Groups Lead Rise of B.C. Liberals: Indo-Canadians, Chinese-Canadians Make Up 66% of Membership Growfh," *Ottawa Citizen*, 26 July 2003, A7.

23 *Edmonton Journal*, "Martin's Surplus Wipes Out Liberal Party Debt," 19 January 2004, A5.

24 *Economist*, "'Mr Dithers' and His Distracting 'Fiscal Cafeteria,'" 17 February 2005; and Frances Russell, "Dither, Doubt, Spin Your Tires," *Winnipeg Free Press*, 16 April 2004, A14.

25 Les Whittington, "RCMP to Probe Federal Ad Deals: Extensive Flouting of Government Guidelines Found in 3 Contracts," *Toronto Star*, 9 May 2002, A29; and Elizabeth Thompson, "'Words Escape Me': Sponsorship Fiasco to Be Probed in Wake of Auditor-General's Scorching Report," *Montreal Gazette*, 11 February 2004, 1.

26 Tim Naumetz, "Gomery Seeks Details of Martin's Role in Ad Decisions," *Ottawa Citizen*, 7 October 2004, A3.

27 Mark Kennedy, "Martin at Mercy of Voters' Thirst for Vengeance: Extent of Desire to Exact a Price for Scandal Will Decide Election," *Edmonton Journal*, 2 November 2005, A1.

28 Melissa Leong, Chris Wattie, and Carrie Tait, "RCMP Probes Suspected Leak at Finance: Goodale Rebuffs Calls to Resign over Alleged Early Release of Tax Policy on Dividends, Income Trusts," *National Post*, 29 December 2005, A1.

29 Wikipedia, "Opinion Polling in the Canadian Federal Election, 2006," https://en.wikipedia.org/wiki/Opinion_polling_in_the_Canadian _federal_election,_2006.

30 Mark Kennedy, Mike Blanchfield, and Anne Dawson, "Reporter 'Clearly Not' a Criminal, Martin Says: Fallout from Raid. We're Not Becoming a Police State: PM," *Montreal Gazette*, 23 January 2004, A12.

31 Ipsos-Reid, "What Do Pharmacists, Doctors, Soldiers, Pilots and Teachers Have in Common? They're among the Most Trusted Professions in Canada," 4 January 2011, 2.

32 Faron Ellis, *The Limits of Participation: Members and Leaders in Canada's Reform Party* (Calgary: University of Calgary Press, 2005), chap. 5.

33 Reform Party of Canada, *Blue Sheet, Principles, Policies, & Election Platform 1993*. (The text used comes from the collection of political texts made available at www.poltext.org by the Center for Public Policy Analysis [CAPP] from Laval University, with the financial support of the Fonds de recherche du Québec – Société et culture [FRQSC]).

34 Miro Cernetig, "Election '93: The Paradox of Manning 'Iron Fist': Confidential Documents Show a Reform Leader Much Different from His Public Image as a Populist," *Globe and Mail*, 20 October 1993, A1.

35 Tom Flanagan, *Waiting for the Wave* (Toronto: Stoddart, 1995), 107.

36 *Blue Book: 1996–1997, Principles and Policies of the Reform Party of Canada* (n.p.), 34; and Frances Russell, "Manning Swats at Bugs: A Bright Light Attracts Bugs," *Winnipeg Free Press*, 20 October 1993, A9.

37 Derek Ferguson, "Reform Party Advertising for Candidates: Replacements Needed for MPs Not Seeking Re-election," *Toronto Star*, 12 November 1996, A9; and Richard Sigurdson, "Preston Manning and the Politics of

Postmodernism in Canada," *Canadian Journal of Political Science* 27, no. 2 (1994): 268.

38 Quoted in Colin Nickerson, "Evolution Views Create Problems for Canadian Premier Candidate," *Boston Globe*, 24 November 2000, A38.

39 Lisa Young, "Representation of Women in the New Canadian Party System," in *Political Parties, Representation, and Electoral Democracy in Canada*, ed. William Cross (Don Mills, ON: Oxford University Press, 2002), 195, 192.

40 *Kitchener-Waterloo Record*, "Manning Ad Takes Shot at Pro-Quebecers," 24 May 1997, A4.

41 Tom Flanagan, *Harper's Team: Behind the Scenes in the Conservative Rise to Power* (Montreal and Kingston: McGill-Queen's University Press, 2007), 24.

42 Flanagan, *Harper's Team*, 107.

43 Manon Cornellier, *The Bloc* (Toronto: James Lorimer, 1995), 157.

44 *Globe and Mail*, "Election '93: Bloc Leader States His Case in His Own Words," 21 September 1993, A8.

45 Richard Mackie, "Keep Bloc Quebecois in Ottawa, Quebecers Say Poll Finds More Than Half of Voters Satisfied with Work of MPs a Year after Election," *Globe and Mail*, 21 October 1994, A1; and Susan Delacourt, "Bloc MPs Feel Their Lives in Ottawa Won't End after Referendum: Role as Defenders of Quebec's Interests in Commons Seen as Fallback Position If Sovereignty Is Rejected," *Globe and Mail*, 31 August 1994, A6.

46 Quoted in Robert McKenzie, "Canada Can Be Divided, Quebec Can't: Bouchard Can Split Nation Because Not a Real Country, New PQ Leader Says," *Toronto Star*, 28 January 1996, A1.

47 Pierrette Venne, "Why Tories Won't Bed the Bloc," *Globe and Mail*, 4 June 2004, A19.

48 André Bernard, "The Bloc Québécois," in *The Canadian General Election of 1997*, ed. Alan Frizzell and Jon H. Pammett (Toronto: Dundurn, 1997), 136.

49 Clement Godbout, quoted in Karen Unland, "Election '97: Duceppe Feels Betrayed by Labour Union Leader Denies Questioning Whether Bloc Quebecois Helps Sovereignty Cause," *Globe and Mail*, 23 May 1997, 14.

50 James Cowan, "Duceppe Wins Novel Support; Atwood Backs Bloc Leader's Defence of the Arts," *National Post*, 4 October 2008, A6.

51 Jane Taber, "Tories, NDP and Bloc Unite to Demand More Clout; They Want Changes to Commons Rules," *Globe and Mail*, 10 September 2004, A1.

52 Peter Woolstencroft, "The Conservatives: Rebuilding and Rebranding Yet Again," in *Canadian Parties in Transition*, ed. Alain-G. Gagnon and A. Brian Tanguay, 4th ed. (Toronto: University of Toronto Press, 2017), 146.

53 Ross Howard, "Conservative Party Closes Offices, Reduces Its Staff: Bigger-Than-Expected Debt, Poor Election Result Blamed," *Globe and Mail*, 19 November 1993, A5.

54 David Heyman, "The Great Divide: Policy Differences among Key Players Still a Sticking Point in Forming New Party," *Calgary Herald*, 3 December 2003, A3.
55 Lowell Murray, "Don't Do It, Peter: There Is No Good Reason for Tories to Climb into Bed with the Alliance, Says Conservative Senator Lowell Murray," *Globe and Mail*, 23 June 2003, A11.
56 Sean Gordon, "Right Votes to Unite: 90% Tory Support. Move Hailed as Step in Journey to Power," *Montreal Gazette*, 7 December 2003, A1.
57 Sean Gordon, "Tories Bar Ex-Saskatchewan Premier from Federal Run: Devine a 'Scapegoat' for Past Ethics Scandal, Supporters Charge," *Ottawa Citizen*, 20 February 2004, A8.
58 Alan Whitehorn, "Alexa McDonough and Atlantic Breakthrough for the New Democratic Party," in Frizzell and Pammett, *Canadian General Election of 1997*, 91.
59 Alan Whitehorn, "Alexa McDonough and NDP Gains in Atlantic Canada," in *Party Politics in Canada*, ed. Hugh G. Thorburn and Alan Whitehorn, 8th ed. (Toronto: Pearson, 2001).
60 Tony Van Alphen, "NDP Kicks Hargrove Out of Party: Veteran Union Leader Says He's 'Shocked' at His Expulsion for Endorsing Some Liberals in the Last Election. But He Says He'd Do It Again," *Toronto Star*, 12 February 2006, A4.
61 *The Elections Finances Act* CCSM c E32 (2006), s 41 (1).
62 David McGrane, "Ideological Moderation and Professionalization: The NDP under Jack Layton and Tom Mulcair," in Gagnon and Tanguay, *Canadian Parties in Transition*, 168.

9. Conservatism: Old and New

1 Stephen Harper, "Rediscovering the Right Agenda," *Citizens Centre Report Magazine*, 10 June 2003, 72–7.
2 Quoted in R.E. Saunders, "Robinson, Christopher," in *DCB*, vol. 4, http://www.biographi.ca/en/bio/robinson_christopher_1763_98_4E.html.
3 Robert E. Saunders, "Robinson, Sir John Beverley," in *DCB*, vol. 9, http://www.biographi.ca/en/bio/robinson_john_beverley_9E.html.
4 Joseph H. Carens, ed., *Democracy and Possessive Individualism: The Intellectual Legacy of C.B. Macpherson* (Albany: State University of New York Press, 1993).
5 Herbert E. Gaston, *The Non-Partisan League* (New York: Harcourt, Brace and Howe, 1920); and W.L. Morton, *The Progressive Party in Canada* (Toronto: University of Toronto Press, 1950).
6 Carolina Armenteros, *The French Idea of History: Joseph de Maistre and His Heirs, 1794–1854* (Ithaca, NY: Cornell University Press, 2011).
7 Quoted in Ramsay Cook, *The Maple Leaf Forever* (Toronto: Macmillan, 1971), 125.
8 Cook, *Maple Leaf Forever*, 121.

9   William Lyon Mackenzie King, *Industry and Humanity: A Study in the Principles Underlying Industrial Reconstruction* (Toronto: Houghton Mifflin, 1918).

10 Stephen McBride and John Shields, *Dismantling a Nation: The Transition to Corporate Rule in Canada*, 2nd ed. (Halifax: Fernwood, 1997), 18; and John Shields and B. Mitchell Evans, *Shrinking the State: Globalization and Public Administration "Reform"* (Halifax: Fernwood, 1998).

11 Quoted in Michael Rustin and Prue Chamberlayne, "Introduction: From Biography to Social Policy," in *Biography and Social Exclusion in Europe: Experiences and Life Journey*, ed. Prue Chamberlayne, Michael Rustin, and Tom Wengraf (Bristol: Policy, 2002), 4.

12 George Grant, *Lament for a Nation: The Defeat of Canadian Nationalism* (Toronto: McClelland and Stewart, 1965).

13 Geoffrey Stevens, *The Player: The Life and Times of Dalton Camp* (Toronto: Key Porter, 2003), 2–3.

14 Thomas Walkom, "Still Feeling Jilted after Right-Wing Marriage: Many Unhappy with PC-Alliance Union," *Toronto Star*, 12 November 2005, F1.

15 D.G. Creighton, "George Brown, Sir John A. Macdonald, and the 'Workingman,'" *Canadian Historical Review* 24, no. 4 (December 1943): 374.

16 Martin Robin, *Radical Politics and Canadian Labour, 1880–1930* (Kingston: Queen's University Press, 1968), 8.

17 Michael Bliss, "The Protective Impulse: An Approach to the Social History of Oliver Mowat's Ontario," in *Oliver Mowat's Ontario*, ed. Donald Swainson, 174–88 (Toronto: Macmillan, 1972).

18 Frank H. Underhill, *The Image of Confederation* (Toronto: CBC Massey Lectures, 1964), 63.

19 "Progressive Conservative Platform of 1949," in *Canadian Party Platforms 1867–1968*, ed. D. Owen Carrigan, 187–8 (Toronto: Copp Clark, 1968).

20 Keith Archer and Alan Whitehorn, *Political Activists: The NDP in Convention* (Toronto: Oxford University Press, 1997), 29, 140.

21 Quoted in Geoffrey York, "Defending the Definition of Poverty: Social Justice Long-time Crusaders for Canada's Poor Are Finding the Foundations of Their Work under Assault by Such Groups as the Reform Party and the Fraser Institute," *Globe and Mail*, 16 July 1992, A1.

22 Quoted in Charles Trueheart, "GOP Victory Encourages Canadians Trying to Steer Ottawa to the Right," *Washington Post*, 14 January 1995, A19.

23 Julian Beltrame, "'Newt of the North' Finds a Soulmate in Gingrich TV Show Turned into a Love-in for Populist Politics," *Hamilton Spectator*, 15 March 1995, A4.

24 Harper, "Rediscovering the Right Agenda," 72–7.

25 Harper, "Rediscovering the Right Agenda."

26 Tom Flanagan, *Harper's Team: Behind the Scenes in the Conservative Rise to Power* (Montreal and Kingston: McGill-Queen's University Press, 2007), 275.

27 Neil Nevitte and Christopher Cochrane, "Value Change and the Dynamics of the Canadian Partisan Landscape," in *Canadian Parties in Transition*, ed. Alain-G. Gagnon and A. Brian Tanguay, 255–75 (Peterborough, ON: Broadview, 2007).

28 Quoted in Bruce Campion-Smith, "Tories Want Fixed Voting Dates: Propose Elections Every Four Years, Senate, Commons Reform on Agenda," *Toronto Star*, 27 May 2006, A6.

29 L. Ian Macdonald, "Happy Birthday, Prime Minister: A Poll Showing the Tories in a Dead Heat with the Bloc Is Good News for Harper," *Montreal Gazette*, 1 May 2008, A21.

30 Bill Curry, "Performance Pay for Senior Bureaucrats Up Sharply," *Globe and Mail*, 13 August 2010, A4; Greg Keenan et al., "Auto Industry: Bailout to Top $17 Billion," *Globe and Mail*, 13 December 2008, A1, A4; and Statistics Canada, "Employment and Average Weekly Earnings (Including Overtime), Public Administration and All Industries," http://www40.statcan.gc.ca /l01/cst01/govt19a-eng.htm.

31 Gerry Nicholls, "Et Tu, Stephen?: Fiscal Conservatives Feel Betrayed by the Man They Thought Was Their Champion," *Montreal Gazette*, 4 February 2009, A17.

32 FilipinoWebChannel, *Jason Kenney: Canada's "King of Multiculturalism,"* 6 March 2011, https://www.youtube.com/watch?v=cNIxsw2sRSc.

33 Quoted in Canadian Press, "Former PC Up-and-Comer Brison Joins Liberals," *Hamilton Spectator*, 11 December 2003, A13.

34 Linda Diebel, "Documents Show How Dion Rejected Warnings from Liberal Pollster on 'Loser' Green Shift," *Toronto Star*, 17 October 2008, A1.

35 Jeffrey Simpson, "What a Difference Five Days Make," *Globe and Mail*, 4 December 2008, A23.

36 Jane Taber, "'Dion Must Go': After a Campaign That Failed to Connect with Canadians, Liberals Lose Seats across the Country and Fall to Historic Lows in Popular Support," *Globe and Mail*, 15 Oct 2008, A12.

37 Quoted in Michael Valpy, "Being Michael Ignatieff; He's known for his charm, good looks and big ideas. But he also admits to ruthlessness. He has hurt those who loved him most. And after decades abroad, he now wants to become the leader of this country," *Globe and Mail*, 26 August 2006, F1.

38 Anne Dawson, "The 'Thinker' in the Wings: Paul Martin has practically only begun his reign, but many senior Liberals are already star-struck over the leadership potential of Michael Ignatieff, an opinion-maker with 'good Canadian genes,'" *Ottawa Citizen*, 4 March 2005, A4; and Caroline Alphonso and Jeff Sallot, "Liberals Miffed by Ignatieff's Candidacy," *Globe and Mail*, 28 November 2005, A1.

39 Barbara Yaffe, "Liberals' First West Coast Convention Draws Few of the Faithful; Gathering aimed at building support in the west suffers from

tight budgets, and with no leader to elect, it'll be all about policy and planning," *Vancouver Sun*, 25 April 2009; and quoted in Bruce Campion-Smith, "Members to Vote on Future Leaders: Party Moves Away from Delegated Conventions," *Toronto Star*, 3 May 2009, A6.

40 Peter Newman, quoted in Jane Taber, "Newman Rewrites Ignatieff's History; Former Liberal leader found to be a brilliant man so full of ideas as to be unfocused, and guilt-ridden to a fault," *Globe and Mail*, 28 May 2011, A17.

41 YouTube, "Conservative ad: Ignatieff Just Visiting – Arrogance (2009)," 26 April 2013, https://www.youtube.com/watch?v=edcpuNB_Zxo.

42 Joan Brydon, "Liberals Struggle to Get Their Voters Out: Less Than 43% Have Registered," *Edmonton Journal*, 23 Mar 2013, A18; and Campbell Clark, "Liberals Need Modern Red Machine," *Globe and Mail*, 22 February 2014, A8.

43 Allan Woods, "NDP Achieving Record Support in Quebec, Holding Lead Nationally, New Polls Show," *Toronto Star*, 21 August 2015.

44 *Toronto Star*, "Brian Mulroney Gives Stephen Harper Piece of His Mind," 4 September 2014.

45 Harold J. Jansen and Lisa Young, "Solidarity Forever? The NDP, Organized Labour, and the Changing Face of Party Finance in Canada," *Canadian Journal of Political Science* 42, no. 3 (September 2009): 657–78; and Dennis Pilon, Stephanie Ross, and Larry Savage, "Solidarity Revisited: Organized Labour and the New Democratic Party," *Canadian Political Science Review* 5, no. 1 (January 2011), 20–37.

46 *Windsor Star*, "NDP Must Repay Union Sponsorship Funds: Tory Complaint after Convention," D3.

47 Quoted in Tonda MacCharles, "'I'll Put Government out of Its Misery,'" *Toronto Star*, 28 April 2005, A1.

48 *Wikipedia*, "Opinion Polling in the Canadian Federal Election, 2011 by Constituency," https://en.wikipedia.org/wiki/Opinion_polling_in_the _Canadian_federal_election,_2011_by_constituency#.

49 Brad Lavigne, *Building the Orange Wave: The Inside Story behind the Historic Rise of Jack Layton and the NDP* (Madeira Park, BC: Douglas and McIntyre, 2013).

50 *Montreal Gazette*, "NDP Bios: Students and a Political Giant-Killer," 7 May 2011, A6.

51 *Hill Times*, "The Ipsos-Reid Numbers," 26 September 2011, 4.

52 Bill Curry, "Mulroney Says Harper Is in for Tough Re-election Fight in 2015," *Globe and Mail*, 4 September 2014.

53 Mark Kennedy, "Leaders Battle to Define Key Issues in 78-Day Campaign," *Ottawa Citizen*, 4 August 2015.

54 CBC, "French-Language Leaders' Debate: 5 Feisty Exchanges: Heated Exchanges on the Niqab, the Clarity Act, Pipelines," http://www.cbc.ca

/news/politics/canada-election-2015-key-exchanges-french-debate
-1.3243081.

55   Éric Bélanger and Richard Nadeau, "The Bloc Québécois: A Sour Tasting
Victory," in *The Canadian General Election of 2006*," ed. Jon H. Pammett and
Christopher Dornan, 122–42 (Toronto: Dundurn, 2006).

56   YouTube, "Culture en peril," n.d., https://www.youtube.com/watch?v
=n3HVFsIQ5M4.

57   Bloc Québécois, "Présent pour le Québec" (2008), and "Thankfully, Here,
It's the Bloc" (2006). (The text used comes from the collection of political
texts made available at www.poltext.org by the Center for Public Policy
Analysis [CAPP] from Laval University, with the financial support of the
Fonds de recherche du Québec – Société et culture [FRQSC]).

58   Alain-G. Gagnon and Jacques Hérivault, "The Bloc Québécois: Charting
New Territories," in *Canadian Parties in Transition*, ed. Alain-G. Gagnon
and A. Brian Tanguay, 3rd ed. (Peterborough, ON: Broadview, 2007),
132.

59   Erin Tolley, "Political Players or Partisan Pawns? Immigrant, Minorities,
and Conservatives in Canada," in *The Blueprint: Conservative Parties and
Their Impact on Canadian Politics*, ed. J.P. Lewis and Joanna Everitt (Toronto:
University of Toronto Press, 2017), 118.

60   *Edmonton Journal*, "Punt Tories, Ignatieff Urges Quebecers," 15 March 2011,
A6.

61   Éric Bédard, "La fin du consensus liberal?," *Policy Options*, June–July 2011,
http://policyoptions.irpp.org/magazines/the-winner/la-fin-du
-consensus-liberal/.

62   Tim Naumetz, "Federal Greens Growing in Popularity: Poll," *Vancouver
Sun*, 14 April 2004, A3.

63   Cara Camcastle, "The Green Party of Canada in Political Space and the
New Middle Class Thesis," *Environmental Politics* 16, no. 4 (2007): 642.

64   Jane Taber, "Elizabeth May Stands Up for Nycole Turmel; Green Party
Chief Defends Interim NDP Leader in Phone Call," *Globe and Mail*, 6 August
2011, A8.

65   *Globe and Mail*, "Anti-Nuclear Fight Wins 11 Candidates," 30 January 1980, 9.

66   Peter C. Newman, *When the Gods Changed: The Death of Liberal Canada*
(Toronto: Random House, 2011); and quoted in Taber, "Newman Rewrites
Ignatieff's History."

67   Darrell Bricker and John Ibbitson, *The Big Shift: The Seismic Change in Canadian
Politics, Business, and Culture and What It Means for Our Future* (Toronto: Harper-
Collins, 2013).

68   Abbas Rana, "'These Ridings Will Elect the Next Government,' Swing
Ridings with Majority Visible Minority Populations Will Tilt 2019 Election,
Say Politicos," *Hill Times*, 20 November 2017, 1, 22.

69 Quoted in Bruce Campion-Smith, "Thomas Mulcair Vows to 'Wipe' Floor with Justin Trudeau," *Toronto Star*, 16 November 2013; and Kory Teneycke, quoted in *National Post*, "Trudeau Will Exceed Expectations 'If He Comes on Stage with His Pants On': Harper Spokesperson on Debate," 5 August 2015.

Conclusion: The Ever-Changing Party

1 Quoted in Gorges Edmond Howard, *Aphorisms and Maxims on Various Subjects for the Good Conduct of Life* (Dublin: Sarah Cotter, 1767), 225.
2 R. Kenneth Carty, "Choosing New Party Leaders," in *Canada at the Polls, 1984,* ed. Howard Penniman (Durham, NC: Duke University Press, 1988), 56.
3 William Cross, *Political Parties* (Vancouver: UBC Press, 2004).
4 Shruti Shekar, "Former Dion Adviser Pens New Book, Could Create a Bit of Drama," *Hill Times*, 9 April 2018, 2.
5 Ian Brodie, "In Defence of Political Staff," *Canadian Parliamentary Review* (Autumn 2012), 34.
6 Elections Canada, "Registered Political Parties and Parties Eligible for Registration," http://www.elections.ca/content.aspx?dir=par&document =index&lang=e&section=pol.
7 Robert Benzie, Brennan Doherty, and Victoria Gibson "Lawyer Seeking Injunction to Extend PC Leadership Race," *Toronto Star*, 8 March 2018; Glen McGregor, "Raid on Tory HQ Included 'Overbroad' Seizure: Lawyers," Canwest News Service, 22 January 2009; Figueroa v Canada (Attorney General), [2003] 1 SCR 912, 2003 SCC 37.
8 Donald Smiley, *Canada in Question: Federalism in the Eighties*, 3rd ed. (Toronto: McGraw-Hill Ryerson, 1980), 137; and Rand Dyck, "Links between Federal and Provincial Parties," in *Representation, Integration and Political Parties in Canada*, ed. Herman Bakvis (Toronto: Dundurn, 1991), 129–77.
9 Anna Esselment, "Fighting Elections: Cross-Level Political Party Integration in Canada," *Canadian Journal of Political Science* 43, no. 4 (2010): 871–92.
10 R.K. Carty, "Three Canadian Party Systems: An Interpretation of the Development of National Parties," in *Party Democracy in Canada*, ed. George Perlin, 15–30 (Scarborough, ON: Prentice-Hall, 1988).
11 S.J.R. Noel, "Leadership and Clientelism," in *The Provincial Political Systems: Comparative Essays*, ed. David J. Bellamy, Jon H. Pammett, and Donald C. Rowat (Toronto: Methuen, 1976), chap. 4.
12 The Legislative Assembly Act, SM 2010, c 33, s 31; and Tobi Cohen, "NDP Bill Seeks to Ban Floor-Crossing," Canada.com, 2 November 2011, http://o.canada.com/news/ndp-bill-seeks-to-ban-floor-crossing.
13 John C. Courtney, "Party Leadership Selection in the New Dominion," in *The Selection of National Party Leaders in Canada*, ed. John C. Courtney, 100–21 (Toronto: Macmillan, 1973).

14 D.V. Smiley, "The National Party Leadership Convention in Canada: A Preliminary Analysis," *Canadian Journal of Political Science* 1, no. 4 (1968): 373.

15 John Courtney, *Do Conventions Matter? Choosing National Party Leaders in Canada* (Montreal and Kingston: McGill-Queen's University Press, 1995), 11.

16 R.K. Carty, Lynda Erickson, and Donald E. Blake, "Parties and Leaders: The Experiences of the Provinces," in *Leaders and Parties in Canadian Politics: Experiences of the Provinces*, ed. R. Kenneth Carty, Lynda Erickson, and Donald E. Blake (Toronto: HBJ Holt, 1992), 4.

17 Nelson Wiseman, "The Pattern of Prairie Leadership," in *Prime Ministers and Premiers: Political Leadership and Public Policy in Canada*, ed. Leslie A. Pal and David Taras (Scarborough, ON: Prentice-Hall, 1988), 180.

18 John McMenemy, "Fragment and Movement Parties," in *Political Parties in Canada*, ed. Conrad Winn and John McMenemy, 29–48 (Toronto: McGraw-Hill Ryerson, 1975).

19 *Toronto Star*, "Savage Survives Vote of Nova Scotia Liberals," 8 July 1995, 8.

20 Robert Benzie, "Liberals Need to Reach Out to the West: Kennedy," *Toronto Star*, 28 March 2006, A6.

21 Daniel Latouche, "Universal Democracy and Effective Leadership: Lessons from the Parti Québécois Experience," in Carty, Erickson, and Blake, *Leaders and Parties in Canadian Politics*, 179.

22 Agar Adamson and Ian Stewart, "Changing Politics in Atlantic Canada," *Party Politics in Canada*, ed. Hugh G. Thorburn and Alan Whitehorn, 8th ed. (Toronto: Prentice Hall, 2001), 313.

23 Hugh Winsor, "Second Fiddle Leads: NDP McDonough Wins, Robinson Gives In," *Globe and Mail*, 16 October 1995, A1.

24 Leonard Preyra, "From Conventions to Closed Primaries? New Politics and Recent Changes in National Party Leadership Selection in Canada," in *Party Politics in Canada*, ed. Thorburn and Whitehorn, 8th ed., 449.

25 Miro Cernetig, "Many Want to Lead, Few Want to Follow: Alberta Tories Seek Members," *Globe and Mail*, 19 November 1972, A1; Allan Fotheringham, "'Instant' Tories Thwart the Bright Betkowski," *Financial Post*, 8 December 1992, 13.

26 R. Kenneth Carty, William Cross, and Lisa Young, *Rebuilding Canadian Party Politics* (Vancouver: UBC Press, 2000), chap. 9.

27 Walter Young, *The Anatomy of a Party: The National CCF, 1932–61* (Toronto: University of Toronto Press), 60.

28 John A. Irving, *The Social Credit Movement in Alberta* (Toronto: University of Toronto Press, 1959), 141.

29 Peter Mair and Ingrid van Biezen, "Party Membership in Twenty European Democracies, 1980–2000," *Party Politics* 7, no. 1 (2001): 5–21.

30 Peter Woolstencroft, "The Progressive Conservative Party, 1984–1993: Government, Party, Members," in *Party Politics in Canada*, ed. Hugh G. Thorburn, 7th ed. (Toronto: Prentice Hall, 1996), 292.

31 *Inside Queen's Park* 17, no. 2 (16 June 2004).
32 David Reevely, "Reevely: Ontario Tories' Voting Turns Up Thousands of 'Missing' Members in Just a Few Ridings," *Ottawa Citizen*, 9 March 2018.
33 Hugh Winsor, "Poor Turnout a Bad Omen for Liberals," *Globe and Mail*, 22 September 2003, A4; Alexander Panetta, "Federal Liberals Now Claim 531,000 Members: A Historic High," Canadian Press, 24 July 2003; and Anne Dawson, "Liberal Ranks Swell to 531,536: Eight-fold Increase in British Columbia Reported in Runup to Leadership Vote," *Ottawa Citizen*, 25 July 2003, A5.
34 CBC, "Justin Trudeau Vows to 'Bring Canadians Together' at Brampton Rally," 4 October 2015, http://www.cbc.ca/news/politics/canada-election-2015-trudeau-brampton-rally-1.3256142.
35 Éric Grenier, "6 Things Fundraising Data Tell Us about NDP Leadership Race," CBC, 27 September 2017, http://www.cbc.ca/news/politics/grenier-ndp-fundraising-1.4305838.
36 World Sikh Organization, "Are There Sikh MPs?," http://www.worldsikh.org/are_there_sikh_mps.
37 Ishaan Tharoor, "Canada Now Has the World's Most Sikh Cabinet," *Washington Post*, 5 November 2015; and Chidanand Rajghatta, "More Sikhs in my Cabinet than Modi's: Trudeau," *Times of India*, 14 March 2016.
38 Canada Elections Act, 1974, s 70.1, as amended by the Election Expenses Act, 1974, s 12.
39 Quoted in Joseph Schull, *Laurier: The First Canadian* (Toronto: MacMillan, 1965), 591–2.
40 Reginald Whitaker, *The Government Party: Organizing and Financing the Liberal Party of Canada, 1930–58* (Toronto: University of Toronto Press, 1978), 12.
41 T.D. Regehr, *The Beauharnois Scandal: A Story of Canadian Entrepreneurship and Politics* (Toronto: University of Toronto Press, 1990).
42 *Report of the Committee on Election Expenses* (Ottawa: Queen's Printer, 1966).
43 Sebastien Spano, "Political Financing," PRB 07-50E, Government of Canada (2008), http://publications.gc.ca/site/eng/9.564093/publication.html.
44 Quoted in Bill Curry, "Liberals Seek Less Debate, More Money: Amendments to Move Up Summer Break, Hike Subsidy," *National Post*, 10 June 2003, 1.
45 Evan Dyer, "NDP Says $9M Raised in 3rd Quarter a Canadian Record – for Now," CBC, 1 October 2015, http://www.cbc.ca/news/politics/canada-election-2015-ndp-fundraising-record-1.3252990.
46 David Coletto, Harold J. Jansen, and Lisa Young, "Stratarchical Party Organization and Party Finance in Canada," *Canadian Journal of Political Science* 44, no. 1 (2011): 111–36.
47 Paul Rutherford, *A Victorian Authority: The Daily Press in Late Nineteenth-Century Canada* (Toronto: University of Toronto Press, 1982); and George

Fetherling, *The Rise of the Canadian Newspaper* (Toronto: Oxford University Press, 1990).

48 Communic@tions Management Inc., "Requiem for the Print Edition," 30 November 2017, figure 2, 4.

49 Murray S. Donnelly, *Dafoe of the Free Press* (Toronto: Macmillan, 1968).

50 John A. Irving, *The Social Credit Movement in Alberta* (Toronto: University of Toronto Press, 1959).

51 Walter C. Soderlund, Walter I. Romanow, E. Donald Briggs, and Ronald H. Wagenberg, *Media & Elections in Canada* (Toronto: Holt, Rinehart and Winston, 1984).

52 Tamara Small, "Two Decades of Digital Party Politics in Canada: An Assessment," in *Canadian Parties in Transition*, ed. Alain-G. Gagnon and A. Brian Tanguay, 4th ed. (Toronto: University of Toronto Press, 2017), 402.

53 Alex Marland, Thierry Giasson, and Anna Lennox Esselment, eds., *Permanent Campaigning in Canada* (Vancouver: UBC Press, 2017).

54 Justice Gary Hearn quoted in Michael Oliveira, "Tory Staffer Sentenced to Nine Months in Robocall Scandal," *Globe and Mail*, 12 May 2018.

55 R. Kenneth Carty, William Cross, and Lisa Young, *Rebuilding Canadian Party Politics* (Vancouver: UBC Press, 2000), chap. 9.

56 Sydney Sharpe, *The Gilded Ghetto: Women and Political Power in Canada* (Toronto: HarperCollins, 1994), 24; and Robert Everett, "Parliament and Politics," in *Canadian Annual Review of Politics and Public Affairs, 1993* (Toronto: University of Toronto Press, 1999), 31–2.

57 *Hamilton Spectator*, "Quotables," 2 January 1995, A8; and *Economist*, "A Balancing Act: Paul Martin Reshapes His Team," 22 July 2004.

58 Tim Harper, "On the India Fiasco, Trudeau Is Looking for Blame in All the Wrong Places," *Toronto Star*, 28 February 2018.

59 Nicholas Kristof, "Thank God for Canada!" *New York Times*, 6 February 2019.

60 André Blais, Elisabeth Gidengil, Richard Nadeau, and Neil Nevitte, "Measuring Party Identification: Britain, Canada, and the United States," *Political Behavior* 23, no. 1 (2001): 5–22; and Laura Stephenson, Thomas J. Scotto, and Allan Kornberg "Slip, Sliding Away or Le Plus Ça Change ... : Canadian and American Partisanship in Comparative Perspective," *American Review of Canadian Studies* 34, no. 2 (2004): 283–312.

61 Harold D. Clarke, Jane Jenson, Lawrence LeDuc, and Jon H. Pammett, *Political Choice in Canada* (Toronto: McGraw-Hill Ryerson, 1979), 303–17.

62 S.M. Lipset, "Democracy in Alberta," *Canadian Forum* 34 (November–December 1954): 175–7, 196–8.

63 Robert Bothwell, *A Short History of Ontario* (Edmonton: Hurtig, 1986), 99.

64 Kyle Kondik and Geoffrey Skelley, "Incumbent Reelection Rates Higher Than Average in 2016," *Rasmusson Reports*, 15 November 2016, http://www.rasmussenreports.com/public_content/political_commentary

/commentary_by_kyle_kondik/incumbent_reelection_rates_higher_than _average_in_2016; and Richard E. Matland and Donley T. Studlar, "Determinants of Legislative Turnover: A Cross-National Analysis," *British Journal of Political Science* 34, no. 1 (2004): 91.

65 Harold D. Clarke, Jane Jenson, Lawrence LeDuc, and Jon H. Pammett, "Absent Mandate: Canadian Electoral Politics in an Age of Restructuring," in *Party Politics in Canada*, ed. Thorburn and Whitehorn, 8th ed., 407.

66 Quoted in Agar Adamson and Ian Stewart, "Changing Party Politics in Atlantic Canada," in *Party Politics in Canada*, ed. Thorburn and Whitehorn, 8th ed., 309.

67 Richard Johnston, "The Reproduction of the Religious Cleavage in Canadian Elections," *Canadian Journal of Political Science* 18, no. 1 (1985): 99.

68 Sarah Wilkins-Laflamme, "The Changing Religious Cleavage in Canadians' Voting Behaviour," *Canadian Journal of Political Science* 49, no. 3 (2016): 499.

69 Frank H. Underhill, *In Search of Canadian Liberalism* (Toronto: Macmillan, 1960), 237.

70 Ian Stewart, "Friends at Court: Federalism and Provincial Elections on Prince Edward Island," *Canadian Journal of Political Science* 19, no. 1 (1986): 132.

71 Vincent Lemieux, "Quebec: Heaven Is Blue and Hell Is Red," in *Canadian Provincial Politics: Party Systems in the Ten Provinces*, ed. Martin Robin, 2nd ed. (Scarborough, ON: Prentice-Hall, 1978), 248; and Alain-G. Gagnon and François Boucher, "Party Politics in a Distinct Society: Two Eras of Block Voting in Quebec," in Gagnon and Tanguay, *Canadian Parties in Transition*, 4th ed., 278.

72 Neil Nevitte and Roger Gibbins, *New Elites in Old States: Ideologies in the Anglo-American Democracies* (Toronto: Oxford University Press, 1990), 127–9.

73 John Meisel, "Decline of Party in Canada," in *Party Politics in Canada*, ed. Hugh G. Thorburn, 5th ed. (Toronto: Prentice-Hall, 1985), chap. 15; Meisel, "The Dysfunctions of Canadian Parties: An Exploratory Mapping," in *Party Politics in Canada*, ed. Thorburn, 6th ed. (Scarborough, ON: Prentice-Hall, 1991), chap. 18; Grant Amyot, "The Waning of Parties?," in Gagnon and Tanguay, *Canadian Parties in Transition*, 4th ed., chap. 5; and Robert D. Putnam, *Bowling Alone: The Collapse and Revival of American Community* (New York: Simon & Schuster, 2000).

74 Nelson Wiseman, *In Search of Canadian Political Culture* (Vancouver: UBC Press, 2007); Jared J. Wesley, ed., *Big Worlds: Politics and Elections in the Canadian Provinces and Territories* (Toronto: University of Toronto Press, 2016).

Index